The
Children
of Master
O'Rourke

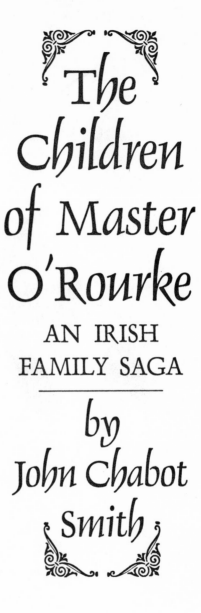

The Children of Master O'Rourke

AN IRISH FAMILY SAGA

by
John Chabot Smith

HOLT, RINEHART
and WINSTON
New York

*The names and faces of most of the people
in this book have been changed to protect
their privacy, and some liberties have
been taken with times, places, and dialogue.
But they are all real people, and with their
help, especially the generosity and
patience of the family called O'Rourke,
I have tried to tell this story as nearly
as possible the way it actually happened.*

*Published simultaneously in Canada by Holt,
Rinehart and Winston of Canada, Limited.*

*Library of Congress Cataloging in Publication
Data
Smith, John Chabot.
 The children of Master O'Rourke.*

 *1. Ireland—Social life and customs
—20th century.*
*2. Ireland—Biography. I. Title.
DA959.1.S56 941.5082'092'2 [B] 77-23278*

ISBN: 0-03-016916-X

First Edition

Designer: Kathy Peck

*Printed in the United States of America
10 9 8 7 6 5 4 3 2 1*

To the Saints and Scholars of Ireland,
especially Patrick, Kevin and Martin,
O'Malley of Ballycarrick,
Maire and Eoin,
and all the others who helped me
write this book.

Contents

PART
I

First
Impressions

I.

The
House at
Saint Patrick's
Well

The O'Rourke family home is in the parish of Saint Columbanus, Ballycarrick, on the northwest coast of Ireland at the entrance to Sligo Bay, where the winds and billows of the Atlantic come ashore bringing the warm, wet breath of the Gulf Stream with them. Ballycarrick is not marked on any tourist road maps, and there isn't any reason why it should be. It's a not particularly wide place in the road from Sligo Town to Ballina, with a handsome Catholic church built of gray stone and plastered over in pink, with tall stained-glass windows and a high gabled roof surmounted by a simple cross, set back from the road behind a gravel parking lot, just beyond the graveyard. Before you come to the church a sign beside the main road points up a lane to the left, saying BALLYCARRICK ½. It's a remarkably straight lane for Ireland, climbing steeply uphill past another graveyard and another church, this one Protestant, an impressive square-turreted building that bears the unmistakable stamp of the Church of Ireland, reminiscent of a fortified castle yet with the same ecclesiastical dignity of design as an American Episcopal church. The high stone walls around it are pierced by a locked and barred gate, with neatly painted notice board proclaiming the hours of Morning Prayer, Holy Communion, and Vespers each Sunday. Facing it across the road behind another wall and another gate, this one wooden and painted white, stands the rectory, its function announced by a polished brass plate on the top bar of the gate, although the house is empty and there is no rector there now.

It was a good half mile from the main road to the Church of Ireland, so we knew when we reached it we must be in Bally-carrick. A huge outcropping of bare rock behind the church seemed to be the "carrick" that gave the place its name. But there was no one about to tell us where to find the O'Rourke home. We continued up the lane, past grazing cattle and a few distant farmhouses, until it ended at another road with another sign, pointing downhill the way we had come, and with the same message as the sign at the bottom of the hill: BALLY-CARRICK ½.

There was nothing to do but turn our little red Fiat around and head back downhill until we came to a track that led to one of the farmhouses.

It was raining as we pulled into the yard, a sudden shower of that soft, warm summer rain that freshens the Irish country-side, not really wet enough to cause any discomfort, and bright-ened by the sunshine slanting down from beyond the edge of the cloud. Only in Ireland can you have sunshine and rain in the same place at the same time, and stand in the rain without getting wet.

A door opened in the low, rambling house, and out from be-tween the white plastered walls stepped a dark-haired young woman, hatless, in a cardigan sweater and skirt, who ran down the steps to our car to see what we wanted and how she could help.

Betty called to her, "Oh, but you mustn't stand there in the rain! Let my husband hold an umbrella for you—we only want to ask the way."

I got out of the car, leaving the umbrella behind because it wasn't really necessary, and followed our hostess back up the steps to the shelter of the open doorway, where a tall, lean, rather gaunt-looking man in his fifties came forward to join us. "The O'Rourke family?" he asked in surprise. "That would be old Master O'Rourke?"

"That's the one," I said, for the father of all the O'Rourkes had been the schoolmaster in Ballycarrick for more than thirty years until his death twenty-seven years ago, and it was he who had built the family home we were looking for. This graying farmer must have been one of his pupils.

"He's dead, you know," said the farmer in a gentle, matter-of-fact tone. It was as though he thought he might be breaking the news to me, and I, too, might be one of Master O'Rourke's old pupils, returning to Ireland after so many years in the hope of seeing him. I reassured him quickly.

"Ah, yes, I know; but his sons are using the house on their holidays."

"Well, then," he said, "I can tell you exactly where that house is, I know it well. Let me see now, what would be the best way to get there, for there are many ways," and he discussed the problem briefly with the dark-haired young woman, who might have been his daughter or his wife. "You go back down the hill to the main road," he decided, "and turn to the right back toward Sligo Town, and a little way on your left you'll see the road to the strand—you know that road?"

"Yes, I think I saw the sign as we came along," I said.

"That's it, then. You go along that road about a mile and you'll come to a turning on the right, it's the only right turn you'll find, and there's a little bridge there—"

"That's the turning," the young woman interrupted. "I remember that wee bridge, you'll see it as you turn."

"You go on a way further until you pass Hogan's shop," the farmer continued, "and a little way beyond the shop you turn again to the left, and go on until you see the house on the right. It's a two-story house, the only one thereabout."

They went over the instructions twice more to be sure I understood them, and the farmer said, "I wonder, can you remember all that and keep it in your head?"

"I think I can," I said, "and if I get lost I can always ask someone to help me as you have done."

"Remember the wee bridge and Hogan's shop," said the young woman, and followed me out to the car as I left. The rain had stopped now; the wild raspberries in the hedgerows were glistening damp in the sunshine, and the moisture was rising in little wisps of steam from the tarred surface of the lane as it dried.

We found the wee bridge without difficulty, and a little while after crossing it we were in open meadowland with the great sky above us, the rounded hump of Slieve Gamh, or Ox Mountain, on our right, and the hills around Sligo Town in the distance straight ahead. On the near horizon was a gentle slope dotted with cows and crisscrossed with stone walls and green hedgerows, rising to a low ridge crowned with a grove of trees, among which we could see our two-story house, with double chimney and steep slate roof, outlined against the sky. The road swerved away from it through a settlement of low gray stone houses bordering the road, where we found a Texaco station and what looked like a little country store with a sign above it saying HOGAN in letters two feet high. Sure enough, a little farther on was a left turn that took us to the O'Rourke house and would have led us, if we'd stayed on it, to the gravel cliffs at the edge of the sea, less than half a mile beyond.

We parked the Fiat in a little walled area across the lane from the house, where it would be safe from the white-faced brown cows, every one of them so much bigger and heavier than the little red car that an inadvertent toss of the head or swish of the tail might have done it fatal damage if they came too close;

there was no other traffic to worry about. Then we got out and looked at the house, wondering about the man who had built it nearly sixty years ago, and lived in it through the Anglo-Irish war that brought Ireland's freedom from British rule, and the civil war that had lasted for one terrible year in the South and was still going on sporadically after more than fifty years in the North; and about the fifteen children who had been born and raised here, the mother who had lived here for nearly thirty years of married life and twenty years of widowhood, and the thirty-four grandchildren who came here from time to time with their parents for their holidays, while the house stood empty the rest of the year.

It didn't look big enough for such a large family; for all that, it was the biggest house for miles around. Master O'Rourke had been thirty-five when he built it for his bride, who was twelve years younger; he had built it of stone, plastered inside and out, with good hardwood floors and a staircase that rose straight up the center from the hallway in front to a small landing in the rear, off which the bathroom had been added after the mother's death. There was money enough to bring in the pipes and electric power long before that, but the widow wouldn't hear of it. She liked the house the way it was, and wouldn't have felt comfortable with the changes.

There were three bedrooms when the house was first built, a large one running from front to back on one side of the staircase, and two smaller ones on the other side. Downstairs were the two main rooms of the house, the kitchen on one side with its great hearth and dining table, where six of us sat down on the day of our visit, leaving room for three or four more if we'd crowded a bit; and on the other side, the sitting room, with carved oak mantelpiece over the hearth, and pictures of the Holy Family, the Sacred Heart, and Pope John XXIII.

As the family grew, a wing had been added at the back of the house with three more bedrooms—still barely enough for a family of seventeen, but they were never all together in the house at the same time. There was twenty years' difference between the eldest child and the youngest, and the two eldest had left home before the two youngest were born.

Only at their mother's death did all the children gather together at the same place at the same time for the first time in their lives, and even then one of them couldn't come to the funeral, for Tony, the fifth to be born, was very ill with multiple sclerosis, and died a few months after his mother, at the age of thirty-nine. The fourteen had their picture taken in a group, and to make it complete the photographer used a head-and-shoulders picture of Tony, taken not long before, which was reduced to the same scale and inserted at the proper place so that he seemed to be standing behind the others, looking over the shoulders of his next elder brother, Charlie, and his next younger brother, Jimmy. It was the only picture of the whole family ever taken, and each of the brothers and sisters had a copy.

I had seen this picture in a small town in Connecticut, where William, the tenth-born O'Rourke and second of the three priests in the family, had shown it to me in his office at Saint Mary's Church. There were too many faces in it to recall, but when Charlie stepped from the doorway of the house at Ballycarrick to welcome me, I had no doubt who he was.

The O'Rourke men were all tall, broad-shouldered, and dark-haired, although Joe, the eldest son, was beginning to gray; they had strong, bony faces, long rather than round, with bright eyes set far apart, and hair trimmed shorter than the modern fashion. They all had the same quiet laugh, which came easily to them, and the same soft voices and rapid Irish diction. Charlie, at five feet ten, was the shortest, but heavyset and looking as though he weighed almost as much as his brother Peter, the tallest at six feet four, who was lean as a string bean and nearly ten years younger. Peter was the youngest of the three priests, a member of the Society of Missionaries to Africa, and had spent three years in Nigeria but returned to teach theology in Ireland's seminaries. When Charlie described him to us, I suggested that it might be his priestly calling that kept him so lean.

"Ah, no," said Charlie, "for the parish priests are as fat as can be, especially in these country parishes. That's because they have so little to do—it's a lazy life in a small country parish, with nothing but a few Masses on Sunday, and the odd wedding or funeral during the week."

"And the odd baptism, too," said his wife, Una, a tall, blond young woman with the same ready laugh as her husband. She laughed now at our puzzlement over the Irish idiom for something that happens only occasionally. "Everything is always odd in Ireland," she said. "But then Peter doesn't have a country parish, and he's a very hard-working man. When he was in Nigeria, like his brother Matt, who's there now, they used to give him only ten shillings for a wedding, the same as our fifty pence, and expect him to do the baptisms for nothing."

It didn't seem fair, since in truth there was nothing either odd or occasional about baptisms in Catholic families, whether in Nigeria or Ireland; they were far more numerous than weddings or even funerals, though not so frequent in Ireland now as they had been forty-five years ago, when Charlie was born. As Charlie said, "People know more about these things now than they used to. We don't have to have such large families anymore, and we can't afford them either."

Charlie and Una had two children, boys six and three years old. The elder boy, Cathal, had already finished second grade; the younger, Liam (short for William, his uncle's name), would start school at four if there was room for him. There probably would be, Charlie said; the national school in the section of North Dublin where they lived was not particularly crowded. They were bright boys, with the same interest in learning as their grandfather, the schoolmaster. Cathal was drawing a picture of a house when we arrived, in red, blue, and green crayon, and his father asked him what house it was.

"Toberpatrick," the boy answered, and his father laughed because that was the name of the house we were in, and the boy's drawing was not a bad likeness, except for the colors he'd used. And then he explained where the name came from—it meant Saint Patrick's Well, because there was a well in the neighborhood that, it was said, good Saint Patrick had blessed some fifteen hundred years ago.

"I don't know whether he really did," said Charlie, "but all over Ireland wherever there is a good well people like to believe Saint Patrick had something to do with it." And indeed, there must be hundreds of places in Ireland called Toberpatrick, or sometimes Tubberpatrick; they are more abundant than the old houses in New Jersey and along the roads to Valley Forge with signs announcing GEORGE WASHINGTON SLEPT HERE.

Una was in the kitchen getting lunch as Charlie and I sat in the living room playing with Cathal, at half past two on a windy afternoon. The family had spent the morning on the beach, returning to the house just a few minutes before we arrived, though they had no way of knowing when to expect us, and no telephone on which we could call them. Telephones are a rare commodity in Ireland, available only in the larger towns and along the busier highways, or after spending months or sometimes years on a waiting list. Charlie had one in his Dublin home, but there had been no answer when I called. His brother Joe, a police sergeant in County Clare, could be reached by phone at the police station, and he had told me where to find Charlie, and promised to send him a postcard to say I was coming.

Joe had invited us to visit him at his home, near the hauntingly beautiful bare limestone hills of the Burren, and on the way we would have to see the Knock Shrine in County Mayo, scene of an apparition of the Blessed Virgin Mary nearly one hundred years ago, where Father Peter O'Rourke, the missionary priest and teacher, was on duty for the summer.

These were to be our first contacts with the Irish branch of the O'Rourke family, brothers and sisters of our friends Patrick and Father William in Connecticut, and of Gertie, Tess, and

Brigid in England, and Father Matt in Nigeria. What started as a friendly errand on a three-week vacation, carrying greetings across the Atlantic from one branch of the family to another, was to grow into a profoundly moving experience, bringing Betty and me back to Ireland that fall for a year's stay, to share the lives of this extraordinary family and explore the mysteries and paradoxes of their country. The seemingly endless guerrilla war in the British-controlled North, the terrorists who carried their attacks sometimes to the Republic and more often to England; the turmoil of changing ideas in the Irish Catholic Church—all these were part of the O'Rourkes' experience of life. Some of them had stayed in Ireland and some had left, some preferred the older ways and some the new, and all in their different ways had had their successes, their disappointments, their faith, and their occasional despairs.

It was an experience of the Ireland that those who love cannot leave for long, and that those who leave cannot return to for long; and a view of the twentieth century from a land where many of the ways of the nineteenth, eighteenth, seventeenth, and even earlier centuries are still practiced, and new ways must stand the test of comparison with the old before they are accepted, however popular they may be in other parts of the world.

Our only introduction to Charlie and Una was a letter they had received from William and the postcard from Joe, neither of which could have given them more than the vaguest idea of when we would arrive. As William had told us, "There's no need to let them know when you're coming; just drop in when you're in the neighborhood." So we had set off from Dublin at a little after nine in the morning, to drive across the whole width of Ireland, from the Irish Sea on the east to the edge of the Atlantic in the west, a journey of almost 150 miles, part of it on broad two-lane highways with an occasional passing lane or four-lane stretch, and the rest on narrow roads confined between stone walls or high, flowering hedgerows.

Often there was barely room for our little Fiat, and beyond every curve or hill we could expect to meet an approaching Morris or Mercedes, bicyclist or pedestrian, donkey cart or herd of cows, hay wagon or broad lorry brushing the twigs off the hedgerows on both sides of the road—or any other surprise that might be waiting for us. It was a beautiful ride, through rolling hills and green pastures with here and there the ivy-covered ruin of an ancient castle tower on the skyline; along the short main streets of the neat villages the plastered houses were dull gray in the poorer districts, bright with pastel colors in the more prosperous. The journey took us just three and a half hours, as we had been told it would.

We stopped for lunch at Ballysodare, the last fork in the road before Ballycarrick, according to the map, though we knew by then that some of the loveliest roads in Ireland were not shown on the maps supplied for tourists. From there on it was a matter of asking the way, with no street name or number to offer, just the name O'Rourke. No one in the inn at Ballysodare knew the family, but they told us how to get to Ballycarrick, and assured us that once we got there we'd have no trouble. And they were right.

It was a country lunch, not at all what we wanted and far too much of it, but, as is the way with country inns in Ireland, we were given no choice. Thick soup, roast lamb, several pounds of soggy boiled potatoes, and mounds of carrots, parsnips, and peas were placed before us, and the rather tubby young girl who brought them without waiting for our order seemed surprised and rather hurt when we turned down the "sweet." A light snack would have served us better, for we knew what lavish hospitality would meet us in Ballycarrick, and what herculean feats of eating were expected of a visitor to an Irish home. That was why we wanted to arrive after lunch rather than before, since "lunch" is the Irish countryman's main meal of the day; besides, after our long drive we needed some refreshment before tackling the sometimes difficult task of asking directions.

It was a bit of a blow to find Una just starting to prepare another lunch as we arrived, with tempting rashers of lean country bacon, fried eggs collected from the hens that same morning, boiled new potatoes with a fresh young shine on them, white bread and brown bread baked in sister Rita's oven, and Rita's own homemade currant cake and black-currant jam, not to mention a pastry-topped fruit pie that nobody quite had room for.

We protested that we had already eaten; Charlie apologized that he had no whiskey to offer us, since he and Una belong to that large and growing army of Irishmen who drink no spirits, and wear little lapel pins with the insignia of the Sacred Heart to let new acquaintances know that no drinks need be offered, and thereby spare all concerned the embarrassment of a kind offer refused. They weren't wearing their pins at home, of course, but William had warned us that they were "Pioneers," as the nondrinkers are called, so we weren't surprised. Charlie felt badly because he always keeps a bottle handy in Dublin for visitors, but had forgotten to bring it with him. We protested that three o'clock in the afternoon was too early for whiskey; but no time was too early for tea, so we sat at the table with them and shared tea from their big pewter pot, and dug into the homemade bread and jam and cake as though we hadn't had a thing to eat all day.

Cathal and Liam sat side by side between their parents, dividing their attention among the food, the visitors, and a little fishnet at the end of a pole that they had taken down to the sea that morning without much luck, and wanted to use again in a little lake not far from the house. The food quickly disappeared from their plates, and three-year-old Liam stood up on his stool and started to wriggle out of his father's grasp.

"Now then, Liam," said Charlie in his soft, gentle voice, "you're not going to be a naughty boy, are you? Mr. Smith's come all the way from America to see us, and if you're not careful he'll take you back there with him. He has a big black bag and he's going to put you in it and tie it up tight and lock you in the back of his car so you'll never get out!"

Liam giggled with delight at this interesting prospect, and said something inscrutable about fetching his sweater, waving his arms about to illustrate the point. His voice was as soft as his father's, and as he squirmed on his stool it was hard to tell whether he was trying to get down to the floor or climb into his father's lap. It was all a game, and his father didn't seem to care which way it would end. His mother pretended to be shocked at such behavior. "Now why must you boys always show off in front of visitors?" she asked, knowing quite well the answer.

Cathal got down and fetched sweaters and boots, and there was some discussion in the same quiet undertones of what the children should wear and how far they might go by themselves. Liam had a little difficulty getting his arms into the sleeves of his cardigan, and wrestled with the buttons, but Cathal helped him while their mother watched, and suddenly they were gone, trailing their fishnet behind them. It was big enough to catch minnows, but if they caught any they'd have to throw them back because they didn't have a bucket to bring them home in. And anyhow, they weren't going to go near the water until their father could come with them.

Charlie wanted to show us the sights of Ballycarrick, the church and the graveyard, the school where his father had taught, the pastures and the view of the hills and the sea, and how to find his sister Rita's house. Una stayed behind with the children; she was packing to return to Dublin the following day, and had to tidy the house and leave it ready for Charlie's brother Christy, who would be coming from Roscommon with his wife and four children to take their place in Toberpatrick. Charlie took his own car, an Irish Ford no bigger than our Fiat, so that he could leave us at Rita's and come home; we followed at a respectful distance. There was no traffic on the roads, but they were narrow and high-walled, with a succession of blind turns that might be hiding cattle or children to bring us to a sudden stop.

A gusty rain gave us an excuse for going by the graveyard without stopping, which suited Betty and me well enough, though we promised to return someday to see the graves of the schoolmaster and his widow. The church doors were closed against the wind, but unlocked; Charlie pushed them open and ushered us in with the air of a man coming home after a long absence, happy to be back and not surprised at the changes that had been made.

It was a big church for such a small parish, with high vaulted roof and enough pews for three hundred people or more; the population in this valley, as in all Ireland, had been much greater when the church was built 150 years ago. The altar was simple and uncluttered, with only candles, a microphone, a small gold crucifix, and a stand for the priest's Mass book on its white cloth, as required by the new rules of the Second Vatican Council. It had been moved forward so that the priest could stand behind it, facing the congregation as he read the prayers of the Mass aloud, in English at some Masses and in Gaelic at others, instead of mumbling inaudible Latin with his face to the far wall and his back to the congregation as he used to do in the old days.

Not everyone in Ireland liked these new ways, which had been introduced in the decade since Vatican II, the great ecumenical council that reformed the liturgy and the practices of the Catholic Church. But Charlie did. "This is really just the same as it always was," he said contentedly as we walked down the aisle between the two rows of pews. "Nothing very much has changed, except they've put in central heating now and moved some of the things around. Up there under the roof those beams used to be open, and you could see the slates between them; now they've put in that wooden ceiling between the beams to keep the warmth in." The ceiling was sky blue, and the walls off white, with the faintest glow of pink in them, except for one solid brick wall that rose up to the high windows behind the altar; it was a bright, cheerful church.

"And you see," Charlie went on, "they've taken away the marble rail that used to run across here, and some of the figures, and moved the tabernacle from the altar to a stand of its own behind. The altar used to be up against that brick wall with the figures on it, the four apostles; now the only figures left are the saints in those stained-glass windows, and these three here in front that were my mother's favorites, Saint Anthony, the Sacred Heart, and the Blessed Virgin. I think they may have moved them; seems to me I remember Saint Anthony on the right, and now he's on the left, but I'm not sure. Mother always used to visit all three, she'd go from one to another and say a prayer and put in an offering and then go on to the next. She wasn't taking any chances," he added with a sudden grin. "Here now, perhaps we'd better light a candle for her while we're here."

He stepped quickly to a vigil-light stand, shaped like an Irish harp of polished bronze, which stood opposite the white marble statue of the Blessed Virgin where Charlie remembered Saint Anthony once had stood. A teen-age girl with a troubled look on her rain-freshened face had been busily engaged in dropping coins in the box and lighting one candle after another while we were talking, but there were still two candles left, and Charlie picked up one of them, dropped in his coin, and lighted the candle from one that the girl had just set in place.

Then he turned and led us back to the church door, remarking on the way that the stairs to the choir had been moved and were now closed in behind a door. "That will be because of the central heating," he said. "Oh! it used to be damp and drafty in here on a cold day. What we really need now is a porch outside the front door, so you don't get hit in the face by rain the moment you open it. We'll have to get some more money from our American friends, though, before we can do it."

"American friends?" I asked. "Did they pay for the rest of it?"

"They did, they did, a great deal of it. There'd never be enough money here in Ballycarrick for all this. But the people who left here and went to America, you know, or whose fathers or mothers did—they remember the old church and help us out when we need it. They've been wonderful to us."

We hurried out through the shower to our cars, and Charlie led us a mile or so along the main road and then down a narrow lane toward the sea, till we came to the school where his father had taught so many years ago. Here the change was much greater—the drafty old two-room building with its narrow windows and open fireplaces that Charlie remembered had disappeared, and in its place was a rambling one-story stucco building in the modern style, with floor-to-ceiling windows in some of the rooms, electricity, running water, central heating, and a small concrete-paved yard to play in.

Charlie pointed to the meadowland around the school, green fields dotted with purple heather and yellow gorse, bordered by hedgerows of wild roses, lavender-headed thistles, raspberry canes with little pink blossoms, and the hawthorn that brightens the world with masses of close-packed delicate white petals for week after week in May and June. "It's a shame," he said, "that they can't make better playing fields out of that."

"But it's so beautiful," I said. "What a lovely place for a child to grow up in!"

"Ah, that it is," he said, lifting his eyes to the green hills that framed the valley, and the rushing sea below them, shining blue now as the shower passed and a wide blue hole in the sky let the sunshine in. "We had a happy time. But you can't stay here, you know. There's no opportunity for the youngsters as they grow up, and we have to go away to Dublin or abroad to make a living."

"I suppose that's true," I said, "but if you made a lot of opportunities here by putting factories and shops and power plants in the valley, what would happen to the beauty of it?"

"Ah! that's the dilemma," he answered, and we got back into the cars to go to Rita's house.

2.

The
Two Who
Stayed

Charlie's sister Rita was the youngest of the O'Rourke girls, born two years before Patrick, the youngest brother, who had gone to America at twenty and seemed likely to stay there for the rest of his life. Rita had tried London for a year, but she was an exception to Charlie's rule; she had preferred to come back to Ballycarrick and live in this rolling meadowland where she had been brought up, with the big sky overhead and the stone walls bordering the fields down to the windy sea a few hundred yards away. Her husband, Tom Brennan, was a dairy farmer with fifty acres and almost as many black cows, more than enough to support a small family in Irish comfort.

Their home was a lime-white cottage of stone and stucco with walls nearly two feet thick, and the thatch on the roof came down so low over the doorway that Charlie had to stoop a little to get in. The wooden ceiling inside went up under the thatch almost to the ridgepole, and the effect was of spacious, high-vaulted rooms. One end of the house was extended by a barn facing the road, and behind were sheds to shelter the cows in winter; a waist-high wall surrounded the lawn in front.

The house was a mile or so from Toberpatrick, where Rita was born, and a scant two miles in the other direction from the farm of her sister Mary, the eldest of the O'Rourkes, who was the other exception to Charlie's rule. The two girls, first and next to last of the family, were the only ones who still lived in Ballycarrick.

No one knew how long Rita's house had stood there; two or three hundred years, she guessed, for Tom had been born in it and his father and grandfather before him; she didn't know how many generations before that. She led us through the little front hall into her kitchen, always the main room of an Irish farmhouse, with its big enameled cast-iron stove warm from the turf burning in it. Her two children, ages about nine and ten, were perched on a cushioned settee under the window on one side, facing an oak table with four chairs.

It was a cozy room, comfortingly dry and warm after the wet gusts outdoors; a passing sunbeam came through the yellow linen curtains and showed everything spick and span as though the room had been hand polished in preparation for our arrival.

"What a lovely room," Betty exclaimed as she sat down in the rocker beside the stove.

"Oh, you must be joking!" said Rita with a sudden blush, studying us with big round brown eyes as though eager to see what kind of people these American visitors might be.

Rita was shorter than her brothers, yet still a tall girl, with her copper-brown hair cut short and curled in tiny ringlets all around her fascinatingly mobile, expressive face. She had a light, girlish bounce to her step that made her seem almost to be dancing as she moved about the room, filling an electric teakettle and plugging it in to boil. We knew we were going to be eating again.

The children were introduced, Belinda the older and Padraig the younger, and they quietly held out their hands to be shaken.

Then, as if he'd been watching from the fields for our arrival, Tom Brennan burst in, a short and stocky man with twinkling blue eyes and a short stubble of beard on his square, wind-reddened face. He bobbed around the room in his loose gray jacket and Wellington boots, shaking hands and talking in the same friendly, rapid style the O'Rourkes used, and took his seat on the corner of the settee next to the children.

"I wonder, now, would you like a little whiskey?" asked Rita with a bit of a wink and a sidelong glance at Charlie, who was sitting with us at the table. It was still only mid-afternoon, and it was hardly a habit of ours to drink neat Irish whiskey between two large doses of Irish afternoon tea, but there was no way to avoid it. I was grateful to Charlie for leaving his bottle in Dublin, but it was clear that Rita wanted to make up for her brother's inhospitable carelessness, and it would have offended them both if we had refused.

"Well, if you're having one I'd be glad to keep you company," I suggested weakly, but it was not to be. Tom sprang from his setttee, bounced out of the room with the same lively step as Rita's, and reappeared in an instant with a freshly opened bottle from which Rita poured two healthy portions in slender bar glasses, leaving Betty's a little less full than mine out of deference to her sex and her protest that she only wanted a tiny bit.

At home in America I think we would have been self-conscious if we'd been asked to drink our host's best whiskey by ourselves, while host and hostess and brother and children looked on, watching to be sure we enjoyed it. But this seemed to be part of the quality of Irish hospitality: a giving that is more than just sharing, and brings a special pleasure to both host and guest. Perhaps it was just a convention of politeness, but we had encountered it before and were to do so many times again in Ireland. I couldn't help thinking that there must have been occasions in the lives of many Irish families when the last drop in the bottle—whether whiskey or milk—had been given to guests and strangers, for such a kindly tradition to be so widely observed.

It was a good whiskey, too, and it put all of us at our ease. We started talking about the farm, and I asked Tom if his cows were responsible for the marvelous butter we had been eating everywhere we went in Ireland, for Irish butter is by far the best in the world, as every experienced traveler knows. Rita responded with a sparkle in her eye and that friendly O'Rourke laughter I was coming to know so well, and suddenly we were being treated to a demonstration of the art of churning butter. Rita had been doing it that morning, by hand in a wooden churn, an experience she had thought to escape forever when electricity came to the valley and the local creamery opened for business. But there had been a power failure at the creamery, or something had gone wrong with the machines, and the Brennans had been left with ten gallons of milk that would have spoiled if they hadn't churned it themselves.

Tom and little Padraig dashed out of the room to find the wooden churn and bring it in for us to see, Tom explaining that it was of a new design, and "after fifty years the Irish have finally invented something useful." Indeed, it didn't look at all like the stand-up churns of American Colonial days so popular in New England antique shops; it was more like a barrel organ made of scrubbed white oak, with a four-bladed paddle wheel inside, slotted to let the milk pass through, and a hand crank outside.

It held about nine or ten gallons, Tom said, although it didn't look that big; from that much whole milk they made four pounds of butter, and could have made more if they had skimmed the milk first, as the creamery does, and used thick cream.

Padraig started turning the crank, to show how it worked the paddle wheel, and Tom remarked, "It doesn't turn as easy as that when there's milk in it, you know, especially when the butter starts forming." Rita had done the churning, and I asked her how long it had taken; only half an hour, she said lightly, but I didn't believe that. It looked like a backbreaking job.

Then Rita brought out the butter she had made, all in one four-pound slab on a wooden board; its surface twirled and peaked like a confection in a bakery window. It was bright yellow, and of that soft and creamy consistency that only the Irish can achieve, neither icebox hard nor melted and runny, but chilly and soft as a spring morning's mist. We had some of it for tea not a moment later.

Belinda ran out at a word from her mother to fetch the damask tablecloth, and with one expert flip laid it on the table, corners neatly matched and the creases where it had been ironed forming a cross exactly in the middle. Then out came the best cups and saucers, delicate bone china with gilded rims, and the white bread and brown bread, currant cake and black-currant jam, and the fresh-churned butter in the place of honor in the middle. Whether it was the whiskey or the fresh gusty air and the raindrops we'd come through on the way from the church, or just the magic of an Irish kitchen and Irish conversation, somehow we ate it all again with as much appetite as before.

In the well-fed warmth of that friendly kitchen I thought again of Charlie's comment that there was no way to make a living in rural Ireland, and I wondered if Tom would agree. If there wasn't enough opportunity to go around in this valley, how did people decide who was to go and who was to stay?

Tom thought about that for a minute, running his hand through his graying hair, and then answered, "Well, you see, if a farm is only big enough to support one family, then one of the brothers stays to work the farm and the others go off."

"You mean the oldest son gets the inheritance and the others have to go out in the world to make their fortunes?"

"It isn't always the oldest son who stays, sometimes it's the older boys who have the drive and go off looking for something better, and leave a younger one at home to do the drudgery."

"Who do you think has the best of it," I asked, "the ones who go or the ones who stay?"

He grinned at that, and leaned forward on the settee. "Oh, I've had some hard times, to be sure, and there have been plenty of days when I wished I'd gone off like some of the others, and earned all the money and had fine cars and a big home and all that. But with them it's all rushing and pushing and beating each other, on the go every minute. I've seen them come home from America and go on the same way here. They've no time to rest or enjoy it, they want to be out of bed at six in the morning in wintertime even, when the sun itself doesn't get up until half-nine or ten."

"Well, then," I said, "in your case, I think on the whole you're glad you stayed."

"Ah, yes, I am," he said, "taking one thing with another."

It wasn't a complete answer, but it was all I could get just then. Tom had something else he wanted to talk about. Did we know an American lady named Quinn, he asked, an artist who had bought a roofless ruin on the shore nearby some dozen years ago, and restored the two ends of the stone house but left the middle in ruins. "Now why would she ever do a thing like that?"

We didn't know the answer, and we didn't know Mrs. Quinn; nothing would do but that we see the place ourselves. Betty demurred, but I went with Tom as he hustled me out the door and climbed into the car beside me to show the way. We went back toward the main road a few hundred yards, and then after a sudden turn we were heading toward the sea, past another farmhouse and an open, windswept meadow until Tom cried, "There it is!" I didn't see what he was pointing to because my eye had been caught by one of those little warning signs that appear on European roads, with stylized pictures instead of words. This was a warning no words could have conveyed so vividly: a steep triangular cliff with a car falling off it, and underneath a wavy line to indicate the sea. I braked in alarm, and there in front of me was indeed the end of the road, with not even a fringe of weeds to mark the spot where it ceased to exist, and a vertical drop of ten feet or so to the splashing waves below.

Ahead was a long finger of Sligo Bay, white breakers sweeping in from the gray Atlantic, and on the other side another hump of a hill like the hump on Ox Mountain behind us, but this one rising directly from the sea, with a neat little knob on top like the handle on the domed lid of a stew pot. This was Knocknarea, which Charlie had already pointed out to me from his own front door, and described how he and Una and the children had climbed it one day; the knob on top was a heap of stones like a gigantic cairn, which legend said had been put there by ancient Gaels in pre-Christian days to mark the grave of their Queen Maeve. "But I don't know whether that's true," Charlie had said in his laughing way. "I suppose they must have been put there for some reason, and it might as well be that as another."

We were in a desolate spot, a road leading nowhere, with only the wind and the waves beyond, and a gap in the stone wall beside the car closed by a tall iron gate painted white. "Who would have put that gate there and what for?" I asked Tom.

"That's what we've come to see," he said. "Come on, now!" We got out of the car and he led the way along the rocks outside a low seawall that stretched back from the road along the top of the little cliff. "There was always a path here that led down to the shore," he went on, "and she had to leave us that, but she built this wall to keep us out. People here don't like that, you know; we're used to coming and going on each other's land, and the walls are just to keep the cattle from straying. But she won't have anyone walking in her fields, oh! no, and she put up these wall to keep us out. No matter, she's away now, and we can go in."

We had arrived at a point where the ground outside the wall rose a little higher, and the outcropping head of a boulder made an easy step up to the top. Tom was over the wall in an instant, and I followed easily; it was as if Mrs. Quinn or

24

her builder had left this informal entrance as a compromise with the customs of the neighborhood, defeating the wall's stated purpose.

We strode through long wet grass where no cattle grazed, a level lawn unmowed for six summer weeks, and I saw at last the peculiar structure that had caught Tom's fancy. It was a square tower of gray weathered stone, three stories high with a pyramid roof of slate, the upper parts of new cut stones with fresh mortar showing where the restoration had been done. Beside it stretched a ruined roofless wall, draped with the vines and moss and lichens that adorn a thousand other such ruins in every part of the Irish countryside. The wall reached perhaps twenty or thirty yards from the tower to a handsome stone house, square like the tower but only two stories high, broad enough for three or four large rooms on each floor, and showing the same outlandish combination of ancient rough-cut, weather-pitted stones and new smooth gray limestone with neatly mortared edges. It looked like a pop-art creation; illogical, yet with a striking, almost melodramatic beauty, challenging the spectator to make out of it what sense he could.

Tom led me around the square tower to the back, more sheltered from the sea wind, where four roofless halls were open to the sky between the tower and the house. Most of the back wall had fallen, so the halls were like three-sided bays, with thistles and gorse growing where the floor used to be, and in one sheltered corner a rhododendron bush, in another a young beech tree. Here the ancient walls had been restored only enough to keep them from falling down; old stones had been used for the repairs, and betrayed their presence by the wet shine on their faces where the moss and lichens had been rubbed off, or a bit of new mortar showing where it was carelessly applied, or an irregularity of shape or size where the replacement stones didn't exactly fit the holes left by the originals.

It was a contrived piece of stage scenery, part genuine ruin, part artist's design; and from the sparse remains of old outbuildings three sheltered garden nooks had been created, with more rhododendrons, roses and lilies, neat graveled paths, and a garden bench whose seat was an ancient gravestone. Clearly Mrs. Quinn, whoever she was, had built a place of beauty; it must have cost a fortune, and after fifteen years of work was still unfinished. Or was it? Perhaps she meant to do no more, or perhaps this was only the beginning of a grander plan.

"She comes here for two weeks every year, all by herself, and then goes away again," said Tom. "She's all over us when there's something she wants, but once she has it, we might as well not be alive." There was a field of two or three acres between the house and the lane, where summer vacationers in gypsy caravans, the big barrel-shaped covered wagons that are rented each year by people who know enough about horses to care for them, used to park within sight of the sea, and turn the horses loose to graze in the pasture. Mrs. Quinn hadn't liked that, Tom said. "She badgered the man who owned the field until he sold it to her, and built that wall around it so the caravans can't come here anymore."

The building looked as if it had been designed originally as a kind of barracks, with lookout tower and armory, and a boathouse on the shore, but no pretensions to architectural elegance or the glamour with which its present owner had invested it. A wrought-iron spiral staircase now led up to the second floor of the tower, where a heavy oak door was double locked and barred; from there a narrow catwalk led along the front wall through the four roofless bays to the house.

"Now why do you suppose she wants to walk this way in the open air from one end of the place to the other?" asked Tom. "An old lady living alone with no one to help her if she falls?"

There was only a single iron handrail to hold on to on the open side of the walk, which was of narrow planks with gaps between them that easily could catch a feminine heel. It was raining again, and I opened my umbrella, which had been useless before because of the gusty winds, but in the shelter of the walls it offered some protection. "You'll never get through here with that," said Tom as we came to the gap in the first of the three cross-walls, but by lifting it high I was just able to get it over the top of the wall.

The door at the other end was locked and barred too, and we made our way back to the spiral staircase, this time with my umbrella folded, and climbed down to make a circuit of the ground floor of the house, peering through uncurtained windows. An elaborate French-style bathroom, with modern fixtures and a bidet; a vast living room with a modern open staircase, all treads with no risers, seeming to hang in mid-air; polished oak floor but no furniture in evidence; double bedroom with the beds made up but no sign of ever being used; closet doors open to disclose nothing but emptiness; that was all we could see. "There's another bedroom upstairs and a studio where she does her drawing or painting or whatever it is," said Tom, and I didn't ask him how he knew.

It was an exciting place, yet sad in its loneliness, and like Tom I was baffled by it. "What was this place before it fell down?" I asked. "What happened to it?"

" 'Twas a customs house," said Tom. "The English built it, in the old days."

"A customs house? Way out here?" There was no port, no harbor, no sign that there ever had been any ships landing on this remote headland.

"Ah, this was a great place for smuggling in the old days. Silk and wine and brandy and all that, from Spain and France, you know. They'd go out from here to catch the ships before they landed. The harbor's in there, by Sligo Town, and this was the outer defense for it. They had big guns here, once."

"So it was knocked down in a war, I suppose. When would that have been?"

"The IRA burned it down," said Tom, with a hint of pride. "The old master had something to do with it, they say, but that was before my time."

"The old master?"

"The schoolmaster, Rita's father. In the Black and Tan war.

That was long before she was born, and she won't talk about it, but one of her brothers told me years ago. I don't know what he did—was he in the IRA or just one of the crowd. Everybody around here was against the Tans then, you know."

That was all Tom would tell me about it, and when we got back to the house and I asked Rita, she only laughed and changed the subject. "Daddy was always mad for politics," she said. "He had politics on the brain, I suppose. It never meant anything to me. People here can get very thick about politics, if you say the thing the wrong way. I never go near it."

It was a long time before I understood why Rita was so shy about her father's politics, and the other O'Rourkes were much the same. But it was part of their lives, and in the end it wasn't difficult to put the story together from the bits and pieces that came out as they talked. The first clue came that same evening, talking to Rita's older sister, Mary.

When Tom and I got back to his house it was already past six, and we wanted to be on our way to the hotel in Sligo, but Mary was expecting us, and we didn't want to disappoint her. Rita would come with us to show us the way; we offered to bring her home afterward, but she wouldn't hear of it.

"I'll get a bike from Mary and come home across the fields," she said. "It's much shorter that way, and you'll be on the main road to Sligo at Mary's house. If you come back here on these little lanes you'll never find your way out again!"

Mary was another who preferred the old ways, as Father William had explained when he told us some of the family history before we left Connecticut. She had left Toberpatrick as a child to live with Aunt Annie and Uncle Pat, who worked the farm that belonged to her mother's family, and had a little tobacco and sweets shop at one end of the old farmhouse that stood by the main road. A few years later Joe, the eldest brother, had joined her there, and Joe might have inherited the farm if he'd wanted to, but he didn't. He'd gone off to join the Garda Síochána, the national police force, while Mary stayed on and was courted by Michael Finnegan, who had some neighboring acres of his own.

When they were married the young couple lived with the old ones and took care of them until they died, and then Mary inherited the farm and it was joined to the Finnegan acres to make quite a substantial property. They raised seven children, the nearest any of the O'Rourkes came to the fifteen in the family they had grown up in. Mary's oldest was twenty-seven, a surveyor who worked in Ballina, twenty miles away in County Mayo. Her second son was in the army, one daughter had a job in Dublin and another in Longford, and one boy was a local truckdriver. Only the two youngest boys were still in school, and neither of them was in evidence when we arrived.

It was a handsome new house of cream stucco, a hundred yards up the road from the old place, which had been abandoned a few years before when the roof fell in, and still stood there, a melancholy ruin half hidden now by vines and brambles. The new house was set back from the road behind a low stucco wall, with a neat plot of lawn and a border of lupins, foxgloves, and yellow snapdragons on either side of the front door. It looked more like a suburban villa than a farmhouse, for it was on the edge of the property and far removed from the animals' sheds and the barn.

As we went in I asked Rita to warn her sister that we had already had two teas that afternoon and didn't want another, and she gave an understanding chuckle and passed the message on. Mary led us into the little front parlor, with its needlepoint chairs and white wooden mantelpiece, though Rita protested that the kitchen would be more comfortable. What would we have instead of tea? I suggested beer, and Betty nodded agreement, and in a moment four bottles of Harp appeared, the popular Irish lager.

Mary was eighteen years older than Rita, but you wouldn't have known it to look at them. Mary was a little shorter, and rounder in both face and figure; Rita's face was truly heart-shaped. They both had the same sparkle in their eyes, and the same vivacious way of talking, ideas and observations pouring out in a torrent.

It was a little while before we got around to the subject of old Master O'Rourke's activities in the IRA, and then Mary turned it aside much as Rita had done.

"We've always been Republicans in our family," she said, "and my father was for the Republic in the hard times of the twenties, I know, before I was born. But he was never a soldier. The old IRA, they were real soldiers, not like these murderers today in the North. They're a different lot entirely. It's so sad, isn't it, all that killing, and it's all for nothing. I think it will be going on for years and years, it will never get any better, you know."

The troubles of the North—the six counties of Northern Ireland still under British rule—filled the Irish newspapers that summer of 1975, as they had done for seven years before and were to go on doing for years after, but it was not a subject the Irish people we had met in the twenty-six-county Republic wanted to talk about. They were watching in helpless agony as people in the North killed one another without bringing their political struggles any closer to solution. It seemed like a continuation of the centuries-old fight between British and Irish, which had ended in the rest of the country fifty years before. But it wasn't the same, we were told; there were half a dozen armed gangs now, killing whoever chanced to be in their way, none of them with any hope of winning control or any idea of how to govern if they had it.

Mary didn't mind talking about it; she'd seen some of it with her own eyes. The road past her house came from the border less than fifty miles away, and beyond that from Enniskillen and Dungannon and Belfast, not so far away as Dublin, though no one in County Sligo would think of going to Belfast unless he wanted to be part of the fight. But there were many in the northern counties who went to Dublin rather than Belfast for their shopping, or streamed across the border for holidays in

County Sligo, to get away from the street fighting, riots, explosions, and assassinations.

"I feel so sorry for them, you know," Mary said, "they're like refugees. There's hardly a one of them that hasn't lost a father or a son in the shooting, or hasn't a brother in prison. I don't care which side they're on, it's a terrible thing that's happening. But there's nothing we can do to help. We want to give something for these poor souls, but you never know who you're giving it to. They come around with their collection boxes and then they use the money to buy guns or spend it on themselves. You feel you're only making things worse unless you give it to somebody you know.

"There was that young man who died in prison in England last year, Michael Gaughan; he died on a hunger strike, and they brought him back here to bury in Ballina. He was a murderer, and they'd caught him and put him in prison and he killed himself there with his hunger strike. I don't know what they do that for. He'd never been in Ballina since he was born, because he'd lived in England all his life, but his family came from there. His father didn't want him brought home to be buried, he was that ashamed, poor man, that his son had been in the IRA and done the bombings in England. But they didn't pay any attention to his father, they brought him back and buried him in Ballina as if he was a hero to his people.

"That's a great center for the IRA, Ballina, they're all there and they had a parade and it was all for the publicity of it; his family and their friends weren't there at all. And with all those gangsters and their guns running around the town, they closed all the pubs and most of the shops closed too, so they wouldn't be stealing things and getting drunk and starting more fights. Oh, it was a terrible day, and all just for the lying publicity of it!"

Mary told us about the annual "marching season" in the northern counties, when the shootings were at their worst, beginning with the march of the Orangemen on July 12, and ending with the march of the Apprentice Boys of Derry on August 12—both celebrating battles nearly three hundred years ago in which the Protestant King William defeated the Catholic King James. The battles were part of the mythology of the Protestants' claim to rule over the Catholics in the six counties, and on the anniversaries the Protestants marched with drums and banners to show their strength and militancy, their obdurate determination to keep the Catholic minority subdued. "If you want to see what it's all about," said Mary, "you can go to Belfast on the Twelfth. But I wouldn't advise it."

"I'd go if I knew someone there I could rely on," I said, "to show me where to go and what to do without getting in trouble."

"Well, I know a man who could do that for you," said Mary. "Did you ever hear of Patrick Riddell? He's a writing man like yourself."

"Patrick Riddell? Yes, I do—in fact I met him once in New York. I'd forgotten he was in Belfast." I had a sudden vision of that engagingly opinionated columnist for the *Belfast Sunday News,* author of *The Irish—Are They Real?,* whose sad face and courtly manner had reminded me of Don Quixote, the Knight of the Sorrowful Countenance. "Do you know him?" I asked.

"He came by here a few years ago when he was writing his book," said Mary. "Oh, he was a kind man, he was. Saw me waiting for the bus to go into Sligo, when he was coming by in that little old car of his, and he stopped and picked me up, and took me all the way into town, though he wasn't intending to go there, I think. You'd want to see him if you go to Belfast, he'll tell you all kinds of things. I never knew such a man for talking. But I wouldn't go there myself, all the bombs and shooting, 'tis worse than we ever had here."

"You may be right," I said, "but just the same I think I'll go, if Patrick will show me around. There's still a week till the Twelfth, time to call him and see if he'll be there."

3.

Knock
and
Glendalough

T*he* next morning, after I had telephoned Patrick Riddell from the hotel and made a date to meet him on the Twelfth, Betty and I headed south toward the village of Knock in County Mayo, which holds a place in Irish life not unlike that of Lourdes in France or Fatima in Portugal. For at Knock on August 21, 1879, an apparition of the Blessed Virgin Mary was seen by fifteen villagers, and ever since, the fame of that event has attracted pilgrims. The little parish church has become Ireland's National Shrine of Our Lady, and it was here that we were to find Father Peter O'Rourke, eleventh of the schoolmaster's children, on duty for a month to serve the spiritual needs of the pilgrims.

It wasn't going to be easy; from the moment we arrived we were lost in a crowd of several thousand people, hundreds of them priests, and there didn't seem to be any office or information booth where we could inquire. We walked up the little town's one main street, lined on both sides with booths selling souvenirs, religious and otherwise, and tea shops crowded with visitors, until we found our way to the church, with its statues and its racks of literature by the door, its collection boxes for the pilgrims to drop in their pennies. We found a schedule of Masses and a leaflet of instructions for pilgrims, but nothing to show where the priests on the staff might be found. So we read the leaflet, and learned the story of Knock.

The apparition was first seen at about eight o'clock on a summer evening, according to the leaflet, while it was still broad daylight in this northern latitude but raining hard. The Blessed Virgin Mary had appeared on the hillside outside the south gable of the church, before the astonished gaze of fifteen parishioners, young and old. With Mary were her husband, Saint Joseph, and the disciple Saint John, the Evangelist who described himself in his Gospel as "the one whom Jesus loved," and who at Jesus' command from the cross took his place as Mary's son, and cared for her thenceforward in his home.

For two hours the villagers had watched the apparition, reciting the rosary in the pouring rain as the light of the summer evening slowly faded until the "visitors" could no longer be seen. One of the watchers, an old lady named Brigid Trench, approached the gable and tried to kiss the Blessed Virgin's feet, but found them impalpable. Yet the ground beneath the feet was dry under Brigid's hands, though Brigid and the other villagers were drenched with the rain.

The Blessed Virgin had her hands and eyes raised toward heaven, as though in prayer, but it is not recorded that the villagers heard her speak. They described her afterward as wearing a large white cloak fastened at the neck, and a brilliant crown. Saint Joseph was at her right, head bowed and turned slightly toward her; Saint John, at her left, was in a bishop's robes, book in hand and right hand raised, as he is so often represented in statues and pictures. A little to the right of the group appeared an altar with a cross and the figure of a lamb.

The news spread through the village that night, and by

morning people were coming from miles around to see the spot and wonder at it, and ask one another what the vision could mean. The witnesses all gave much the same description of what they had seen, and when a formal commission of inquiry examined them six weeks later on the authority of the archbishop of Tuam, the Most Reverend Dr. John McHale, the commission found that the "testimony of all taken as a whole was trustworthy and satisfactory."

As the weeks passed, thousands of pilgrims began to arrive at Knock from all over Ireland, England, continental Europe, and the United States. Many invalids brought to the spot found themselves cured; three were archbishops, two from Australia and one from Canada, and all three presented paintings to the new shrine in thanksgiving. In due course the shrine received formal recognition from the Vatican, and special honors and privileges have been accorded to it by each of the three recent Popes, Piux XII, John XXIII, and Paul VI.

In subsequent years the number of pilgrims increased until in 1975 there were well over three-quarters of a million. Yet the Knock Shrine was not as well known throughout the world as France's Grotto of Lourdes, where the Blessed Virgin appeared before the child Bernadette Soubirous in 1858 to give her blessing to the then-new doctrine of the Immaculate Conception; nor as Portugal's Shrine of Our Lady of Fatima, where in 1913 three children were commanded by the Blessed Virgin to pray for the conversion of Russia. There was no spoken message of theological or political importance at Knock; only the simplicity of a visual demonstration of Catholic faith. And it occurred in a land then ruled by a Protestant government with a Protestant Established Church, where Catholics were tolerated only grudgingly by their rulers, no longer persecuted and oppressed as they had been in earlier times but not yet free to govern their own affairs.

Nevertheless, three-quarters of a million pilgrims a year is a lot of people for a little village with only one narrow main street, especially on Sundays, holy days, and the anniversary of the apparition, now celebrated as the Feast of Our Lady of Knock. It was a Thursday when we arrived, which was a big day too, because every Thursday there was a special sacrament of anointing the sick after the Gospel at each of the five Masses of the day. We did not know it yet, but Father Peter, whom we had come to see, was to be the celebrant at the three o'clock Mass.

Over the years some provision had been made for the pilgrims, but Knock was still far from the magnificence of better-known shrines. The old parish church, not as large as the one we had seen at Ballycarrick, was still in use, the chief addition to it being a glass enclosure outside the south gate to protect life-size statues of Our Lady and her companions as they were described by the fifteen witnesses to the apparition. A vast new church, with room for as many pilgrims as America's Shrine of the Immaculate Conception in Washington, was under construction, but wouldn't be ready until the following summer.

In the center of a paved courtyard sloping southward from the church was another glass enclosure, of octagonal design, known to the priests who used it as "our bandstand." It sheltered an altar large enough for eight priests to stand together, and had a cluster of loudspeakers on the roof pointing in every direction. Here the priests and the Blessed Sacrament were protected from the rain, and the wind could not blow into the microphones and drown the voices of the celebrant and lector as they read the prayers and lessons of the Mass. Around the enclosure on all sides were rows of wooden pews, with an iron railing around the front pews on the west side to mark the section reserved for the sick, the aged, and the infirm. On busy days the overflow congregation would stand in the parking lot beyond the fence, and the cars and buses would park in the even larger lot beyond the new church that was being built.

Across the street was the new Confessional Chapel, where teams of priests were on duty in relays all day every day to hear from the pilgrims about the sins they could not bring themselves to confess to their parish priests at home, and the feelings of guilt or exaltation, despair or hope, that led them to make this pilgrimage and seek the special intercession of Our Lady at Knock. Next to it was Saint Mary's Hostel, a kind of inn operated by nuns, where the priests lived and took their meals, and lunches and teas were served to hundreds of pilgrims every day.

We asked for Father Peter at the hostel after lunch, and one of the nuns went into the priests' refectory and interrupted him as he was finishing his coffee. He was indeed the tallest of the O'Rourkes, as we had been told, a towering man with gentle eyes in a handsome chiseled face, and a lean, athletic figure. He had a way of looking at you that made you feel as tall as he.

He led us upstairs to a wide sitting room, with a fire laid at one end but not lighted, and an aged nun working at a sewing machine by the window.

"This is Sister Gabrielle," he said, "whose fingers never stop working. Don't let us disturb you, Sister. We're only going to sit here and chat quietly for a few moments, and you can go on with your work if you please."

Sister Gabrielle would not allow that; she rose to her feet and gathered yards of blue linen from the machine, first inviting us to put a match to the fire and be more comfortable. There was no need for that, we told her, and she slipped quietly from the room.

Peter talked of his work at the shrine and inquired after his brother William in America, and we told him of our visit to Toberpatrick. It was a respite for him from the endless confessions, free time he was allowed before he was to celebrate the Mass.

"It's a new experience for me, listening to the pilgrims who come here," he said. "Not at all what you would hear in a home parish, where you know everybody, or they think you do, and there is a certain shyness, a reticence, in spite of the privacy of the confession. I've been hearing things I've never heard from a penitent before, and it isn't always easy to know what to say to them. It's made me more realistic, I think, about the Church, and what it can do for people."

"What kind of things?"

"They're burdened with such feelings of guilt, when they've done nothing to deserve it. They have such confused ideas about sex, and it's their own parish priests who have so often caused the confusion. The women have more children already than they can care for, and not the strength to have more, but they've been taught they must give themselves to their husbands, it's a sin not to, and they must do nothing to prevent another child, that would be a sin too. They cannot see that having too many children can also be a sin, for it can mean harming themselves, and their other children, and their husbands. Yet, if I tell them that, they can see no way out, and it is more than they can bear."

"What do you do?"

"You try to help them understand their own problem, reassure them that they have the power to choose. You give them absolution where their own priest sometimes would not do it. You help them see that when it is not a sin in their own conscience they need not confess it, even though there might be others who would call it a sin. The laws of the Church are not so inflexible as some people, even some priests and schoolteachers, try to make them."

Contraception was still technically against the laws of both the state and church in Ireland, Peter explained, but the ban was no longer enforced by either. In 1974 an Irish court had found it unconstitutional, and after a long debate the Dáil had defeated a substitute law, the prime minister himself voting against his own cabinet's proposal. There the matter rested; the law was not enforced and could not be, although some people chose to obey it and some priests still preached that it should be obeyed. Father Peter was not one of them.

These were common problems; far more difficult was the plight of the young men who confessed that they had joined the IRA, and found out too late what they were in for. They were idealists who thought they'd be fighting a noble and heroic war against the Protestant persecutors of the North, and discovered instead that they were in a tiny band of outlaws hated and feared by the very people they were supposed to be protecting, and that their "war" consisted of murdering defenseless civilians on the streets and in their homes, killing people at random by leaving bombs in pubs and hotels and cars abandoned on the street, setting booby traps and land mines that would be criminal enough if they only killed the soldiers and police for whom they were intended, but that often went off at the wrong time and killed others instead.

Peter told us of a disillusioned teen-ager who had come to him in the Confessional Chapel of the shrine with just such a story, not only repentant but horrified at what he had been trapped into, and afraid for his life.

"The boy had no way of getting out of the box he was in," Peter said. "If he broke away from the IRA, or even let drop a hint that he wanted to, he would be shot, there was no doubt of that. What should he do? What could he do?"

"What did you tell him?" I asked.

"Well, I counseled him. I reminded him that getting himself shot wouldn't solve anything, for this too would do harm, to his family and friends as well as himself, and that wrong wouldn't make up for the other. I suggested emigration, but that could be difficult for him, and might involve some wrong to others and not save him. I think in such cases emigration is probably the only way, but it can be a terrible thing, and even a danger to his parents, unless they go with him.

"There is no practical answer, it is a dilemma he must live with and resolve in his own conscience. So I gave him absolution and sent him away to think out what he may find best and how to do the least harm to others."

It seemed an inadequate answer, but we didn't know of any better one. We had heard a similar story before, from a

Passionist father who had a quite saintly style of devotion to his faith, a kind of euphoria that shone in his eyes and sounded in his voice.

His name was Father Martin, and we had met him on our first visit to Glendalough, that most famous of Ireland's ancient monastic ruins, set in the loveliest of all the lovely glens in Ireland. Two small lakes lie in a narrow cleft between steep-sided mountains, their slopes showing golden green in the sunshine and darker where they are striped by the shadow of passing clouds; a bright torrent of water tumbles down in a narrow white stream at one end, a slanting waterfall lying against bare black rock, to keep the lakes full; and on the slopes are every variety of cover from moss on the shining rock to grass and ferns in the shallow soil, and great forests of pine, fir, oak, birch, and holly trees where their roots find deeper footing.

To this quiet spot Saint Kevin had come about the year 520, according to legend, and lived as a hermit in a curious rectangular hole in the face of a stone cliff thirty feet above the waters of the upper lake. His sanctity attracted many disciples, and he was obliged to give up his inaccessible retreat and build himself first a hut, then a chapel, then a church. In time he became the founder of Ireland's first great monastic city and center of learning, to which came scholars from all the known world, and from which missionaries carried Irish Christian teaching for more than six centuries to the barbarian lands of continental Europe, where the fall of the Roman Empire had produced what historians call the Dark Ages. This was the period of Ireland's greatest glory, when it was known as the Island of Saints and Scholars, and the missionary traditions were begun that Father Peter O'Rourke and his brother Matt followed in Nigeria.

To this spot also Father Martin had come as a boy in his teens, and fallen in love with it; now at forty-four he was still coming whenever he could, often pedaling his bicycle the thirty-odd miles from his monastery in Dublin to be near the saint who had for so long been his inspiration. When we found him he was squatting on the wharf at the edge of the lake, holding the bow of a little boat with an electric-powered motor that could carry a half dozen tourists or pilgrims across the water to look at "Saint Kevin's Bed," the hole in the rock where the holy man had lived.

Father Martin was a short, wiry man, with the pointed nose and agile legs of a leprechaun, though his face was clear and tanned and young with not a wrinkle except for his smiles. He helped us into the little boat with the air of one who owned it—three English teen-age girls, two small Irish boys, a black priest from Uganda, Betty and me, and the skipper of the craft—and then he climbed in too.

"Is it safe?" asked Betty when the overloaded boat rocked from side to side, splashing water into our laps as it headed across the wind-whipped lake.

"What does it matter, you're safe in God's hands," said Father Martin. "This is holy water here, you can get out and walk on it if you like. Don't be afraid!"

We didn't know what to make of that; was he teasing, or was there some serious meaning in that mellow, laughing voice? Father Martin was exulting, serene, as though only his faith were real, and the world around him an illusion.

"Drink the holy water," he commanded, and dipping his hand into the lake beside the boat he scooped up a mouthful and bent down to sip it, splashing his face as it spilled. He wiped his lips and grinned. "It's the most delicious water in the world," he said, "the true water of heaven. Why don't you drink some?" And we did, following his example, and found it delicious water indeed, cold as a mountain spring and with a faint smoky taste of the bog, like Irish whiskey.

Father Martin and his Ugandan companion started singing together, the happy, exuberant singing of small boys let out of school on a fine summer day. They sang psalms and Mass prayers in Latin, they intoned Gregorian chants, they sang the new hymns of the Folk Mass in English—"Whatever you do to the least of My brothers, that you do unto Me"—and the black priest sang a hymn in the Ugandan tongue, and then translated it for us; it was the same theme of brotherly love. He was a happy man, a seminarian whose examinations for the priesthood had just been completed, a man now a priest in all but the formal ordination ceremony, which would take place in Uganda, where he was to return the next day. An occasion for celebration; part explanation, perhaps, of the pair's euphoria; yet there was more to it than that.

We reached the far side of the lake, directly under Saint Kevin's Bed, which wasn't at all where the tour guide had pointed when we had heard him lecturing to a busload of tourists besides the road, but as Father Martin said, "It's no use listening to those fancy liars, they'll tell you anything they have a mind to if they think you'll enjoy it. Half the legends about Saint Kevin are lies like that, or maybe the whole of them for all I know, for nobody wrote any down until he was nearly five hundred years dead, and then whoever it was could have made them all up. But there is truth in them too, if you've a mind to look for it.

"Now I'll tell you what I believe about Saint Kevin," he went on, in half-serious, half-joking tones, more like a barstool raconteur than a priest setting out on a homily. "He was tempted by the beautiful Kathleen—ah, what a terrible thing for a man to be tempted by a woman!" And he gazed into the eyes of Betty and the three English girls to set them laughing. "They tell all kinds of stories about how he treated her, and all of them make him sound like an unpleasant sort of a person; some say he beat her with nettles, and some say he pushed her off the cliff to her death, and some say she was so horrified at her own sin for trying to tempt such a holy man—or so angry when she found she couldn't stop him from becoming a monk— that she turned around and dove off the cliff and swam away."

"Swam away?" I asked. "After diving from that high cliff onto those rocks?"

"Ah, she was a great swimmer," said Father Martin. "Won the quarter-mile in the All-Ireland finals that year!"

Father Martin grinned at his own invention; in the usual version the spurned temptress drowned, and Saint Kevin was so stricken with remorse that he blessed the lake and asked God to see that no one else ever drowned in it. Tradition had it that no one had ever drowned there from that day to this, and the fringes of the lake were thick with No Swimming and No Boating signs, and life preservers hung from a hundred trees in case some unbelieving visitor might put Saint Kevin's blessing to the test.

"Tell me, Father," I asked, "why did people in those days think it was a saintly thing to spend seven years alone in a hole in a cliff?"

"I still think it's a saintly thing," he shot back. "Don't ask me for reasons—why, what's reason good for? You have to put reason in a box and nail the lid on hard and toss the box into the water if you want to know the truth, for it's only by faith that the truth can be known. God doesn't ask you for reasons, or give you reason for what He does; God acts by his own will, and you have to learn of it by prayer."

On shore after the boat ride, Father Martin told us why he had chosen to become a priest, and the story had something in it of Saint Kevin, and something of the problems Father Peter was wrestling with at Knock. Father Martin had his Kathleen who pestered him for years to marry her, while he studied and worked at secular jobs and listened to advice pro and con, but the moment of decision came during a conversation with a young man in the IRA. Like the boy who had gone to Father Peter, he was seeking a way out, and his friend Martin had urged him to start by going to confession. In those days the IRA was under a formal ban of excommunication, but that could not apply to a man who repented and was willing to leave the forbidden organization, if he could find a way to do so.

As Martin waited, the boy came out of the confessional haggard and shaken, his eyes black and lifeless like unlighted coals. He blurted out, "The priest won't listen to me—he said, 'You murderer, get out of the box!'"

The "box" was the confessional box, in the sense the priest had used the word, but it suited as well as Father Peter's metaphor to describe the prison he was in. This boy's box was even more hopeless, for he was cut off from the help of the Church, and unable to escape from the way of life he found himself in.

"I wanted to do something for that boy, to help him," Father Martin said, "but as it was there was nothing I could do. I decided in that moment that if I was ever to be of help to men such as he I would have to become a saint." It was a serious statement of a realizable goal that Father Martin had set for himself, one that I had never heard anyone else bold enough to make.

When I mentioned this story to Father Peter, in the upper room at Saint Mary's Hostel in Knock, he smiled sadly. "In a certain sense he is right, of course," he said. "But we do what we can. That was a long time ago, and the Church has changed since then. But there are still many of the old priests who haven't heard of the changes, or can't accept them."

He looked at his watch, and it was time to go back to the "bandstand" and prepare for the three o'clock Mass. We followed Peter down the stairs, and waited while he found his umbrella, wondering if it might rain and drive us into the shelter of the little church, or if the crowd would be so great we'd have no choice but to stay outdoors. And so it was; the church wouldn't have held a quarter of the throng, but the weather held, and only a moment's light sprinkle freshened our faces as we knelt on the hard wooden benches.

Seven priests in white vestments followed Father Peter in his green and gold as they moved in procession from the church across the sloping courtyard to the glass-enclosed altar, and we marveled at such an impressive staff; but they were visitors, parish priests from all corners of Ireland and England who had come with their bands of pilgrims.

They took their places beside tall Father Peter at the altar, reciting the consecration prayers in unison; the eight different accents gave a choral richness to the words, and Father Peter's Irish tenor was no longer soft as moss, as it had been in the nun's sitting room, but bold and firm and strong. The altar in its octagonal enclosure was raised high above the courtyard, reached by a flight of six steps, so that all the worshipers could see above one another's heads, and the eight priests looked out through the eight glass sides to all the corners of the earth.

After the Gospel they emerged, again in procession, carrying glass bowls with cotton soaked in sacramental oil, and walked to the railed-in area to the west of the altar, where the aged, sick, and infirm were waiting to receive their anointing. Earlier, nuns had moved through the crowd seeking out pilgrims who might need this special blessing, and helping them to find their places, so the enclosure was quite full. Each was blessed by name, and anointed on the forehead and both outstretched palms, and as the priests passed among them others in the congregation rose from their pews and moved forward, overcoming whatever hesitation had held them back before, to receive the same blessing. Then they returned to the altar, and Father Peter led the whole congregation in the prayers for the sick, thousands of voices together offering encouragement and the reassurance of a shared faith to those who were living in pain or facing the prospect of death.

After the Mass came Benediction, that ancient ritual of song and praise, part in English and part in Latin, which was so refreshing in the old days because of the English, and is still today because of the Latin. A choir and organist had been recruited from among the pilgrims, and the music came over the loudspeakers from some seemingly invisible source.

Betty and I followed along as best we could, stumbling over words we hadn't heard or said since Vatican II. Betty mentioned this to Father Peter afterward, as we had tea together in the refectory, and he said only, "I had the same trouble, for it's eight years since I did the Benediction last," and left unanswered our unspoken question—why had this pleasant custom so fallen out of use, to be revived again at Knock? Perhaps the answer was in the lameness of our knees when we had risen at last from those hard wooden kneeling benches; only at such a shrine or celebration could so much be endured.

4.

The
Policeman

Joseph O'Rourke of Killimor, County Clare, the police
sergeant of nearby Ennis, had been referred to by his brother
William in Connecticut as "the patriarch of the family," not
because of his age, which was barely fifty, but because he was
the eldest son, and had carried the responsibility of seeing that
their widowed mother was properly cared for, and the younger
brothers and sisters adequately helped in their education and
other needs. It was Joe who had inherited the house called
Toberpatrick, and paid the rates and fitted it up with electricity
and indoor plumbing for the use of his brothers and sisters and
their families as well as his own; Rita, because she lived nearest
to it, kept the key.

Joe didn't look much like a patriarch when he opened his
door to us the day after our visit to Knock; he looked much
like his brother Charlie, a little taller and heavier, a little
rounder of face, and with a little gray in his brush-cut hair, but
not much; the same bright eyes, the same broad smile and ready

laugh. And like Charlie he was about to sit down to lunch—
we'd made the same mistake again, and this time we should
have known better.

We hadn't really noticed the time, and hadn't expected to
find Joe's house so easily. We'd brought a box lunch in the car,
and eaten it picnic style in a green pasture with a view of the
distant limestone hills of the Burren, lingering over it but not
long enough. In Killimor I had walked into the first pub we
came to and asked the bartender if he knew Joe O'Rourke.

"You mean the sergeant?" he'd said, and leading me out the
door had pointed to the house, not fifty yards away. "It's that
gray one with the black door where the hill slopes down, just
beyond the railing there. Not the house behind the railing, but
the one beyond it." It was a two-story house like his father's,
of stuccoed brick, but in the center of town instead of the
windswept hilltop at Toberpatrick, and on one of the main
tourist routes that lead from Ennis across the Burren to Lis-
doonvarna, Ballyvaughan, and the Cliffs of Moher.

We were tired when we climbed the steep stone steps to Joe's
house, and our heads were full of the experiences of the past
two days. It was a relief to sink down in the comfortable arm-
chairs beside the hearth in the big front room, as the children
were brought forth one by one to meet us. There was Owen, the
eldest, ten going on eleven, a wiry little version of his father,
all arms and legs with slender shoulders; two roly-poly girls,
Maura and Therese; and little Joseph. Their mother was
Breda, a young woman about Rita's age, with blue eyes behind
big round glasses, a round face like Mary's, and bright golden
hair as curly as Rita's but hanging more loosely and a little
longer. Breda was as vivacious as Rita, and as soft-spoken as
Charlie and Joe, with the competent, confident air of a woman
who might as well be running an office as a family of four
children.

We talked about William in America, whom Charlie had
called Liam, and Rita had called Willie, and Joe now called
Bill, and we talked about Toberpatrick and Knock and the

48

O'Rourkes we had met and the things we had seen. Joe laughed at my description of mad Mrs. Quinn's romantic ruin and said he did, indeed, know her, and she wasn't mad at all; he knew the architect who had designed the restoration for her, and would introduce us to him if we stayed long enough or came back.

Suddenly we were talking about coming back in the fall, for this quick trip was too brief, and too crowded with impressions that cried out for further attention. Betty asked Breda about rents, and the prices of blankets and crockery, and we found that Breda and Joe were house hunting too, for the children were growing too big for the Killimor house, and Joe hoped he could find a place nearer Ennis.

"That's why we've let this place get into such a mess," he said, waving his arm vaguely at the four corners of a room that was no more untidy than one might expect of a combination dining room, sitting room, kitchen, and hall, where four children played their games, watched their television, and on occasion did their lessons for school. "It's only rented and we're soon to move out, and you don't take the same care as if it were your own."

Joe hadn't found what he wanted yet, but there were some houses for rent that he wanted us to see—new thatched cottages, traditional in design but all modern inside, with central heating and electric cookers and vinyl tile floors, which the Irish Tourist Board had built for tourists to rent by the week, with comfort and convenience in colorful surroundings, but at commensurate expense. They were beautiful places, but they were not, alas, for us.

No matter, said Joe, we would surely find what we wanted, and he drove us on in his pale blue Volkswagen to see the bare crags of the Burren and the corkscrew road that twists down the mountainside to Ballyvaughan. From the top of the mountain we could see the Aran Islands far out in the Atlantic, and on each side the empty rock, a wasteland in pastel shades of blue and pink and green, where nothing grows but tiny wild flowers that find minute patches of soil in the cracks between the rocks. Once we saw a horse standing riderless on the very summit, silhouetted against the sky as if posing for a Maxfield Parrish picture; how he got there so far above any edible pasture or why he should have climbed the bare rock we couldn't imagine.

"You know what Cromwell is supposed to have said about the Burren?" Joe remarked. "He called it a useless place, without water enough to drown a man, trees enough to hang a man, or ground enough to bury a man. Or so they say," he added, with the same quick skepticism as his brother Charlie and Father Martin. "Whether Cromwell ever said that or not I don't know, but it's true he didn't stay here long." No place for invading soldiers, to be sure; but a good place for defenders to hide in, and a place of rare beauty.

As we drove along, Joe chatted about his work, the orderly routine of a provincial police station with no crime to speak of and none of the troubles of the North or the IRA hotbeds near the border. "Police work in a small town, it's not really hard, you know," he said. "The thing is, you can never see an end product in a policeman's work. You can do wonderful work, you can prevent crime just by being there, being seen. You make people happy; you could be making them sad, as the case may be, if you're too severe on them. But it's not like a man making something in a factory or where you can see your pupils, like my father. You cannot be judging yourself on your work. Preventing crime and things like that, in a policeman's life—it's different."

"You mean it's a dull life preventing things, because nothing ever happens?"

"Yes, and you don't know if you're a good policeman or a bad one. And then it's hard to get ahead, you know. I was qualified for sergeant years before they gave it to me, and I've tried to get transferred to a bigger town, but there's been no chance. Well, I'm happy enough as it is; looking back from this position now, I'm happy enough, but I'd say I'd like to have more teaching; I'd have made a good go.

"You see, I missed out on a secondary education, which I have regretted in a big way. My father was a good teacher, a dedicated teacher, but he couldn't really afford to send me to a secondary school, with all the kids that were coming on behind. That wasn't paid for by the government then, as it is now, not at all. Charlie didn't go to a secondary, nor did Mick, none of us did until the three priests. Even Chris, now, he joined the Garda a long time after I did, because he's so much younger, but he didn't have any secondary education either."

Joe always enjoyed the change when he was assigned to border duty, which both he and Chris had done several times in recent years. But it was still routine work, checking cars as they went back and forth between Donegal and Derry. The border was hundreds of miles long, though it enclosed an area no larger than Connecticut, and was half surrounded by the sea; the land frontier followed the twists and turns of old county lines, cutting through farms and sometimes farmhouses, and was crossed by innumerable little roads and footpaths, so it was quite impossible to prevent anyone from going secretly from one side to the other.

From time to time the British army would put up barricades at some of the minor crossing points, or blow holes in the roads to make them impassable, but the local people would take down the barricades or fill in the holes as soon as the soldiers went away. There would never be enough troops to guard a frontier shaped like pieces of a jigsaw puzzle, but checkpoints had to be maintained on some of the major roads if only as a matter of form.

"We were there and when the cars came through we stopped them and searched for whatever they were carrying," Joe said. "The boot was opened and searched, and if the bonnet needed to be lifted we did that. If he was clean his name was noted and his number, and he passed through. He was on record, there was nothing on him. And if he came across ten times during the day it was the same routine."

"Ten times?"

"They would, yes, because in that village where we were, they brought the cows across in the morning and again in the evening; it was a rural area, and people had fields on both sides. If a farmer leaves his house in the morning to fodder his cattle, and has some of them in stables on the other side of the border line, he is going to walk across the line to fodder them, and nobody is going to stop him.

"Now the Bogside in Derry, that was different. When I was in Donegal we used to go into it, it was just across the river. But it was a nonpolice area, the IRA Provisionals were running it, and when you went through this gate into the terrace you took a chance. Once inside, they'd say, 'We want your car for a job tonight, you're not getting it and you go without it.' Well, if you objected they might just put two bullets through the tires and say, 'Now do you give it or don't you?' "

"They'd hijack a police car that way?"

"Not a police car, no; we didn't go there in police cars, nor in uniform either. Ten years ago you could do that, a Garda in uniform could travel anywhere in the North, once you passed the checkpoint and showed your ID card you were cleared straightaway and you were gone. But you don't do that now, you'd be a marked man. No, I went with some lads that were there, that were known to them. One of them, his girl friend was there; he used to go in and out all the time, he was known. The other way I wouldn't have chanced it, even though I probably would have had no reason to worry either, but then you don't know. What looks like an innocent, empty street could be the greatest flashpoint for danger. You'd be in it and caught in a cross fire before you know it."

I didn't like the sound of that, and wondered if I'd be running the same risk in Belfast on the Twelfth.

"I don't know about Belfast," said Joe, "I've never been

there. But you'll be all right with Mr. Riddell, I would think, especially while they're all marching. It's after the marching stops that there's trouble, unless they march right through one of the flashpoints, as they did a couple of years ago. I don't think they'll do that this year, but Mr. Riddell will know where you can go.

"There's another man you ought to know if you're going to Belfast," he went on. "The lad I was telling you about that I knew in Donegal. His name's Gerry Byrne, and he runs a taxi now in Belfast. He drives the government fellows when they go there investigating these things, and he'll know where he can take you without being apprehensive at all. When we get back to the house I'll find his address for you, and if you tell him you know me he'll take care of you. You won't be taking your own car up there anyhow, will you?"

"Not if it's going to get taken from me by the IRA."

"It would, it would. You hired that car in Dublin, didn't you? I can tell by the number tag. If you leave a car with a Dublin number tag on the street anywhere in the North it will be gone by the time you come back. They steal them and put bombs in them, you know, that's what they call car bombs. Blow up the car and the building it's standing next to."

I didn't doubt that Joe knew what he was talking about, nor did Betty. She thought I was mad even to think of going to Belfast, and flatly refused to come with me. "That's all right," I said. "You probably wouldn't enjoy it, but I'm not coming all the way to Ireland and then going home without seeing the main event. I'll be all right with a couple of experienced guides like Pat Riddell and Gerry Byrne."

"Sure he will," said Joe, quick to steer the subject into safer channels. "Safer in Gerry's car than driving yourself around the roads of Ireland. Have you noticed that the Irish are terrible bad drivers?"

We hadn't thought of that; our preoccupation had been with the narrow roads, the blind curves and hills, and remembering to keep our tiny car on the left side of the road. But we had to admit that driving in Ireland was a more sporting enterprise and called for a lot more skill and care than at home. We'd been warned to stay off the roads at night for a good hour after the pubs' closing time at eleven-thirty, and Joe confirmed that that was the most dangerous hour.

Nobody ever seemed to leave a pub before closing time in Ireland, and we'd often heard that in country pubs people didn't leave even then, but went into a back room and continued drinking while the local constabulary turned a blind eye. We didn't ask Joe about that, though, because we didn't think it would happen in Ennis.

Breda added another comment on Irish drinking habits a little later, when we got back to the house for tea. "The men leave when the pubs close, and not a moment before, not even the young ones," she said firmly. "I knew that before I was married, when I used to go to the dances at the dancing hall in Ennis. The dance would be from ten till one, and all the girls would be there at ten o'clock sharp, lined up against the wall and waiting for the boys to come in. But not a one of them would arrive until the pubs closed, and then they would drift in toward midnight, and walk up and down in front of the line of girls, looking us over. They were half jarred or worse, the boys, all of them, and they wouldn't ask you to dance politely; they'd just grab you by the arm without saying anything, and point to the floor."

"Too drunk to say a word, some of them," Joe said. "They still do that, too, the young ones, and worse."

"Kick me in the shins or step on my toe instead of saying, 'Will you dance?'" Breda went on with a half-indignant chuckle. "Now why would I want to dance with a young man who'd do that!"

Somehow I couldn't imagine Joe, with his gentle, courteous ways, ever behaving in such a fashion, but from the reminiscent glint in his eye I judged that he might have done so thirty years ago, long before he'd met Breda. No wonder so many girls in Ireland don't marry boys of their own age, I thought; they look for men who've grown old enough to learn manners. It was something I wanted to find out more about.

We were about to leave when the outer door opened and I heard another voice, new to me yet with a familiar ring to it, calling, "Any O'Rourkes in here?" The children rushed to the door and Joe said, "It's Jimmy!"

In came another tall, lean O'Rourke, looking very like Father Peter but a few years older, preceded by his plump blond wife and three children. "Just passing by," said Jimmy, "on our way to Galway for the holidays, and since we hadn't seen you in two or three years we thought we'd drop in. I see you haven't found the place you want in Ennis yet, since you're still here."

"That's Jimmy," said Joe. "Never writes to say he's coming, and doesn't often come; but, Jimmy, it's good to see you." Then he introduced us, to Jimmy's evident surprise, and when I asked if he'd heard about us from William, as the others had, he answered, "William never writes to me—I hear from him Christmas and Easter, that's all." To which William replied, when I reported it to him later, "That's because Jimmy never writes to me, any more than he does to Joe."

There were seven children and six grownups in the room now, but chairs were found for them all, and Breda put the kettle on again and started setting the table for another tea. Hilary, Jimmy's eight-year-old, had a cast on her leg, the result of a playground accident the very last day of school, but there were no autographs on it because it was a new cast, replacement for the autographed one, which had broken. This time her mother had put a sock over the cast to protect it, and insisted that it be kept clean and white.

Patricia, the elder daughter, had been trying to make a list of all her cousins and aunts and uncles on both sides, and there were so many of them that it looked as though she'd never be finished. The youngest of Jimmy's children was some-where in the room playing with Owen, but by this time I'd lost track and wasn't sure which was which.

It was time for us to go, or we'd be there to the end like the half-jarred boys in the pub. Jimmy gave us his address in Cobh, where we promised to visit him in the fall, and by slow degrees, with many farewells and handshakings all around, we made our way to the door.

5.

The
Orangemen

On the Twelfth of July, I left Betty sightseeing in Dublin and took the eight-thirty train from Connolly Station to Belfast, a journey of two hours and a quarter when the train is on time. That Saturday morning it was only about fifteen minutes late, though it seemed to crawl most of the way after crossing the border, with unexplained stops that made me wonder if the tracks were being searched for booby traps. A land mine had exploded on the line two weeks before, just after a special train loaded with IRA supporters had passed, and I hoped that if any surprises were in store for this journey, they would be similarly inept. The train I was on didn't seem worth attacking; it was almost empty, for everyone in Dublin who cared about the Twelfth had already gone north to see the bonfires the night before.

To some people in Northern Ireland the Twelfth may seem a little like the Fourth of July in the United States, for it is a national holiday with parades and picnics and patriotic oratory, it commemorates a historic event, and it falls in July. But there the similarities end. The event that is celebrated—the victory of Protestant King William in the Battle of the Boyne, on July 12, 1690—was not the beginning of national independence but a stage in an unending struggle. It is remembered as a symbol of the great change that took place in that struggle after the wars of the Protestant Reformation, when the ancient fight between Irish natives and British invaders became a battle of the Catholic Irish against the Protestant British.

When the Irish finally won their independence 232 years after the Boyne, it did not extend to the six counties of the north, where the Protestant British were strongest. There the struggle has continued. A two-to-one majority in their tiny British province did not make the Protestants feel secure; they resorted to oppression, and the minority to rebellion, and the annual commemoration of the Boyne became an occasion for provoking each other to new fighting.

This was not an event that Patrick Riddell, my Belfast newspaper friend, ever took part in, but he was glad to act as guide for an American visitor. "There's only one problem," he had said when I telephoned him. "The marchers go right past the end of the street where we live, but we're on one side of the line of march and when you get off the train you'll be on the other."

"Don't they have places where you can cross?"

"Not while they're marching, and it takes them about three hours to go by. But no matter. There's a hotel next door to the station, the Europa. I'll go there before the march begins and have a cup of coffee while I'm waiting for you. Then we can watch as much of it as you want to, and they should all have passed our house in time for us to get there for lunch. I hope you won't mind walking, but there'll be no other way. It's only a mile or so."

To walk a mile is nothing in Ireland, and Patrick regarded the prospect with pleasure in spite of arthritis in his leg. When he visited New York he had walked from Times Square to City Hall without thinking it anything unusual, and declared New

York to be the finest city he'd ever seen. He was seventy years old, a retired civil servant who had been writing his free-swinging column in the *Belfast Sunday News* for ten years. He attacked both sides of Northern Ireland's anachronistic battles with a hot and balanced anger, but his peppery column was imaginative, well-informed, and witty. If such a man had not yet been assassinated by either side, it was because he knew how to take care of himself.

When the train reached Belfast I passed through customs without trouble, having brought nothing with me but an umbrella; even a camera might have attracted unfriendly suspicions. The inspector on the train had not asked for my passport; it was enough that I had a return ticket. In the station, twisted steel beams dangled from a large hole in the roof, and a crudely chalked notice on a blackboard announced: WE REGRET THAT THE PUBLIC TOILETS ARE CLOSED BECAUSE OF BOMB DAMAGE.

The Belfast Europa Hotel was, as Patrick had said, right next to the station. There was a chain-link fence around it with barred gates, and the only entrance was through a little wooden shack that looked like a foreman's hut for the construction work at the side of the building. This was the security post, where a courteous guard in uniform patted my sides from hips to armpits, glanced at my umbrella, and ushered me to the rear door with a mumbled word of politeness, as though he expected everyone to be accustomed to such things. One becomes accustomed to them very quickly in Belfast.

The hotel, like the train, was virtually empty. Patrick was sitting alone in the coffee shop, his back to a dividing partition so he could neither be seen through the window nor look out. His gray beard added distinction to his long tanned face, and his blue jeans belied his age and his dignity. He pressed me to join him in coffee, and we chatted awhile about Mary Finnegan and our friends in New York before he was ready to talk about the events I had come to see.

"Provocation, that's all it is," he said bitterly. "This damned Orange procession angers every civilized Ulsterman who wants his country to grow up." Patrick was a Protestant, a Church of Ireland man, but he was no longer a churchgoer and professed only dislike of all the perennially divided churches in Ireland. They were too political, he said, too irreconcilable where they should be forging Christian bonds between divided people.

"We're sick of Orange fanatics," he went on. "We're sick of their damned drums and banners, sick of their arrogance, their deliberate public taunting of our minority group. That's what this march is, believe me, it's deliberate taunting of the losers by the winners. It brings no honor to the name of decent Ulster Protestants. Don't judge us by the Twelfth procession, John."

He rose from the table. "Come on," he said, "let's take a look at it."

We walked out through the security shack, the guard greeting Patrick as an old friend but searching him just the same, as he searched me, in case we might have picked up guns in the hotel. Patrick had a permit for a gun, since he had been publicly threatened with assassination by some of the Protestant "paramilitary" leaders, but he wasn't carrying it today; it would have been too dangerous.

We walked across the empty street in front of the hotel under the empty bombed-out windows of the abandoned stores it faced, and down an empty side street past the Crown Bar and some buildings under construction, to Bedford Street, a block from City Hall. We saw nothing moving until we got there; all traffic was banned from the streets on either side of the line of march, taxis immobilized and bus service suspended.

The procession was coming from High Street, down Donegall Place and Donegall Square, and out along the Dublin Road and Lisburn Road to a field at Edenderry, outside the city, where the speeches would be made; for the three hours it took to pass, and the three hours it would take to pass again on the way back from the field, traffic could not move in downtown Belfast, and there was no way to cross from one side of the city to the other.

Patrick didn't expect any trouble, because the route of the procession led only through safe Protestant territory; there had been serious riots a few years before, he said, when "those lunatics" led their parade through the Catholic ghetto of Falls Road. "They were asking for trouble, and they got it," he said.

"Why were they allowed to do it?" I asked. "Aren't there laws and city permits for parades, somebody at City Hall to control the route they'd take?"

"They didn't dare," he said. "The Orangemen run City Hall, they run everything here, they do what they want and nothing can stop them. This year they may have learned some sense, but I doubt it."

And there were the Orangemen parading before us, armed not with guns, as far as we could see, but with fifes and drums, big bass drums carried by stalwart young men who swaggered from side to side and pounded with all their might, swinging first one arm and then the other, as though the drum were the enemy the drummer wanted to fight; and little snare drums hanging from the shoulders of grown men and small boys and sometimes girls, with their harsh high-pitched rattle as the marchers showed off the machine-gun rhythms they'd been practicing all year.

Behind each group of drummers came the huge banner of the Orange Lodge they represented, stretched between flag-poles carried by two men, each silken banner fringed with braided gold and bearing an almost life-size painting of King Billy on his white horse, or fat Queen Victoria on her throne, or on a smaller scale the burning walls of Derry under siege by James's troops, and the heroic Apprentice Boys at the gates. They are costly, those banners, glorious to the Orangemen and the watchers on the sidewalk, hideous to the eyes of Belfast Catholics.

Behind the banners came platoons of marching men, with orange shirts or orange sashes around their necks and hanging down across the breast, sashes passed on from father to son as the proudest heirloom of the family. Some were hatless, some wore bowler hats, but all plodded solemnly on, with six miles to walk before lunch and six more miles back home again, their vacant faces showing no expression except a kind of tired determination.

How many lodges were there? Patrick didn't know, but the newspapers said there were 100,000 marchers, some from England and America and some from as far away as Australia and New Zealand. At a guess there seemed no more than a hundred marchers to each lodge, and each exactly like the other, except for the paintings on the banners. The same drums, the same rhythms, the same songs played on the fifes; no floats, no baton twirling, no pretty girls in costume, no comedy to lighten the solemn mood.

"Is Saint Patrick's Day in New York anything like this?" asked Patrick.

"Not in the least," I said, and he seemed pleased.

The watching crowd stood two or three deep along the curb on each side; no need for barriers to restrain them, and plenty of room to walk behind, for along a six-mile line of march there were places enough for all who wanted them. Farther out, the parade would march through residential neighborhoods, where householders put folding chairs on their front lawns for friends and neighbors, and the local churches earned funds by renting chairs and selling teas, ices, and home-baked cakes. Here at the city center the watchers had to stand, with the same tired, expressionless faces as the marchers, and the children grew bored and restless.

"It's a dull thing to watch," said Patrick. "Have you seen enough?"

"In a minute," I replied. "First, tell me what brings these people here to see it. They don't seem to be enjoying it much. Is it because there's nothing else to do, nowhere they can go, because they're trapped by the marchers, no shops open, and

62

if they stay home and watch television all they'll see is the same thing they're watching here?"

"They're a mindless crowd," said Patrick. "These are slum people, for we've Protestant slums here as well as Catholic. Look around, you won't see anyone well dressed, or with an eye in his head of any learning. They're frightened people, and these marchers are their boys, out to put on a show of strength, so they come to watch, and show support."

"It's reassurance for them, then?"

"Aye, you could say that."

We walked up to Donegall Square, and over the heads of the crowd and the marchers Patrick pointed out City Hall and Linenhall Library, as though this were an ordinary sightseeing trip and nobody in our way. Then down Wellington Place, past an alley blocked by another chain-link fence, with two British soldiers in battle dress on guard at the gate, carrying automatic rifles. Patrick, a veteran of the Royal Marines, stopped to chat with them and ask if there'd been any trouble that day. No, all was calm, one of the soldiers said; he was a fresh-faced youngster who looked no more than twenty.

"I don't think they'll try anything today," he said, "there's too many of us about."

And indeed there were; around the corner on Fisherwick Place we came upon two more soldiers in a weapons carrier, their radio crackling with intermittent jargon to which they seemed to pay no attention. Patrick asked them how they liked being in Ireland.

"It's not a bad duty as long as nothing's going on," the older one said. "It's quiet today. But it can be tricky when we're out on patrol, especially at night. Snipers—they can be anywhere."

"Better than Africa, anyhow," said Patrick.

"Yes, but not so good as Berlin," said the boy. "That's where you've got it made. Good pay, bright lights, plenty to do, no fighting."

Patrick reflected rather sadly as we walked off that British troops were not as busy all over the world as they used to be, but the army was still a good career. And there was still a little action in Ireland, which some people thought was good for training, even if it wasn't accomplishing anything else.

Farther on, a single soldier stood in a doorway, his eyes roving over rooftops and broken windows where snipers might hide, his hand on his rifle. He looked pale, and gave only a brief acknowledgment to Patrick's greeting as we passed.

We made our way back to the hotel and had more coffee while Patrick telephoned his wife at home and was told that she was planning lunch for one-thirty, by which time the parade would have passed their road. "Do you mind the walk?" Patrick asked me again. "It's a mile and a half."

"Not if you can manage it on that game leg of yours," I said.

"It's nothing," said Patrick. "I'd walk ten times as far if it weren't bothering me a little."

The crowds did not disperse after the marchers passed; they simply milled around in the street now that they were no longer confined to the sidewalk. There was still no traffic to speak of; nobody wanted to go anywhere, they had brought their lunches or were buying them from tea shops and refreshment vans, to eat while they waited for the marchers to come back. The gutters were full of empty beer bottles and soft-drink cans, and ice-cream wrappers were blowing about in the street, but nobody seemed to mind. It was too soon to start cleaning up; the day wasn't over yet.

Patrick discouraged me from following the marchers to their field for the speeches; there was no way to get there except on foot, nothing worth listening to when I got there, and nobody else would be listening to it either. They'd be resting and drinking, and maybe having a little something to eat, and the speeches and resolutions they were to adopt would all be in the afternoon papers, even before the speeches were made and the resolutions unanimously voted.

So I had lunch with Patrick and his wife, Eileen, and we

talked of Irish politics and how Patrick had fallen in love with New York, and after that he introduced me by telephone to some of his friends, including Monsignor Ryan, the only churchman of either faith that he seemed to admire. Monsignor Ryan's Catholic church at one end of Patrick's road was balanced by the Protestant church at the other; Patrick attended neither, and professed to believe in neither, but he believed in Father Ryan as one of the wisest and most levelheaded men he knew. Over the telephone Father Ryan invited me to see him the following Saturday.

"Don't forget to ring him on Saturday morning to remind him," said Patrick, "for he's an old man of nearly eighty, and he'll forget all about it if you don't. And bring your wife next time, and come and have lunch with us again. She'll be perfectly safe."

6.

Prods
and
Taigs

I *had* to be out of Patrick's house and across Lisburn Road by four o'clock, when the marchers would be back, or I'd never make the last train back to Dublin, which was to leave at five-thirty. Patrick tried to telephone for a taxi, but none would come. I didn't mind, there was plenty of time to walk. On the way I picked up an evening paper, to find the morning's events described under the headline CAREFREE TWELFTH, in letters two inches high; no one had been killed so far, and it had been the quietest Twelfth in seven years.

Betty was a little dubious about Patrick's invitation, but when I got home safely and showed her the paper, she agreed to come. The next Saturday we took the same morning train, which was quite full this time, and when we reached Belfast and called Father Ryan, we were given an appointment for four o'clock. Too bad it wasn't earlier, but it couldn't be helped. And there was plenty of time for us to explore Belfast on a normal Saturday, without the excitement of the marching Orangemen.

Yet Belfast on a normal Saturday was not as different as we had expected. The same search at the security shack outside the Europa Hotel, when we went in to use the telephone; a woman in nurse's uniform searched Betty in a separate room while the expressionless guard I'd met before searched me. The same empty street, or nearly the same; the buses were running now, but not many of them, and a few private cars, all with their windows rolled up tight, though it was a warm day. No pedestrians near the hotel, which was fortunate, because we had left Betty's raincoat in the hotel coffee shop, and a few minutes later the waitress came out with it, saw us walking down the empty pavement a hundred yards away, and came running up. "They're as friendly here as in Dublin," Betty remarked with pleasure.

There was no one on Bedford Street, where the marchers had been the week before, but a line of cement-filled oil drums stood in the street outside the Arts Council building, protection against the "car bombs" that Joe O'Rourke had told us about. A successful car bomb was simply a stolen car with a time bomb locked inside it, parked in front of some building that a terrorist wanted to wreck. An anonymous call to the police would identify the car, the place, and when the bomb was to go off, in time for the building to be evacuated. No time would be allowed for towing the car to a safe place or breaking the lock to get the bomb out; only a few minutes' warning was ever given, and sometimes the bombs went off before the time was up.

Because of the cement-filled oil drums lining the curb, any terrorist would have to leave his car in the middle of the street, too far away from the building to cause it much damage with a small homemade bomb; the car would then draw attention by blocking the street, so the police might have time to tow it away and explode it safely before the bomb went off. The protective drums were a comforting sight.

We saw these drums outside all the major buildings in downtown Belfast. Around the main entrance to City Hall and the fashionable shops on Donegall Square they did double duty as flower planters, as though their function were merely decorative. They were an ugly reminder to us of why cars were so scarce in Belfast's streets; they couldn't be left unattended except in a guarded parking lot or other secure place.

There were some pedestrians on the main shopping streets, however, and the buses were running. Only the main streets were open; the narrower back streets were blocked with high steel fences, guarded by soldiers, and posted with black and yellow signs announcing the hours during which pedestrians would be allowed in, after being searched, and the routes that could be used by cars and trucks to reach the buildings being guarded. We walked hastily by, and passed a large department store whose locked doors were marked, PLEASE GO ROUND THE CORNER FOR ENTRANCE.

We obeyed, joined the queue at the one open door, and in due course were admitted to a security lobby, searched again for weapons, and allowed to enter the store. We were not surprised to find more merchandise there than customers, but it was a blow when Betty asked for the ladies' room and was told, "I'm sorry, madam, all the toilets are closed for security." Convenient places for planting bombs, apparently; we remembered the chalked notice at the railway station.

It was a grim morning, but the bright spot was our discovery of an empty taxi in the rank outside City Hall. Patrick had told us that taxis in Belfast never cruised for passengers, and when you called one by phone you had to order either a Catholic or a Protestant cab, depending on which part of the city you were going to. We didn't know which kind the cab in the rank was, but for this trip it didn't matter, because Patrick's home was in neutral territory, one of the few remaining mixed neighborhoods.

From Patrick's home it was only a short walk after lunch to Monsignor Ryan's, and once he started talking to us we forgot about such small problems. He was a man of great gentleness and dignity, his tall frame slightly stooped with age, his hair sparse and his face deeply lined, but his eyes still bright behind his gold-rimmed spectacles.

His church had been bombed twice, he said, and once a parishioner had been assassinated on the steps as he was coming out after Mass. The man had been one of the first to leave the church, as Monsignor Ryan was leaving the altar, and when the elderly priest reached the front door, not having heard the shot, his first knowledge of what had happened was when he found himself standing in a pool of blood. There had been Protestants shot in the same street, too; one of them, he said, a very fair-minded judge.

"Now why should they kill a fine man like that?" he asked sadly. Perhaps because he was so fair-minded, I thought, and had sent one of the murderers to jail. The elderly priest shook his head; it wasn't as simple as that.

"It's the young boys who do it," he said, "and it's hardest on the young. Think what it means to be growing up in this terrible atmosphere of hatred and fear. I see the little ones imitating their elders with the bombs and the guns, and it breaks my heart.

"And yet there are some graces and mercies that come with the horror too," he went on. "One of my parishioners, whose son had been killed before her eyes, told me she was visited by the mother of a Protestant boy who had been killed some time before, and she said to her, 'I know how you must feel holding the dead body of your son in your arms, for it's happened to me too, but I know you'd a million times rather have that than be the mother of the one who killed him!' "

The Protestant church at the other end of the road had sent him contributions to help repair his church after it was bombed, and both churches took up collections for the relief of each other's bereaved families. "This is not a quarrel between the churches," he said with an edge of bitterness in his gentle, contemplative voice, "we're all victims of it together.

"It's only two percent of the population on each side that is doing the killing. They're the illiterates who don't go to church

69

and don't know anything at all. But it's all very well to say they're only the illiterate two percent; if they're a hundred men with a hundred guns it doesn't matter what percent they are."

Where do they get their support, I wondered; why did the Catholics in Belfast and Derry support the IRA, instead of turning them over to the police?

"Because they're terrorized," Father Ryan said. "These gangs are terrorizing their own people. They knock on your door and demand money and if you don't give it to them they tell you to your face that they'll kill you, or they'll kill your mother or your children, or kidnap them or burn your house down—and they do that, too. Those collection boxes for the 'prisoners' families' aren't that at all; these men are lining their own pockets and living off the fat of the land. And all these bank robberies, who do you suppose is doing them and what are they doing with the money? There's a lot of the criminal element among them now."

So that was it—the protection racket of Chicago gangland days, but on a wider scale and under the color of patriotism and sometimes the name of God. No wonder the aging priest was angry.

But he hadn't lost his sense of humor, or his hope. "We'd be better off if we could laugh at them," he said. "I'd like to ask those Orangemen to do their marching around my church; they could march round and round and bang their drums all day and it wouldn't hurt us, we'd laugh at them until they went home."

It was almost five o'clock, and the last train for Dublin left at five-thirty. Could Father Ryan get us a taxi? We didn't want to spend the night in this frightened city, behind the security guards in that beleaguered hotel, already bombed twenty-seven times and expecting a twenty-eighth.

He was on the telephone at once. A taxi was promised, but Father Ryan wouldn't leave us at the door. He came with us out to the empty street and stood watching, waiting, shading his eyes with his hand against the afternoon sun. "It shouldn't take long, you know," he said. "They usually come quite quickly. But then you never know; sometimes they're held up, and never get here at all."

"Is there a bus?" I asked, and there was, but before we got to the bus stop it had sailed past, unheeding, and there wouldn't be another for half an hour. "I really think perhaps we'd better walk," I said.

"Run, you mean," said Betty. "Let's not wait here another minute."

"Perhaps you should," said Father Ryan. "Stay on this side of the road all the way down, and if the taxi does come, I'll describe what you look like, so he can catch up with you." Without much faith in this arrangement, we thanked him and hurried off.

It was downhill all the way, a gentle slope, but we now had only twenty minutes to go a mile and a half, and neither Betty nor I was in much shape for running, or even a fast walk. We didn't dare ask a passing motorist for a ride; what kind of murderer might he be, or why should he stop for a stranger when even taxis wouldn't do that? We tried to flag down an army lorry, but it was going the wrong way and didn't see us.

Then at last we came to University Road, where there were more buses, and caught one that carried us the last few blocks. We got to the station on time, with a minute or two to spare— and too exhausted to care that the train was, after all, going to be half an hour late.

Betty had had enough of Belfast after that, but I returned once more for a tour of the battle zone with Joe O'Rourke's friend Gerry Byrne. He was a dark-haired young man with a long nose and nervous eyes, which shifted constantly from side to side as if he felt it was a dangerous handicap to have only one pair. He let me know promptly that he was Catholic; in Northern Ireland you have to know who you're dealing with, he explained. I appreciated the courtesy, though it was hardly necessary—his loyalties were clear enough from his conversation.

The ride lasted four hours, and Gerry seem preoccupied with showing me wreckage—homes and shops leveled, streets littered with rubble, abandoned homes with bricked-up windows to prevent them from being used by snipers, homes with gaping holes in the roof, bombed and burned homes being slowly restored by their owners or tenants. He showed me barriers in the streets to stop hit-and-run bombers, barriers around pubs and shops to fend off car bombs, "dragon's teeth" of steel and concrete to bar streets from even the heaviest lorries, and the British army forts in Catholic neighborhoods, hidden behind palisades of corrugated steel sheets, surmounted by chain-link fencing and barbed wire.

They were peculiarly menacing, untidy and unmilitary-looking, these forts. There were no signs to identify the military units installed in them, no dress-uniformed sentries or MPs at the entrances to turn away visitors and salute those who arrived on military business. There was often no entrance to be seen by the passerby; you had to know how to find it.

Nothing could be seen of what went on inside these forts— no buildings, no vehicles, no weapons, no soldiers. Those in the neighborhood who kept a watch on such things would have a pretty good idea of the strength they concealed, but nothing more; these were secret forts, a constant reminder that the armed forces inside them were in hostile territory.

Ostensibly the army had been brought to Belfast to protect the Catholic population against Protestant attacks, and that was why the forts had been built in Catholic neighborhoods. But now this was IRA country, and there was war between the British army and the IRA. A truce of sorts had been proclaimed, but it didn't seem very effective; every few days there would be another "incident"—a bombing, an ambush, a land mine that killed two or three British soldiers. The IRA would call it retaliation and blame the British for provoking it, and the army would react with arrests and firefights, "responding to the level of violence" in accordance with the British government's stated policy.

"Things aren't so bad now as they were," Gerry said. "The truce has helped; it's stabilized the situation a bit. But it's only a truce between the IRA and the British army; there isn't any truce on the Protestant side. The UDA and the UVF and the UDR and all the rest of them, they're at it as much as ever. They're what they call paramilitaries, the Ulster Defense Association and Volunteer Force and Defense Reserve, but they're just armed civilians really. And mostly they kill other civilians, and so do the IRA."

"It really is a religious war then," I said, thinking of Monsignor Ryan's comments, "whether the churches take sides or not."

"Not at all," Gerry interrupted. "I say Protestant and Catholic because you have to have some kind of names for them, but that isn't what the fighting is about. It's their homes they're fighting for, and their jobs. The Prods have all the good jobs, and they don't want the Taigs to take them away."

"Taigs?" I asked in surprise. "Prods" was clear enough—short for Protestant, with a Gaelic accent turning the *t* into a *d*. But where did "Taigs" come from?

"It's just a word they use," said Gerry. "An old word the Prods use to show their contempt and hatred for us. Taig is an old Gaelic name, like Jack or Jim or Tim in English—I guess it means Tim, really. There's a character in one of Yeats's plays called Taig, and he was a fool, see, so the Prods think they're calling us fools when they call us Taigs. But it's older than that; it goes back to when the Protestant thing got started. The fighting is tribal, it's the old Protestant families against the old Catholic families, and they go on with it today even though the ones who are doing it don't care anything about religion at all, don't know what it means.

"When you look at the politics of it," he went on, "there isn't any better way you can describe the two sides. They're both so split up you can't tell who's who anymore. Some of the

Prods call themselves Unionists; they say they want to keep the union with Britain. But even some of the Unionists don't want to do that if it means sharing power with the Taigs, which is what Britain wants them to do. And then there's Prods that call themselves Loyalists, and talk about loyalty to the British crown, but they're not loyal when the Brits do something they don't like. They want the Brits to be loyal to them. On the Taig side, there's Nationalists and Republicans, who want us to be part of the Irish Republic, make Ireland a united nation. But a lot of Taigs are against that too, because the Prods would go right on fighting, and the Republic would be even less able to stop it than the Brits. So the names don't mean anything when it comes to the fighting, the names is just politics."

Our tour had begun at the bottom of Falls Road, where the Taigs come out of the comparative safety of their own neighborhood and mingle with the Prods on Divis Street, as they go to their jobs in shops and factories owned by Prods. Two hefty policemen in the black uniform of the Royal Ulster Constabulary were directing traffic in the morning rush hour.

"You'll see no more police in the Falls after we pass these two," said Gerry. "This is as close as they can come; it's the boundary, so to speak. They'll go in sometimes with an army patrol, but from here on it's mainly the IRA in control.

"Notice those old cabs," he went on, pointing to a line of ancient taxis, all painted black, at the curb waiting for fares. "You'll see more of them in the Falls. This is the end of the line for them; they have to turn here and go back. They're the buses the Taigs ride to come to work in, but they can't go further than this because they don't have police licenses. They're licensed by the IRA—owned by them, too. One of the big sources of IRA money here, along with the pubs and nightclubs they run, and the hijacking and bank robbings, and the money they get from the States."

"From the States?"

"Ah, they do. They've got a big committee there, to raise money for them. Have you not heard of it?"

"Sure I have, but I thought that was for prisoners' relief, and widows and orphans."

"There's some of it goes for that, I'd say, but a lot of it goes straight to the IRA. I don't know how much, of course; nobody knows that. But they wouldn't get far without it. These taxis, now, how much do they pay the IRA? Maybe ten quid a week on the average, and there's maybe a couple of hundred of them. You can't keep an army going on that."

The black taxis started, Gerry said, soon after the Belfast riots of 1969. A lot of city buses were bombed, burned, overturned, or smashed in the fighting, and the city responded by discontinuing service to the Taig districts. Left with no public service, the Taigs organized their own. When the fighting subsided and the streets were safe again, the city restored bus service; but by this time the black taxis were well established, and what Taig rider wanted to go back to the Prods' buses if he could help it? Besides, the black taxis were cheaper, and gave better service. So the big city double-decker buses lumbered empty up and down the Falls at twenty-minute intervals, while the crowded black taxis worked the bus stops, following so close you never had to wait more than a minute or two.

Falls Road was the main artery of a whole series of Taig neighborhoods, beginning near the city center in a working-class community where perhaps half the men or more were unemployed, living on the dole. The brick houses were old and rundown, mean two-story affairs, strung together in long rows with a common roof and only thin partition walls dividing them, their front doors opening directly onto the narrow pavement at the edge of the street. There was none of the noise and filth and smells that might be expected in such slums, the children playing in the street, the loungers in the doorways. The doors and windows were closed, where they were not bricked up; no children were to be seen, and the litter in the streets was the debris of battle, broken glass and crumbled brick. The living was done indoors, where it was safer.

The side streets connecting Falls Road with the Prod district of Shankill Road were blocked by the "Peace Line," a barricade of corrugated steel and barbed wire that followed the line of backyard walls between Prod and Taig houses to keep the warring neighbors apart. On the Prod side the streets looked much the same, though the signs of damage were not so common, and the streets were swept. There was a little more evidence of fresh paint on the houses, and more of the damage had been repaired. More of the Prods had jobs, and therefore money. Here the black taxis were run by the UVF and UDA, in imitation of the Taigs, but they didn't seem to be doing so well; there were fewer of them, and the city buses were comfortably filled with passengers.

Bus service had never been withdrawn from the Shankill, Gerry explained, because the riots of 1969 were essentially a Prod attack on the Taigs, and the fighting took place mainly in Taig territory. But the Prod paramilitaries needed money for the same reason as the IRA, and though the Shankill was theoretically under police control, no effort was made to stop the illegal taxis.

The Shankill and the Falls districts stretched side by side along the Peace Line from the city center out to the more attractive suburban districts on the slopes below Black Mountain, where the line between Prod and Taig districts was not always as clearly drawn, and no palisades separated them. To go out on the streets at night in these neighborhoods was dangerous; it invited assassination or at least a shot in the leg if you strayed out of your own street or came across somebody who didn't know you. On some streets, where a Prod neighborhood stood as an enclave between two parts of Taig territory, there were men, Gerry said, who would look out a darkened window and shoot anything that moved.

"Anything that moves?" I asked. "Why?"

"Because anyone who lives there knows better than to go out on the street at night, so anybody on the street must be a Taig from the next street on one side or the other."

"And I suppose the Taigs do the same in their own enclaves?"

"Not at all! The IRA doesn't allow that, it's not worth the retaliation, unless there's somebody in particular they're after, and that's not always Prods. It could be one of their own that's gone back on them, or one of the other IRA—there's two IRAs now, you know, the Officials and the Provos, and sometimes they go for each other. They'll sometimes do retaliation, too, like the others. But mainly they want to hit the Prods where it hurts them, in the pocketbook. They put a bomb in a building; you see, whether it's a shop or a factory or a government building, it's the Prods that own it. They give warning so the people can get away, and the building is blown up, and the Prods have to spend the money to fix it up, or maybe go out of business.

"But the Prods can't do that to the Taigs, because the Taigs don't own any buildings, or not much. They don't even own the homes they live in, they rent them from Prods or the Prod government. About all a Taig ever owns is a pub, and that's why sometimes you'll find the Prods will blow up a Taig pub. But they won't give any warning, because they want to kill the Taigs that are in it. That's the only wealth a Taig ever has, your man and his family. So the Prods don't care who they kill, so long as it's a Taig."

"It doesn't make sense," I said.

"Oh, I'd say it makes sense. Where did the Prods get their property? They got it by driving the Taigs off their land three hundred years ago, and they're still trying to drive out the Taigs that are still here. So they kill the few of us that they can, and hope that will frighten the rest away. They're afraid we'll outnumber them someday if they don't, because Taigs have more children than Prods do. And the Taigs can't get their land back, but they can wreck the buildings the Prods have put on it. Mainly it isn't supposed to make sense; they just hate each other. There's nobody can hate like the Irish.

"A couple of them nearly got me one night," he went on. "They were young fellows I'd picked up in my cab on a Protestant streetcorner, and as we rode along they started loading a gun and talking about what they were going to do with it to the first Taig they met. They didn't care who it was, they were just out looking for a Taig to kill. If they'd known I was one, they'd have shot me then and there."

He paused, as though that were the end of the story; a routine incident for Belfast, the sort of thing anyone might expect. I tried to imagine myself in such a situation, and couldn't.

"What did you do?" I asked.

"Just kept my mouth shut and drove on to where they wanted to go," he said cheerfully. "I didn't say a word for fear they might find out, or anyway decide I was as good a one to kill as the next one."

"But how could they talk like that in your cab, not knowing who you were?"

"Oh, sure, they were both jarred. Drunk as could be. And they thought I was a Prod because of where I had picked them up. What would I have been doing there if I wasn't?"

And suddenly I remembered what Patrick had told me about finding the right kind of taxi driver for the address you were going to.

"So what were you doing there?" I asked.

"Ah, well, in those days . . ." he said, and didn't finish the sentence. "I don't do it anymore, I'll tell you. That was the last time. I sold my taxi business after that, and now I only do private-hire work for people I know. My wife had been after me to do that for a long time. She was always afraid I'd get killed one night, and she'd be sitting up waiting and worrying every night until I got home. It was no life."

I'd had enough by then, and there was not much time left to catch the last train back to the peace and safety of Dublin. Gerry took me back to the station and we parted. As I walked down the platform past the charred brick walls and the twisted girders hanging from the hole in the roof, I thought of the customs house that Eoin O'Rourke had helped burn down in the days when this kind of thing was going on all over Ireland. Not much difference, I thought; it's all part of the same thing.

The thought stayed with me all the way back to Dublin, as I looked out the window at the roofless buildings in the Belfast suburbs, the hand-lettered sign on the back of a tenement house proclaiming PREPARE TO MEET THY GOD, the rival wall slogans, JOIN THE PROVOS and JOIN THE UVF, the men with guns striding across peaceful fields, the British flags fluttering defiantly from Irish houses, and finally the wild, barren hills on each side of the track as the train climbed slowly up to the invisible border and then down the other side, where the fields and sheep and cattle looked the same, but the houses showed no flags and no holes in their roofs, and the sense of peace and release from tension was so strong that suddenly everyone on the train seemed to relax, and people started talking to one another.

I remembered Mary Finnegan's comment that the battle of Belfast was worse than anything that had happened in her father's day, and I was inclined to agree. But was it really? It was here and now, and no end of it was in sight, but that was true in Eoin's day too. Yet it had ended for most of Ireland, and no doubt in the fullness of time it would end in the northern counties, though there was no telling how. Would one side eventually drive the other out? Could they ever learn to live together in peace, after so much hatred? What was there about the Irish people, so kind and friendly when they weren't fighting, so deeply trained in the teaching of Christian peace and love, yet capable of such stubborn, murderous hatred?

I put the question to Charlie O'Rourke when I got back to

Dublin, and we talked about it for a long time. It was the way he summed it up that day that led me to prolong my stay in Ireland for more than a year, and from it gain a whole new insight into modern Irish life.

"I can't answer you, really, John," he said. "You have so many elements involved in the thing, I cannot fathom it in my life. But we had those hatreds in the civil war; they went on in our lives though the war was over when I was born. We tended as a family to be on the side of de Valera, the Fianna Fáil. We grew up with that, and if you are committed to one side you will blind yourself, true. It's only as you've gone along that you can see this is all wrong; there are two sides to everything.

"It's not the same now in Ireland, in the Republic, as it was in my father's day, and it won't always be the same in the North, will it? I can tell you how it was with my father, and with us as we grew up—I can tell you part of it, anyhow; you'll have to get the rest from the others. And you'll see how different things can be. . . ."

PART
II

The
Schoolmaster

7.

Beginnings

Master O'Rourke never told his children much about himself or his early life, nor did his wife; that wasn't the way of it in those days. The children weren't allowed to ask questions, and they were sent out of the room when important visitors called, and when their mother and father discussed family affairs. So a lot of details in this part of the story are missing. Others have been supplied from imagination, or put together from little things overheard by the children, or noticed as they played, and then pondered in later years.

They were bright children, as different from one another as members of one family can be, yet they were as one in their fascination with what was going on around them. They all grew up with the same rather fearful regard for their stubborn and hot-tempered father, and sympathy for their harassed and tough-minded mother, with her many changes of mood and her old-fashioned country ideas.

When their mother was in a good mood, she would tell them

tales of her own childhood while they cleaned up after dinner, or sat around the fire after the evening rosary. Some of the tales sounded rather fanciful, like the ones about haunted houses and fairy trees; if there was a lone thorn bush in a field, the children were warned not to go near it. Their mother was afraid to look at the new moon through a glass, or throw out the dishwater on New Year's Day for fear of throwing out the year's luck with it. She wouldn't let them pare their nails on Fridays or Sundays, and they thought it was the same kind of superstition when she taught them always to sweep toward the fireplace, never away from it. She had a funny way of misremembering dates; she always said she was born in 1900 and married before she was eighteen, but in the parish registry of Saint Columbanus her baptism was recorded in 1899 and her wedding in 1922.

There are differences in the way the others recall these things, too, for everyone in the family remembers different parts of the story, and no one knows it all. What follows is a composite, not quite the way any of the O'Rourkes would tell it, but true to what they all have said.

Eoin O'Rourke was born in 1887, in a little village in the mountains above Collooney, where the view of Sligo Bay is grander than anything a tourist sees in Killarney or Tralee. On a fine day you can see beyond Knocknarea to Coney Island, where the rabbits frisk in the sun and a donkey cart can cross the sands at low tide from Rosses Point. Some say it's the same Coney Island for which Brooklyn's beach was named, by a Sligo man who once owned it and gave it the name of the island he had loved as a child. It might have been an O'Rourke who did that, if the story is true, for three of Eoin's brothers and sisters emigrated to America and never came back, and many of his uncles and aunts did too.

Eoin had "a good few" brothers and sisters; just how many nobody knows. A lot of them died young. One sister became a nun, and one brother remained at home to work the farm; one of the brothers in America is said to have been knifed in a street brawl, and another may have been a Democratic politician, but nobody knows for sure. When Eoin's sons William and Patrick went to America after Eoin's death, they couldn't trace any of their relatives there. Only one aunt, Doty, had kept in touch, sending parcels of food and clothing to the family during World War II and paying for the education of Eoin's sixth son, Matt, to be a priest. And she died within a year of Eoin.

There was nothing unusual about Eoin's family background, for a Catholic country boy in the west of Ireland in the last years of the nineteenth century. Children died young because the farm families were poor, and those who survived left home because there was nothing there for them, only for the one who might work the family's land and hope to inherit it. The holdings were pitifully small, and the land in the west yielded very little. It was no use going to Dublin for work; the Dublin poor were even worse off, and on their way to becoming the most miserable in Europe. Those who could were leaving Dublin to seek jobs in England; most Sligo farm boys preferred to go to America, if they could raise the passage money.

Eoin had an advantage that some others lacked—brains, and a taste for schooling. From some mysterious source—genes, instinct, perhaps the friendship of a good teacher who encouraged him—he acquired an understanding of how the mind can be disciplined to learn, and how learning can open up new possibilities, create new opportunities even in an oppressed and poverty-stricken world.

At thirteen, when he completed the rudimentary lessons offered by the local school, he became apprenticed to the schoolmaster as a "monitor." It was not much of a job, but it helped him to eat regularly, and it kept him in school. He learned something about how a school is run, how to keep order in the classroom, take attendance, keep track of books and papers and chalk and slates; how to keep the floors and blackboards clean, even something of the art of teaching. And it qualified him after a few years to go to a teacher-training college in Waterford, and then come back to County Sligo to be assistant teacher in the town of Ballymote, not far from where he was born.

He was in his early twenties then, a tall young man with reddish brown hair, blue eyes set far apart under level eyebrows, and a rather long, lean, square-jawed face. He had long legs and a broad back, and he'd been about and seen a little of the world outside the green hills of Sligo. His ideas were molded by the literary fashions of the time, Yeats's *Cathleen ni Houlihan* and the revival of Ireland's Gaelic traditions. He had started to learn Gaelic, though it was not his family's tongue and not yet taught in the national school at Ballymote; later, when he was at Ballycarrick, it would become compulsory, and he would have to master the language so that he could teach it.

He had come in contact with the political movements of the day, too, the new Sinn Fein and the older Irish Republican Brotherhood. He was excited by their dreams of freeing Ireland from its English rulers, of destroying the system that kept the Irish poor while the English grew rich. Whenever he could get a copy, Eoin read the IRB paper, *Irish Freedom,* and from the ferocious rhetoric of men like Padhraic Pearse he absorbed the simple lesson taught by Wolfe Tone more than a hundred years before—England was the enemy, England's hold of Ireland must be broken, the English must be driven out.

Pearse spoke of the shedding of blood in almost mystical terms, as though somehow it was a holy thing to do, promising peace and happiness to Ireland and glory to those who died. Many young hearts responded to such themes in those days, and not only in Ireland; Eoin could not deny the practical realities of Ireland's history that seemed to justify them. For it was by shedding blood that the English had conquered the Irish and taken away their lands and livelihoods; submission and peaceful protest had brought starvation in the famine years of his grandfather's life, but rioting and rebellion in the next generation had brought

86

land reforms in his childhood. Ireland was still unfree; and as Padhraic Pearse proclaimed, "Ireland unfree shall never be at peace."

By the time Eoin was transferred to Ballycarrick, and promoted to the dignity of principal teacher in a two-teacher school, he was a thorough Sinn Feiner. He argued politics in the local "cumann" and drilled with the Irish Volunteers, marching up and down the rocky beach with spades and pitchforks for weapons, but he never had a gun in his hand, and wouldn't have known how to use it if he had.

In the spring of 1916, Ballycarrick heard with a kind of horrified excitement the news of the Easter Rising in Dublin. Padhraic Pearse had put his rhetoric to the test, and for a week a few hundred amateur riflemen of the Volunteers, the IRB, and the Citizens' Army had battled the full might of British military power. Pearse had raised the Tricolour, the green, white, and orange banner of Ireland's hopes, over the General Post Office on O'Connell Street, and proclaimed the new Republic of Ireland. He died before a firing squad when it was over, and so did fourteen others; no one knew how many had been killed in the fighting, but the center of Dublin was in ruins, it was said, leveled by British artillery. There had been no hope that Pearse and his men would survive that moment of heroic madness; they had been willing martyrs, dying to arouse a nation's passions.

What did it mean? There were arguments, quarrels, fistfights in the pubs and quiet lanes of Ballycarrick as people tried to sort it out. Eoin O'Rourke, at twenty-nine, was no romantic, to believe with Pearse that the deaths of martyrs would have some kind of magic power in a stubborn world. The Volunteers had fought bravely in Dublin, and were no doubt better armed and trained than the farm boys he drilled with on the beach; but what had they gained? It was murder and foolishness, some people were saying; good men going to their deaths for no real purpose, many a widow and orphan left to starve, and no good could come of it. It was hopeless, it was sinful.

Yet, in all fairness, it would take fighting to break the power of Britain over Ireland, whatever the cost. Eoin longed to get into the fight, but in his schoolroom in Ballycarrick there was no way he could do it. All he could do was teach the children what he knew about Britain, how the British had enslaved Ireland and how Ireland could not rest until they were driven out.

Soon the troubles of the outside world were being felt in the Sligo hills in a more immediate way. In the final year of World War I, Britain was threatening to draft young Irishmen into her armies. Many had already volunteered, men who had English blood or close ties to England; sons of tradesmen, merchants, and rich men who benefited from English rule; political-minded men who trusted England's Liberal party, and believed in their promise of "Home Rule" for Ireland when the war was over; and thousands of unemployed in Dublin, who at least were being offered jobs in the army, and found it better to fight for England than to go on starving. But the volunteers were not enough; the draft had been introduced in England and it was proposed to apply it in Ireland too.

All over the country young men organized in protest—those like Eoin who hated England, and hoped the war would so weaken her that another Easter Rising would have some chance of success; those who cared little for politics but saw no reason to fight for England, and didn't want to be drafted. A great mass meeting was organized at Strandhill outside Sligo Town, and Eamon de Valera, one of the heroes of the Easter Rising, was coming to address it.

Eoin went to the meeting, as did every young man he knew, from Ballycarrick and Collooney and Ballymote and every other town and village and farm around Sligo Bay. He set off at dawn with a dozen friends, pulling an oar in a fishing boat across the narrow mouth of the estuary where the tide flows in to Bally- sodare, then walking up the strand and around the headland to the field where a platform had been set up and banners flapped in the breeze, above big painted signs reading NO CONSCRIPTION —STAND UNITED. All morning long the crowd streamed in, farmers and fishermen and workmen in their caps, young men of the wealthier sort in straw hats and beavers, all pushing and crowding together to get close enough to hear the speakers, until Eoin found himself so tightly hemmed in that his long arms were pinned to his sides, and his broad shoulders ached from the pressure of those behind and beside him. The platform began to fill up too, with citified-looking men in business suits, and from among them appeared de Valera, the man they had come to see. Eoin joined in the tumultuous roar that went up from the crowd, and suddenly people were moving, even in that tight press, and Eoin was able to pull his arm up and snatch off his cap and wave it as the others were doing.

He was surprised and a little disappointed to find that de Valera didn't look like a very big man, standing there at the front of the platform with so many taller around him. He had a sad-looking face, and a rather diffident way about him as he started talking, but then his voice rose and the words of confidence and courage and determination came out, words that Eoin didn't pay much attention to because he had heard them all before and knew what they meant, but there was something in the man's voice that made him seem ten times bigger than anyone around. And as Eoin stood there in the crowd, shoulder pressed to shoulder and his chin brushing the cap of the man in front of him, all leaning forward together, listening and cheering in unison and all of one mind about what they were to do, his doubts and uncertainties suddenly ebbed, and he knew he was on the right side and would never change. England must be resisted, England must be driven out, Irishmen must stand united and win! It was an experience he would never forget.

By the end of the year the war was over, and Britain had no more interest in trying to draft Irishmen to fight her battles.

But there was a general election that involved Ireland, because as long as Ireland was part of Britain, there were Irish representatives elected to the British Parliament. And suddenly Sinn Fein, the party that had never before won a single seat in Parliament, became the party of Eamon de Valera and the Republicans, the party that stood for Ireland's freedom.

Their program satisfied Eoin's longings, and it was simplicity itself. If elected, the Sinn Feiners would refuse to sit in England's Parliament; they would organize a new Irish Parliament in Dublin, to govern Ireland under the authority of the Republic proclaimed by Padhraic Pearse two and a half years before. If England objected, it would be the English rebelling against a properly constituted native government of Ireland—a government legitimized by the votes cast in a lawful election, and sanctified by the blood of Pearse and the martyrs who had fallen in the Easter Rising.

Eoin was not well enough known nor active enough in politics to be a candidate, but he could be a campaigner. Night after night at meetings of the cumann, and on Sundays after Mass in front of Saint Columbanus's Church in Ballycarrick, or Saint Adamnan's in nearby Skreen, or even further afield in Collooney and Ballysodare, Eoin harangued and exhorted his neighbors, standing bareheaded in rain or sun, lifting his voice as he had heard Eamon de Valera do, applying his schoolmaster's knowledge of rhetoric to produce a countryman's version of the great leader's power and style. He was a good speaker, with a deep bass voice that carried like the bellow of a bull, and at every meeting the crowds grew larger and the shouts of approval grew louder.

Some of the older men in Ballycarrick were horrified by Eoin's ideas, and none more so than the parish priest of Saint Columbanus, a man of equally strong voice and opinions, who could be stubborn if he was crossed. Father O'Malley had more learning and more understanding of the world and its ways than was common among country priests, and his authority over the souls in his charge was unquestioned. He was in a special position of authority over Eoin the schoolmaster, for the parish priests of Ireland then as now were the managers of the local schools.

"You're preaching riot and rebellion, young man, that's what you're doing," he said to Eoin one Sunday morning after listening to his campaign speech. "It will go hard with you if it isn't stopped."

"Not at all, Father," said Eoin. "This is a proper lawful election and I'm doing my duty as an Irishman."

"Well, you're not doing your duty as a Christian schoolmaster," the priest snapped. "Trying to get a crowd of fools to start another Easter Rising, that's all it is! How is the Sinn Fein going to pay for your school, will you tell me that? You talk of a new Irish Republic, and your man has neither the right nor the power to do it, nor the money nor any way to get it."

"Oh, they'll do it, Father, they'll do it. Because we're all with them, you see, we're all behind them."

"You're behind them, what can you do? 'Twill be all over in a week, like the other time, and you've done nothing but send good men to their deaths. I won't have it, I won't, not in my church and not in my school."

"Then I'll stand outside your gates when I make my speeches, and I'll say no word to the kiddies in school," Eoin answered. "But you can't stop me, and you can't stop Ireland, and by the Holy Mother of God if you were a man you'd be on our side."

It was a stubborn thing to say, but Eoin was a stubborn man, and he knew Father O'Malley well enough to guess that in his heart he was on Sinn Fein's side, though neither his practical responsibilities nor the doctrines of his Church would let him admit it. So Eoin gave the priest a friendly if somewhat disrespectful parting grin, and strode off up the road after his friends the O'Connors, with whom he was living as a boarder.

The O'Connors had a fairly large farm, as farms go in the west of Ireland, acres enough to support a dozen dairy cattle and grow hay, oats, cabbages, and potatoes for market as well as their own use. They were Sinn Feiners like Eoin, and their farm was high in the hills above the main road, under the huge gray outcropping of limestone that gave Ballycarrick its name. On the way to it was a little tobacco and sweets shop in a thatched cottage beside the road, where a cousin of the O'Connors, Maire Kilcullen, lived with a spinster aunt and bachelor uncle. Eoin stopped in for a packet of Sweet Afton cigarettes, not because he needed them just then, but because he wanted to tell Maire how he had stood up to Father O'Malley. The reaction he got was a surprise.

"You didn't!" she exclaimed, a sudden look of horror in her shy, gray-green eyes. "You shouldn't say such things to Father O'Malley, and him such a saintly man."

"But he's all wrong, Maire," said Eoin. "What does he know about politics, blathering about my Christian duties and all. If the English ever did their Christian duty, they'd be out of Ireland tomorrow and there'd be no more trouble, but would your Father O'Malley ever think of that? Let him stick to his preaching and I'll do my politicking, he won't bother me at all, not at all."

Maire shook her head in dismay, and the two long braids of shiny black hair danced on the countertop, at her waist. Eoin wanted to take them in his hands, pull out the blue satin ribbons and undo the braids, let that soft, silky hair hang loose over her shoulders. But he couldn't do that. She was not yet twenty, and he was thirty-two; a beautiful girl like Maire with her aunt's shop and her uncle's farm to inherit could have her pick of the young men in all of County Sligo. But he had a little money put by and was ready to think about marriage—and maybe Jack O'Connor would put in a word for him. After all, Eoin wasn't a bad catch himself, a man of learning and position—better off as a schoolmaster than he would have been if he'd stayed on his father's boggy acres on the mountain.

"There's to be a big meeting in Dromard tonight," Eoin said to Maire. "Will you come with me? 'Tis at Farrell's lodge, and there'll be a band, and speeches, and we can walk together on the strand after. We won't even listen to the speeches if you don't want to."

Maire blushed and looked down. "You won't be speaking yourself?" she asked.

"Not this time. It's all big fellows from Sligo Town, and there's someone coming from Athlone and maybe even Dublin."

"Then I'll tell Auntie you're behaving yourself. I'll tell her Father O'Malley has talked to you—that's true, isn't it, he really did—and I won't tell her you didn't listen! Now you be off before she comes."

Eoin bounded out the door and raced up the hill to his dinner, reflecting on how lucky it was that Maire was here with her aunt and uncle instead of in County Mayo with her parents. Maire's father was a policeman, a member of the Royal Irish Constabulary, and he had been transferred from Ballycarrick to a larger town in Mayo soon after Maire was born, but Maire had been left here to grow up on the old family place and live with her father's unmarried brother and sister.

She was a lonely child, and very pious, with a special deep devotion to the Blessed Virgin Mary, for whom she had been named, though she used the old Gaelic form of the name. She was a great admirer of Father O'Malley, and seemed to worship the ground he walked on, but Eoin didn't mind that, he rather liked the old priest too. In truth, Eoin had no strong feelings about the Church one way or the other, but he thought it right that women be concerned in such things, and was sure a pious woman would make a good wife and mother. As for Father O'Malley, Eoin thought it was enough to be responsible to him for the running of the school, without also going to confession to him.

Still, there was much to be done before Eoin could get married, and the first step was to have a home of his own. He had borrowed fifty pounds from the bank in Sligo Town, and bought three acres of land near the shore, where he was building a fine two-story house under the beech trees. He had drawn the plans himself, and designed a big house, because he wanted a big family; Maire would want children too, because she was so lonely. He would call the house Toberpatrick, after the holy well what Maire had told him about it. It was nowhere near the house, but that didn't matter, Maire would like the name. And he could do most of the work himself, for he was strong enough and had the skill to lay one stone on another and the mortar between; the brickwork would be even easier.

He cleared the ground that fall, ready to start building in spring, but meanwhile the election campaign in which he had worked so hard ended with a Sinn Fein victory so overwhelming that it changed everything. The promised Dáil Éireann came into being in January, and the struggle with England began.

Eoin was elated at the change in Ireland's fortune, but Father O'Malley was depressed. "You'll see," the priest said.

And as the inevitable war developed between England and the new Irish Republican Army, embracing the old Volunteers, the Citizens' Army, and the IRB, Eoin did see. This was a far more bitter thing than he had ever dreamed, and more than the week of slaughter Father O'Malley had first predicted. It was a guerrilla war of raids and ambushes, with no clear battle lines, no distinction between soldiers and civilians, no safety for anyone, a time of burning, looting, and murder.

Eoin had no training for such a war, but he was part of it; there was no way out. The IRA had few arms and no organized supply of ammunition, food, or uniforms. They took what they could get, raiding police barracks, customs houses, coast-guard stations, any center of British power they could reach. Between excursions they hid in barns and haycocks and the homes of men like Jack O'Connor. The British answer was the Black and Tans, combat veterans wearing a mixture of police and army uniforms, but under the discipline of neither, conducting a war of indiscriminate retaliation more ferocious than anything Britain had ever done before, at least in living memory. It was a war no one could escape.

One night Eoin joined a raid on the customs house at the mouth of the estuary, only a mile or two from the house he was building. The Black and Tans had been driven out, and the mob smashed windows, poured kerosene on the wooden floors and furniture, and set a blaze that lasted the whole night, till the slate roof collapsed and the upper floor broke under its weight. Then the whole wall along the landward side of the building caved in, leaving the gaping ruin that was to be partly restored by an eccentric American woman so many years later, to the amazement of Eoin's son-in-law.

The Black and Tans knew who were the leaders of that night's work, or thought they did, and hunted for them in all the farms along the shore and in the hills beyond. It was a frosty night in November when they came to the O'Connors' place on the hillside a little before dawn, and burst in to search the house from end to end, rousing the family and Eoin from their beds and herding them outside in their bare feet and nightshirts while the men went through the house, overturning wardrobes, smashing chairs and tables, but not finding the men they were after.

Then they went for the "haggard," the open-sided barnlike structure at the far end of the field where the year's harvest was stored, the hay and oats and cabbages and potatoes to serve the family and their animals through the winter. Prodding with their bayonets, they drove the shivering group across the sharp stubble of the frozen fields, eight children, the mother and father, and Eoin in his helpless rage, wondering if they were all to be murdered. But it didn't happen; the Tans poked in the hay, scattered cabbages and potatoes and sacks of oats, and found no one hiding; then they set fire to the lot and held the family at gunpoint so that they could do nothing to put out the fire, only watch in despair.

The Tans left, and Eoin ran back to the house to put on shoes, trousers, and a coat, and then down the hill through the pasture, avoiding the lane where the Tans were riding, to the cottage where Maire lived. He was too late, of course; by the time he came in sight of it the Tans were already there. As he approached through the field he could see Maire up against the wall at the side of the cottage, her arms outstretched like Christ on the cross, a Tan's bayonet at her breast, and her aunt lying at her feet, sobbing.

Eoin ducked behind the stone fence, and pulled out a sharp rock, just fist-size, right for throwing, but then reason stopped him. What good would it do? Even if he was lucky enough to kill the Tan, or at least brain him and knock him out, there would be another in the house, and they'd shoot Maire and her aunt at once and come after him. As he hesitated, the other Tan came out of the house and called to his mate, who brought his bayonet up with a quick tug that ripped Maire's flannel nightgown off her shoulder, and then strode off with him, laughing, as Maire dropped to the ground and knelt by her aunt.

Eoin vaulted the fence and ran to them. "Sweet Jesus!" he cried. "Did they hurt you, Maire?"

"Thanks be to God, they didn't. Help me get Aunt Annie into the house."

"Where's your uncle?"

"At Grannie's. He'll be home this evening."

"He never should have left you!"

"Grannie sent for him. He had to go. We're well enough."

"But, Maire, you're not safe here, alone in this house by the road."

"It's all the same wherever we are, may God and his Holy Mother protect us!" Maire said.

Aunt Annie, pulling herself to her feet with Eoin's help, caught sight of Maire's bare shoulder and ran her hand over it quickly to make sure there was no wound. "Cover yourself up, child," she said, and pulled the ripped nightgown together with a quick, fussy movement. "Into the house, now. Run." Blushing, Maire ran, while Eoin offered Annie his arm, but she brushed him aside and stalked into the kitchen to rake the ashes off the embers in the fireplace, and add a little kindling and some fresh turf to get the fire going for the day. Before the kettle was warm Maire reappeared, in fresh blouse and skirt, and set teacups on the table while her aunt withdrew to dress.

"It's not right, Maire," Eoin said to her. "Look, the ground floor of Toberpatrick is nearly finished. I can roof it over and we can move in, and you can bring Annie and Pat with you, till all this is over. There'll be time enough to build the second story later. We shouldn't wait."

"Eoin, they wouldn't have it. And I wouldn't either. I want no talk of living in an unfinished house with the wind blowing in and me choking in the dust and plaster while you're tramping about overhead building the upper story. We can wait. The Tans have been here now, they won't come again."

"They will, Maire, you know they will."

"Look here, then, and see what saved us!" She pointed to the back of the kitchen door, where an old police uniform of her father's hung on a peg, and the black beret with the British crown on it that the Tans wore. "You see, they saw that and thought we were on their side."

"That'll do you no good if the others come; they'll do for you instead," said Eoin.

"Then we'll hide it!"

"Be serious, Maire! If you think that old uniform is protecting you, bring it with you to Toberpatrick."

"But everybody knows Daddy never lived there, and isn't there now," she said. "This was his house, and this is Aunt Annie and Uncle Pat's house, and it's my house, and I'm going to stay here till yours is finished!"

Eoin went on with the building, and in the summer there was a truce, and the fighting dwindled and gradually stopped. Then after months of argument there was a treaty, but it wasn't the kind that Eoin or his idol, de Valera, wanted at all, for it left Ireland still subject to the British king, not a republic but a dominion in the British Empire, like Canada. Was that all the IRA had won from the bloody fighting, the raids and ambushes, the burning of the customs house and the loss of Jack O'Connor's haggard? The treaty didn't even cover the six counties of the North; they would be cut off from the rest of Ireland now, and be part of England still. This was no victory, it was a defeat.

That was how Eoin O'Rourke felt about it, and so did Jack O'Connor and most of Eoin's neighbors. So did de Valera and most of the IRA, but not all of Ireland, not even a majority. In the elections that June the treaty supporters won, and the new "Irish Free State" came into being. Padhraic Pearse's Irish Republic ceased to be, except in the eyes of de Valera and his IRA supporters. The war began again, but it was a civil war now, the IRA fighting guerrilla fashion as before, but against an Irish government instead of the British. It was more terrible and bitter even than the war against the Tans, for now families that had been friends for generations became enemies, or split in enmity among themselves.

It was a war the IRA could not win, and Eoin knew that. He took no active part, but when his house was finished, and he and Maire were married and moved into it, the IRA men knew they could find shelter there when they were "on the run," as they did at Jack O'Connor's too.

Maire allowed them to hide there during the day, but at night they had to go. She remembered too well what had happened that frosty dawn at Aunt Annie's house, when the boy the Tans were after had been cowering behind a store of potatoes in the cellar, rigid and motionless for fear of discovery, wetting his pants in his terror. She hadn't told Eoin about that at the time, but she told him now.

8.

Growing Family

T*here* was a coolness between Eoin O'Rourke and Father O'Malley as long as the civil war lasted, and they kept their distance from each other. The priest was too wise a man to condemn the IRA from the pulpit, or let politics be mentioned in confessions. The sin was the same, whatever the end in view, and among his penitents were many on both sides, and more caught bewildered in the middle.

The schoolmaster could not let politics into his schoolroom, for he knew too well which side the father of each child was on. There was no way to teach modern history without incurring the wrath of one side or the other; the solution was to drop the subject altogether, and teach ancient history only: the Gaelic kingdoms, the coming of Saint Patrick, the Age of Saints and Scholars, the Viking raiders, the Norman invasion, the Tudor wars, the devastation wrought by Cromwell, when the Irish Catholics were driven from their lands; the penal laws that made the priests subject to hanging or deportation; the famines, coercions, and rack rents of the eighteenth century.

All that had happened since then, a century and a half of Irish struggle for freedom, was involved in what the IRA were fighting about, and as long as men were fighting there was no sense talking about it to children. Even when the war officially ended, the fighting didn't stop altogether, and for years thereafter it was too sore a subject to mention in the school.

Maire was happy in her new life, and went to Mass every morning that she could, weekdays as well as Sundays, until in the spring her first child grew big within her, and she couldn't walk so far. Then she returned to her aunt's cottage to have her baby, where she herself had been born, and was there a month before she came back to Eoin at Toberpatrick with their daughter. They named her Mary, like her mother but in the English form, because Father O'Malley refused to use the Gaelic when he baptized her.

Eoin hired a girl from one of the neighboring farms to help Maire with the baby and the housework, as befitted a schoolmaster's wife. This was fortunate for Maire, who as yet knew nothing of such things. Aunt Annie had brought her up to be a lady, with no household chores to do and no knowledge of what marriage and parenthood were like.

Annie had a spinster's strict and unchanging ways; she always wore black, her long skirt reaching down to her ankles over tightly laced boots that came up halfway to her knees, a style that had gone out of fashion when Maire was a baby. She taught Maire to milk the cows and feed the chickens, but she didn't teach her to cook or make beds, because it never occurred to her that Maire would need to know such things. She couldn't teach her how to get along with a husband, since she had none of her own, or how to feed a baby or change its nappies. Maire hadn't even learned how children get along with their brothers and sisters, because all of hers were thirty miles away in Crossmolina, an impossible distance to walk. For all she saw of her family, Maire might have been an orphaned only child.

After her first child was born, Maire was "poorly" for a long time, or at least that was the explanation she would give in later years for the two-year gap between Mary and Joseph. In the next two years two more sons, Michael and Charlie, were born, bonny boys with their father's big bones and square, even features. Then came Annie Philomena, who had a difficult birth, leaving Maire exhausted and anxious.

There was something wrong with the child, or the mother; the baby couldn't take the mother's milk. Maire wanted to see Father O'Malley about it, but was too weak to go to the church. So Eoin went to fetch him, and the priest came and comforted Maire, telling her to trust in God. The little innocent would go straight to heaven, he said; God's ways were sometimes hard to understand, but perhaps He had a special place in heaven for the child, and wanted her there at once. Such things were not unusual; Maire was not alone. She had other children to console her, and there would no doubt be more.

So little Annie Philomena died, and when Tony was born the next year, he, too, was sickly at first, but he survived and grew stronger. Jimmy, who followed, was as healthy and active a boy as anyone would want, and after him came Gertie, Maire's second daughter.

There were now seven children to feed and clothe, and Eoin's salary had not increased proportionately. Nor did it seem likely to, for the school population was beginning to drop; farm families all around them were feeling the hard times, giving up their land to look for work in the cities. Soon Eoin would lose his other teacher, and be principal of a one-teacher school.

They couldn't afford full-time help anymore, but Mrs. Kelly came in once a week to do the wash. Maire learned to cook in the big open fireplace in the kitchen, boiling the cabbage and bacon and potatoes together in the big iron pot that hung from the crane over the glowing turf. She baked soda bread in the "pot oven," with burning coals heaped on the lid while it hung over the fire beneath. It wasn't easy, especially when a gust of wind blowing down the chimney would loosen a block of accumulated soot in the flue, and send it cascading down on top of the cooking pots. There was always a baby in the cradle and another crawling on the floor, and Maire was heavy most months with the next child coming on, so if the older children didn't look after the smaller ones there could be a lot of wailing and howling before the babies were attended to.

Mary, the eldest, was eight, old enough to help with the babies' bottles and nappies. Maire was grateful for that, but as she watched her little daughter and thought of the comfort and ease of her own childhood with Aunt Annie, she wondered if it was fair. Mary might grow up to be her mother's main reliance, the children's nurse and assistant housekeeper, but it would be no life for such a pretty one. Mary had her mother's raven hair and gray-green eyes, the same heart-shaped face and happy smile that Maire used to have; was it right for her to grow up a drudge, too busy to meet a nice boy and get married, live out her days at home and end by caring for her parents in their old age?

That was the old way, but Maire didn't care for it. Aunt Annie had started out that way, that's why she had never married; and it would have happened to Maire if her parents had taken her to Crossmolina instead of leaving her with Annie and Uncle Pat. She'd been free, then, to marry, and now Annie and Pat were alone again, with no one to look after them as they grew older. If Mary took her mother's place on the farm, Annie and Pat could bring her up, and she would have only the two old ones to look after instead of her younger brothers and sisters. It would be an easier life, with more advantages, and Mary could marry a farmer and the family land would eventually be hers. Maire would miss her, of course, but she owed it to Annie and Pat; they had no one else, and they couldn't be left alone.

Little Mary moved into the old thatched cottage by the roadside, and the next year Matt was born, and there were seven again in Toberpatrick, and afterward came Tess and Willie and Peter and Christy, making eleven children in one house, nine boys and two girls. Gertie, now six, was already quite a tomboy; it was Joe and Mick, the two eldest boys, who helped with the housework and gave the babies their bottles and changed their nappies.

Mick didn't mind doing that sort of thing: he learned to make a tastier soda bread than his mother, and was always patient and gentle with the younger children. Joe hated it; he would rush through his chores and hurry the other boys along too, organizing them and assigning tasks, Mick to clear off the table, Charlie to fetch water from the well, Tony to dry the dishes and put them away while Joe washed them, and then they'd all run outside for boxing matches or races that Joe would direct, acting as judge and referee and scorekeeper because, after all, he was too big to be just a competitor, he'd win every time. Joe was twelve years old and dreamed of being a sports writer; he used to sit on his stool in the evenings writing stories in his copy books about the races his brothers had run during the day, and they called him "Green Flag," the name used by the sports writer in the *Sligo Champion.*

On bright summer days the boys would go down to the rocky shore with their father, to bathe in the warm pools left by the tide in the big potholes, while the older ones ventured out into the sea to learn to swim. There was no such thing as bathing suits, of course, but nobody minded that; when Gertie and Tess were old enough to bathe they would go to another part of the shore and find potholes of their own where they couldn't be seen by the boys. The mother never went near the shore; even the father, as the boys grew old enough to notice such things, withdrew to his own pothole to hide his "privates" from their eyes. The boys wondered about that, sometimes, but that was the way of it in those days.

It was a glorious life for the children, and it never occurred to them that such things wouldn't go happily on forever. But the mother was worried. Sometimes as they walked home from Mass on Sunday mornings across the fields, their father wouldn't be with them, and she would be cross.

"Where's your father?" she would say to Joe. "In O'Riordan's again?" O'Riordan's was the pub just down the road from the church, where the young bachelors went after Mass for their morning pint, and sometimes stayed all day. It might be all right for them, but for a father and a schoolmaster it was different.

"Run in and tell him we're waiting," Maire would say. She never set foot in a pub herself, it wasn't seemly. But small boys could run in and out without harm. Joe would dutifully run in, and reappear a minute later.

"Daddy says he'll be along and not to wait," Joe would say, and the little procession would move in silence across the field, the mother's lips set in a hard, tight line, till the children grew bored with the silence and ran on ahead, laughing and teasing one another.

One such Sunday, when Eoin missed his dinner altogether and didn't come home till late in the evening, too sozzled to do anything but go to bed, Maire confided to the older children that it was the drink that had cost him a promotion.

"He could have been an inspector, with a motorcar to drive when he visited all the schools," she said. "But he'd have to take the pledge, and he wouldn't do it. It's the booze that's keeping him tied to that little school, and where are we going to get the money for you all growing up like you are? Look at you, Joe, you're out of them pants already!"

Not that Eoin O'Rourke drank at home in those days, or drank much more than other schoolmasters or the farmers in the neighborhood. But it was true that he stopped in O'Riordan's more often than Maire liked, and when he went to Sligo Town sometimes, for a meeting with other teachers or just an evening with his friends after payday, he'd have a skinful when he came back.

And there were other things that troubled Maire. She had

never been very careful with money, she would as soon give it away as spend it, but whether she gave it or spent it she couldn't hold on to it. Eoin decided quite soon after their marriage that it was no use giving her money on his payday once a month to run the household; what he gave her wouldn't last, and there would be the rest of the month ahead of him before he was paid again. So he kept the money himself, and gave it to her in small sums as she asked for it, to buy a loaf of bread or a jug of milk or whatever, and he bought and paid for the clothes himself. Sometimes, if the two weren't speaking because of some quarrel between them, she'd send one of the children to him to ask for the money. They didn't like that; nor did she, nor he.

The quarrels often started over little things, as such quarrels do. Eoin wore stiff white collars on his shirts, the detachable kind with big studs in front and back. He kept the studs and collars in a tin box on his dresser, and the collars had to be washed and ironed so that there would always be a fresh one for him each morning. But often enough in the morning the box was empty; somebody had forgotten, there had been too much to do—or one of the little ones had climbed up and upset the box, playing with its contents until the collars were grubby and the little shiny round studs had rolled away.

Then there would be a row and a rushing about the house until Mick found a fresh collar and ironed it, and the mother dug out fresh studs from her secret hiding place, and the children were scolded and sometimes slapped if any were incautious enough to linger within reach. And the father would go off to school, a little late but natty as usual, pedaling his bicycle down the road in his stiff white collar, black coat, and trilby hat, with elastic garters around his trouser cuffs to keep them from catching in the wheels, and his children running barefoot the shorter way across the fields to get there before him.

There would be trouble sometimes in the evening, too, if the children took advantage of a moment of Maire's inattention to run out and play before they'd done their chores, leaving the kitchen a mess and the floor unswept. Maire would call in the offenders and line them up in front of her with their hands held out to be caned. She used the same kind of birch rod Eoin used in school, slapping their hands to make them smart, before they were dismissed to do the chores they'd left undone.

Jimmy was the one who resisted; at school he learned the trick of holding a horsehair across his palm, believing that it would split the rod or at least soften the blow; at home he ducked behind the cradle whenever he could, so that Maire's blow would miss. For more serious offenses, or when she lost her temper, she would go after the children with a broom handle on their backsides, or wherever she could reach; Eoin used his leather razor strop at home, and in severe cases could give a boy a right good tanning with it.

Peace always returned with the family rosary, last thing at night before the younger children went to bed—or in later years, if teen-agers were going out for the evening, before they left the house. Not a day of her life did Maire omit the rosary, nor was anyone in the household allowed to be absent. For some of the children, particularly Charlie, Willie, and Peter, it became a central part of their lives; for Jimmy the rebel there always seemed to be something false about it. An interruption of what he was doing at the time, whatever it might be; a suspension of hostilities, which would be resumed immediately afterward; a recitation of phrases he had to learn by heart—if that was what Christianity was all about, Jimmy didn't see the point in it. As a child he'd rather run out and play, and didn't see why his mother wouldn't let him.

The year Chris was born, Uncle Pat was taken ill, and Mary and Aunt Annie needed help on the farm. Joe was twelve years old, a stocky, round-faced boy with strong arms and back who had learned to plant potatoes and cabbages in the Toberpatrick kitchen garden and milk the family's one cow, so he was sent to join Mary in the thatched cottage and learn to be a real farmer. It wasn't much to his taste, but he had no choice, and when Uncle Pat died a few months later he stayed on, at Aunt Annie's suggestion. That made a little more room at Tober-patrick for Brigid, who was born the next year; and Mick and Charlie were old enough now to take on Joe's chores. It was Joe's last year at school, and for the first time Eoin faced the problem of secondary education for his children.

There weren't many secondary schools in Ireland in 1938, and none of them were free, except the vocational schools where boys learned such trades as carpentry and bricklaying, but little else. Eoin couldn't afford a private school for Joe, and there were no scholarships available for which Joe would be eligible and qualified. Eoin tried to make up for it by teaching Joe him-self, coaching him in algebra and geometry at the school during his lunch hour, and at Toberpatrick in the evening when Joe would walk the mile or two from the farm after the day's work was done. But it wasn't a great success, and Joe always felt in later years that he could have made more of himself if he'd had more education.

Joe wasn't the only one to feel that. Mick missed a lot of school because he had to stay home to help with the children in those months of special strain when a new one had just been born, or was about to be, or Maire was poorly for other reasons. It was especially hard for him in his last three years of school, in some ways the most important of all, for by that time Joe had left and Mick was the eldest in the house. Gertie had the same experience a few years later, when Rita and Pat were born; Jimmy missed a lot of school too, but that was just playing hooky. He didn't care much for school; he was better at fishing and catching rabbits. He was quick to learn what he wanted to know, and always prided himself that if he was shown how to do something once, he'd get it.

The mother's conscience bothered her about these missed school days, and she reacted in a way that Jimmy could never understand. One day after school, when Eoin had gone home and left Jimmy and some of the other boys to sweep the school-room floor and wash the blackboards, Maire came in and started looking through the roll-call book. A good attendance record was important to a schoolmaster, for it earned him an annual bonus added to his pay. The more faithful his pupils in coming to school, the higher was his efficiency rating with the school inspector, and the better his chances of promotion. Naturally, when Mick or Gertie was at home helping their mother, their father marked them present in his roll-call book at school; after all, they were doing their duty, so their absence was excused. Perhaps Jimmy's truancies were excused in the same way—he'd never dared to look in the roll-call book, but he hoped so. Anyhow, Maire looked, and what she saw appalled her.

She didn't say anything about it to Eoin, for he wouldn't have listened. She reported the matter instead to Father O'Malley, her confessor in matters of conscience and her husband's supervisor in matters of school administration. Father O'Malley absolved her of any sin, and reassured her that Eoin's departure from the strict rule of school management was based on sound moral principles and deserved forgiveness; indeed, if she had not mentioned it to him, he would not have inquired into it.

"If a child stays home from school to help the mother," he said gently, "are there not lessons learned of a higher order, duties performed of a higher nature? You must not be too harsh about these things, you know; one can fall into the sin of pride by being overscrupulous. Surely it would be unfair for your husband to discourage such a worthy practice and penalize a child by marking him absent when he was present with his own mother. And remember, it is not only your own children who must do this—such needs arise in other families too. Would you have your husband treat his own children more harshly than the others?"

Maire listened obediently to this homily, but found no reassurance in it. Indeed, the priest's last comment only seemed to make the matter worse. Although she had the highest respect for Father O'Malley, and regarded him as a truly saintly man, she would not take the word even of a saint in matters where she felt she was right and the saint was wrong. One of her uncles was the bishop of Kerry, and she thought of writing to him about it, feeling sure he would agree with her. But he was in another diocese, at the other end of Ireland, she reflected; much better to write to her own bishop at Killala, in County Mayo. So that is what she did, and though the only answer she received was noncommittal, and nothing was done to change her husband's behavior, at least she felt she had done all she could, and her conscience was clear.

Jimmy's conscience, meanwhile, remained untroubled, and he went on playing hooky when the weather was good. But in later years he wondered why his mother had done such things, and whether they might have had more to do with denying Eoin his promotion than the drink his mother complained of. It must be hard for a man to get ahead, he thought, when his wife won't back him up.

Jimmy was a mischievous youngster, and so were the two others nearest him in age—Tony, his elder brother, and Gertie the tomboy, his younger sister. Annie Philomena's death had left a gap between these three and the two older boys, Mick and Charlie, who were the responsible ones in the house after Joe went to Aunt Annie's. Matt, who came after Gertie, was quite a different personality; he set the example for the younger children, who led quite different lives, more sober and obedient than the three rapscallions in the middle.

When Jimmy and Tony were small boys their mother used to send them sometimes to Hogan's little shop for messages, a few loaves of bread, or some milk on a winter evening, when their cow wasn't producing. On the way the boys would spot some farmer's horse grazing alone in a field, and climb over the fence to chase the horse in the gathering dark. The poor old horse would trot off in alarm when he saw the young tormentors charging after him, throwing sticks and sods or whatever they could find, trying to urge him into a gallop. They were lucky the horse didn't step in a rabbit hole and break his leg—and that they didn't either. Once they ran a horse right out over a gate into the road, and left him to canter off alone, and find his way back as best he could. One night a farmer caught them at it, and started to scold, but Jimmy answered, never at a loss for an excuse, "He's stepped in a snare, sir, and tangled it on his foot; we're trying to catch him to get it off."

Then there was the day Tony and Jimmy were taking their turn at scrubbing the bare wooden floor of the schoolhouse. There was no paid help to keep the school clean; Father O'Malley, as the school manager, was supposed to see to the cleaning and heating of the school, but there was no money for it. The children brought their own fuel at the start of winter, turf cut by each family from the bog and loaded in a donkey cart, for the open fire that gave the drafty old building its only heat. There were two rooms in the schoolhouse, but now that there was only one teacher the second room was used only for storage. Its windows were broken and there were no stools or desks in it; all the children, forty or fifty of them from five or six to fourteen years old, did their studying together in the other big room with the warm fire. And every evening when school was over one or two of the older children would stay behind to clean up, taking turns at it.

Sweeping was good enough for the daily cleanup, but during the holidays the floor had to be scrubbed so that the school would be fresh and clean when the children came back for the next term. One mild spring day Tony and Jimmy were sent over with their mother's scrubbing brush and bucket and some old cloths to do the job. On the way they had a go at one of the horses they were so fond of teasing in the fields, but in broad daylight the old fellow recognized them and knew what the game was, and wouldn't play.

In exasperation one of the boys threw the scrubbing brush at him, and the horse bolted off in surprise and irritation, with the two young clowns haring after him. Only when they tumbled in a clump of prickly yellow gorse, too full of laughter and out of breath to run anymore, did they realize they'd lost the scrubbing brush. They didn't want their stern schoolmaster dad saying to them, "What happened to the scrubbing brush, lads, where is it?" They couldn't go home for another, and they couldn't leave that schoolroom floor unscrubbed.

There was nothing to do but hunt around in the storage room at the school to see what they could find. They discovered a hearth brush, not as stiff as a proper scrubbing brush, and thoroughly blackened with soot, but a little soaking in the suds took care of that, and though the job took longer, and left long black streaks on the floor, they were having too much fun to care. Their mother never found out how her scrubbing brush was lost, and by the time school opened again in September the streaks on the floor had faded, and nobody knew the difference.

That fall Gertie missed quite a lot of school, for the mother was expecting again and for the first time in many years something seemed to be giving her trouble. She felt poorly, and the doctor told her to be careful; she was forty now, and couldn't expect pregnancy to be as easy as it used to be. And the little ones needed attention—four-year-old Willie had a cold, Peter was a toddler and into everything, Christy was still crawling, and Brigid was in the cradle.

One wet day in October while the rest of the older children were in school, Gertie was giving Brigid her bottle beside the kitchen fire while the mother sat beside her, cutting old flannelette sheets into nappies for the baby on the way. Suddenly Maire got up off her chair with a cry of pain and fear, and Gertie, who was eight years old, turned to see her clutching at her dress, and blood pouring out. She dropped the bottle and ran to her mother in terror, as she collapsed on the floor. Gertie had never seen a miscarriage before, nor even heard of one, and she thought her mother was going to die. She grabbed the sheets her mother had been cutting up, and awkwardly tried to wipe up the blood and "tidy her up."

"Get the doctor," her mother whispered, and Gertie bustled the little ones out of the kitchen and into the sitting room and closed the door, then ran the two hundred yards up the road to the nearest house, where Tom Finnegan was forking hay in his cow shed. Finnegan hopped on his bike and was off through the rain, with the message, and Gertie ran back to the house and quieted her terrified brothers and sister until the doctor arrived, and then her father. Maire was carried upstairs to bed and stayed there for a long time, three months or more. Even then she came downstairs too soon, and after a day or two had to go back into bed, and the doctor was sent for again.

She got her strength back slowly, while Christy learned to walk and Brigid to crawl, and the old oaken cradle was empty for the first time since Annie Philomena had died, twelve years before. Even Charlie and Mick couldn't remember that, for they'd been too young. Gertie wanted to put the cradle away, to make room in the kitchen, but her mother wouldn't hear of it. Eoin was building a new wing on the back of the house, with another kitchen in it and another bedroom upstairs. There would soon be plenty of room.

Still, there was an air of finality that year, of a stage passed, of the family growing up instead of just growing. Charlie and Mick had finished school, and were starting to do occasional work for the neighboring farmers, spading turf, planting potatoes, cutting hay according to the season. Their own kitchen garden was a sight to be proud of, with so many strong boys to hoe it; the rows of potatoes, cabbages, onions, and turnips were mathematically straight and evenly spaced, for the schoolmaster himself had laid them out, while Gertie held the string for him, fearing he'd chop her fingers off if it was the slightest bit out of line.

The cow gave five gallons of milk a day, more than enough for the whole family, and when she was in calf and dried up, they had a nanny goat instead. The goat's milk was strong in flavor and smell, but money was scarce and Maire O'Rourke didn't like to accept gifts of milk from their richer neighbors, the Farrells, who had dozens of cows. In spite of the goat's milk, it was a good year.

Then one day Gertie, now nearly ten and more aware of the process of birth, though still not understanding it, noticed her mother getting big again. She didn't dare mention it to the others, but she kept saying to herself, day by day, as she watched the change in her mother, Oh, no, not another baby! Soon Maire began cutting up old sheets for nappies again, and then everybody knew.

Jimmy came bursting into the room and stopped short at the sight of the nappies, staring at them with such a look that his mother guessed what he was thinking, and raised her hand to give him a wallop. Jimmy ducked, escaped the blow, and ran out, banging the door behind him, and Gertie said to herself, well, I'm going to say it, anyway. And she said to her mother, "Why does the doctor bring so many kids to our house, why doesn't he bring some more to Mrs. Finnegan?"

This time Maire didn't miss, and Gertie got a slap on the face for her question, but no answer.

It was a moment of puzzlement and inquiry, never to be repeated; when Rita was born a little while later, Gertie was delighted to have another sister. Now it was four girls and eight boys in the crowded house, much better than the nine against two of a few years before. And Gertie was beginning to think of herself as a girl now, although she was still a bit of a tomboy and played with Jimmy and Tony more than with her younger sister Tess.

9.

Children, Politics, and Neighbors

Eoin O'Rourke and Father O'Malley were great friends, in spite of their political differences. They were two of a kind, big men with strong backs and strong voices, who never hesitated to stand up and say what they thought, whether people liked it or not. Father O'Malley was a fine-looking man, with iron-gray hair over a square face with a high forehead, and under the straight line of his black eyebrows his deep-set eyes bored into his parishioners from behind steel-rimmed glasses. He used to come often to the school to talk with the teacher about school business or with the children about their faith. Once at Christmastime he drew a picture of Santa Claus on the blackboard, and talked of the kindly bishop whose love of children had started the Santa Claus legend so many hundreds of years ago. The schoolmaster used to visit the priest at his house sometimes in the evening, or so he would say when he got home afterward, though Maire was never sure he hadn't been at O'Riordan's instead, or stopped there on his way home. Father O'Malley, she was sure, would never give him a drink.

The good priest was a great one for talking about drink in his sermons, and of other occasions of sin as well. He would start calmly, in a soft, gentle voice, lamenting the weakness of man and the presence of old Adam in each of us, and build up his theme slowly, warning of the dangers and pitfalls of life, and the fires of hell that await the unfaithful. Soon he would begin to shout, and the words would come faster and more boldly, and a lock of his hair would fall down from his neatly combed pate and dangle like a wagging dog's tail over his glasses as he tossed his head to and fro.

Anyone who came into the church on Sunday morning thinking he was free from all sin and grateful for a week without temptation, was sure by the time Father O'Malley finished, that he had committed all the sins in the book, in thought if not in word or deed, in the past years of his life if not in the days of that week. It was an exciting experience that filled the children's minds with wonder and their mother's heart with devotion and strengthened resolution; after it Eoin would pass the collection plate, for he, too, was a man of authority, and all the congregation were his pupils or former pupils or their parents.

Father O'Malley was not much older than the schoolmaster, but his blood pressure was uncomfortably high, and in spite of his doctor's warnings he put extraordinary vigor into everything he did. He was sixty-one when he was struck down by a heart attack one day in County Mayo, climbing Saint Patrick's holy mountain not on a pilgrimage but a holiday.

Maire was overcome when she heard of it, for so sudden a death was doubly tragic, but as she said to Eoin, "There's no fear for such a holy man. 'Tis a saint he is, and 'twas a saint he lived. He was always ready, and that day God was ready for him."

When the body was brought back to Saint Columbanus's to

lie in a flower-decked coffin before the altar, the O'Rourkes and their fourteen children were first in the throng of parishioners who knelt beside it to say the parting rosary. Maire mourned her loss, and in her prayers from that day on she prayed not so much for her old confessor as to him.

The funeral Mass the next day was the finest Saint Columbanus's had ever seen, with the bishop in his tall miter, carrying his massive golden crosier, at the head of the procession. Two canons and three curates assisted him, and the nuns from the convent on the hilltop joined in singing the Gregorian chants. The church was so crowded that there was barely room to breathe; the smaller children were packed into the choir loft for safety, with a perfect view of all the goings-on.

Willie, just turned seven and only recently admitted to his First Communion, was filled with wonder and delight. He thought what a grand place heaven must be, if this was the way they celebrated a man's entering into it. And what a great man Father O'Malley must be, if this was the way they said goodbye to him. Willie hadn't thought much about him before; he remembered him drawing the Santa Claus on the blackboard, though he had never quite understood what that had to do with the Holy Mother and the Baby Jesus; he had learned the prayers Father O'Malley taught him for his First Communion, and he had known that the priest was important, because his mother seemed to be nicer to him than she was to his own father, and talked about him more, too.

Willie knew he had been baptized by Father O'Malley, and that was important; Father O'Malley had baptized all his brothers and sisters, and he remembered how it was with his baby sister, Rita; that was only a little while ago. Gradually Willie realized that all this was because Father O'Malley was a priest, not just an ordinary man like his own father. What a wonderful thing it must be, he thought, to be a priest!

After that for a long time the only game that Willie wanted to play was pretending to be a priest. He would get Gertie and Matt to help him, because they were older, and they would build an altar with stones, and put more stones around it to show where the rest of the church was, and the statues. Gertie would find bits of old dresses and towels and scraps of waste material from her mother's sewing box, and drape them over him for his vestments. Then they'd summon the younger ones, Tess and Peter and Christy and Brigid, to join the congregation and play at being worshipers. They'd all kneel down on the ground behind Willie while he bent over his play altar and mumbled words that sounded like Latin, spread his arms as though in prayer, and raised his little cup in both hands over his head, then set it down and knelt before it.

What Father O'Malley would have thought of all this nobody knew, but Willie's mother never interfered. There was no irreverent mockery in this; it wasn't just children playing. Willie had a true vocation, she was sure, and her heart rejoiced.

Gertie soon tired of Willie's game, and Jimmy refused to have any part in it. He and Tony were having more fun chasing horses in the fields, setting snares for rabbits, and running races steeplechase-style, scrambling through the tall brambled hedges and jumping over the low stone fences that divided the fields. Gertie liked to join them, for she could run almost as fast and jump almost as high, or climb over the fences that were too high to jump, though she was hampered by the long braids of raven hair that she still wore in the same style as her mother had as a young girl—two braids, one on each side, long enough to reach her waist, tied at the ends with big bows of shiny pink ribbon.

Those hair ribbons were the bane of Gertie's existence, for they were forever getting caught in the brambles and pulling off. Then her hair would fall loose, and she would brush it out of her eyes and toss her head so it would stream behind her in the wind as she ran. That was much nicer, though she wished her hair wasn't so long; the trouble was combing it to get the snags out when she got home, and finding those blasted ribbons.

"Where's your ribbons?" her mother would call the moment she caught sight of her. "You fetch them before I—" But Gertie wouldn't wait for the rest.

"Ooh! I forgot!" she'd plead. "C'mon, Jimmy!" And the two of them would race back to the fields, still breathless, to run again to each hedge they'd been through and each bush they'd skirted to see if a bit of tattered pink could be seen hanging from a thorn. In the gathering darkness of evening it wasn't easy, and how could they remember where they'd been? Often as not, Gertie had to run home without the ribbons, to be clouted for her carelessness and tortured by the comb pulling at the snags in her hair, until a new pair of ribbons were in place and she'd been warned for the hundredth time not to do that again.

One day when her mother and father were in Sligo Town for their monthly shopping trip, Gertie stopped her brother as he was heading out toward the fields.

"Jimmy," she said, "I've got an idea. Will you cut my hair for me?"

"What for?"

"It's too terrible long. Think how lovely I'd be if it only came to here—" and she sliced at it with her hand, just above the shoulder, the fashionable length she'd seen in a magazine picture.

"Mummy would give us a flaking if we ever did that," Jimmy said doubtfully.

"I don't care. I get a flaking anyhow, every time I lose the ribbons."

So they hunted through the house for their mother's scissors, and couldn't find them. Gertie began to lose her nerve, but once Jimmy got started on something he couldn't be stopped.

"I know what," he said. "Daddy's razor!"

"Don't you touch that; he'll wallop you with the strop."

"No, he won't. He'll never know. He'll sharpen it up like he always does and not know what we've been doing."

So they went to the razor case on the windowsill where it was always kept, and pulled out the long, wicked-looking blade with the folding handle that their father had used all their lives, and Jimmy sliced neatly through the two long braids without even undoing them, fascinated at the way each strand severed neatly as he drew the sharp blade across them. Gertie stood stock still, petrified with anxiety, and could barely feel what he was doing. It was over almost before she knew he'd started.

Then she ran her fingers through the shortened braids to loosen them, and tossed her head to let the hair fall naturally. She peered into her father's shaving mirror to study the result, and gave a whoop of delight.

"You've done it!" she cried. "Oooh! It's lovely! Come on!" And they dashed out to the fields, carrying the hated pigtails with them, flinging them back and forth to each other till they, too, got lost in the brambles to join the old pink ribbons.

They'd forgotten to put the razor away, of course, and Daddy knew as well as Mummy what had happened when the two of them got home. Jimmy and Gertie got their "flaking," but that was the end of it; afterward Maire found her sewing scissors and trimmed the ends of Gertie's hair evenly, getting rid of the ragged places Jimmy had left. Gertie had a natural wave in her hair, and her mother curled it in little rolls and ringlets, thinking as she worked that it looked quite nice that way after all, and made Gertie look more grown-up.

It was her husband that Maire O'Rourke was worried about that evening. Eoin was getting mixed up in politics again, not just campaigning for his friends as he had done so often over the years, but planning to run for office himself. The local elections were coming up, and Eoin was going to stand for the County Council. He hadn't said anything to her about it; he never did that, but she had heard it in Sligo Town. She had seen his name on a poster, with those of the other candidates, and it wasn't simply listed under the Fianna Fáil party, where it belonged; it was all by itself at the bottom of the sheet, under the heading INDEPENDENT FIANNA FÁIL.

Maire had never liked Eoin's political campaigning; she sometimes thought he only did it as an excuse for spending more time in the pubs, drinking with his political cronies. They were always after him for support because of his position in the community; next to the priest, the schoolmaster was the most important figure in the parish, a man of learning and authority who had power over the future of people's children.

But it was one thing to allow your name to be used as a supporter of so-and-so the Fianna Fáil candidate, whoever he might be; nobody objected to that. A man was allowed to have his political views if he didn't make too much of them. Eoin went too far, his wife thought, and it made him more enemies than friends. He was forever making speeches about de Valera—as though Dev had anything to do with local affairs in County Sligo—and raking up old memories of the troubled years. When he talked about the IRA, it brought up memories of the Tans, the civil war, and the terrible test of which-side-were-you-on-then. It was not a thing to talk about, but when the passion of politics was on him, Eoin wouldn't stop.

And what had he ever gotten for it? They'd made him a peace commissioner, to make a shilling now and again for signing a paper, or writing wills for men who had less learning but more money, and little gain did Maire or his family ever get from it. Eoin could quote the Gaelic poets as well as the Latin and Greek; he could stride out into the fields with his long surveyor's chain to measure the crooked fences and figure the rods and furlongs and acres. Surely he could make more of himself than schoolmaster if he weren't so bent on politics, and the booze that went with it. What good would it do him to be county councillor?

Politics was a dirty business, Maire felt, and anyone who got mixed up in it was a fool. And what was Eoin doing calling himself "Independent" instead of staying with the Fianna Fáil he'd always believed in?

If Father O'Malley were alive, Maire reflected, she'd go to him and he'd talk some sense into her husband, but it was too late for that now. The new priest was an awkward, bumbling man, all right in his own way, no doubt, but never the inspiration Father O'Malley had been, and he and Eoin didn't get on at all. So Maire put her question directly to Eoin, and he tried to explain, but Maire couldn't make any sense of it.

Joe Brennan had asked him to stand for the council a month ago; Higgins wanted to retire, or the party wanted him to retire, because he was getting old, and had said or done something they didn't like. Eoin had said he'd do it, and he'd asked his friends for support and begun writing speeches and preparing broadsides for the printers; and then Higgins had changed his mind, or the party had changed their minds, and Eoin had been told he wasn't wanted after all and wasn't going to get the party endorsement; it was going to Higgins. And Eoin was angry, for once he had put his hand to doing something, the tide and the sea couldn't stop him from getting ahead with it. Nor could Maire.

It seemed for the next few weeks that politics was all Eoin O'Rourke lived for. He was on his bicycle every evening after school, from one end of the district to the other, uphill and down, stopping at every farmhouse and pub, arguing and haranguing, standing bareheaded in the rain on the steps of a different church after each Mass, coming home at two or three in the morning soaked to the skin, breathless and coughing with fatigue. It was a passionate, personal campaign; there were no great issues at stake in the County Council, but loyalty to the old dream of the 1916 Irish Republic was still a smoldering fire in people's hearts, revived now by Britain's difficulties in another world war. The year was 1942; fifty miles away across the border there were Irishmen involved in Britain's war, and the Americans, who had done so much for Ireland and for Sligo families like the O'Rourkes, were in it on Britain's side too. Talk of the Republic in this new wartime stirred old fears and angers, and brought conflicts of old loves and loyalties.

Eoin wasn't forgiven for splitting his own party, and there were complaints that a schoolmaster had no business in politics, that at best he was neglecting his young charges, at worst corrupting them. It was said that he drank too much; a common sin among politicians, but not to be forgiven in a schoolmaster.

Eoin had no hope of winning that election, and probably never expected to; he campaigned as a matter of principle. What hurt him most was that even his own parish of Ballycarrick didn't give him a majority; he did better in neighboring Skreen and Dromard. He went there first when the election was over, to thank the voters as they came from church after Mass. They had stood by him when his friends let him down.

At first the defeat didn't seem to make much difference, though Eoin's cough didn't get any better. Once or twice he had a blackout in the schoolroom; he would sit down heavily at his desk, his eyes closed and his face as pale as wax, while the children whispered anxiously among themselves, and pretty soon one of the older ones would take charge, and Eoin would shake his head wearily and walk out into the fresh air, to stand gazing at the sea for a long time, until he summoned the strength to mount his bicycle and pedal home, without a word to anybody.

He was smoking heavily, too, even in the schoolroom, although it was against the rules. He would sit at his desk while the children were reading or reciting, lighting one Sweet Afton after another and tossing them into the fireplace before they were half finished. He generally missed, because he never looked, and when school was over for the day there would be a litter of fag-ends around the grate. Some of the older boys would pick them up after the master left, and hide them in their pockets to smoke when they were away by themselves, behind haystacks or stone fences. That was how Jimmy first learned to smoke at thirteen; later he would sneak a pack of ten out of the store his father kept at home, and when Gertie caught him one day he gave her one of the cigarettes and showed her how to smoke it. She coughed and spluttered and refused to try it again, but she never told on him. One day his father caught him, and that was the end of that.

Tony was the one who was most excited by the election campaign. He had helped with the canvassing, going door-to-door like his father and telling the neighbors what a grand man his daddy was; he had a drawerful of leaflets and newspaper clippings and pictures of de Valera, and he talked about the IRA as though it were still the real army of Ireland. When his father was defeated, Tony resolved to run for the council himself when he was old enough; meanwhile he made up political speeches of his own, and climbed on the dunghill behind the house to deliver them, waving his arms and shouting above the wind to his brothers and sisters. They laughed at him, but Tony didn't mind; he was training for his future career.

Eoin was amused by all this, but it didn't improve his health or his prospects. He was drinking more heavily, and the tensions at home were increasing. The sixteenth child, Patrick, was born when Maire was forty-four years old, though she wouldn't admit it. No one knew then that he was to be her last. The children were growing up, but none of them was yet old enough to leave home, unless money could be found to send them away to secondary school, and there was no way of doing that.

Mary and Joe were with the old aunt, and Annie Philomena had died, and that left thirteen at home. Mick, at seventeen, was his mother's main reliance for running the household; Charlie and Tony and Jim, with some help from Mick, took care of the vegetable garden and the cow and the goat, and worked for other farmers when they got a chance. One year they rented a field and planted potatoes, and got a pretty good crop, but when they dug them up and took them to market they didn't know how to sell them, and came home with barely enough money to pay their expenses. In their innocence they had loaded their sacks too full, and sold long weight for short price; and when the buyers argued that there was too much soil in the sack with the spuds, and the weight wasn't true, the boys believed them and lowered the price still more, not knowing that their spuds were cleaner and their weight more honest than the older farmers were offering.

It was a hard way to learn, and what they learned was not to bother with that again. Jimmy could earn more money catching rabbits and selling them for their meat.

It was a difficult time, and the tempers of father and mother grew shorter. The children never knew what the quarrels were about, but they ended too often with Eoin leaving the house, and there was never any doubt where he was going. In earlier days he would sit of an evening by the kitchen fire, playing Irish jigs and reels on his old tin whistle, and when Maire was in a good mood and not too heavy with child she would do the old step-dancing round and round the kitchen, while the youngsters clapped their hands and did their best to learn the fast steps. That never happened anymore; Eoin in his fifties was too old, and so was Maire in her forties, and her health was not much better than his. So Eoin drank for comfort, and Maire scolded but never moaned.

Then there was trouble with their neighbors the Farrells, who owned one hundred acres of land or more and were the richest people for miles around. The Farrells had always been kind to the O'Rourkes, especially old Mother Farrell, who was always glad to give them a jug of milk when the O'Rourkes' cow was dry. Maire hated accepting that kind of charity, and it embarrassed the children to ask for it, but it was better than drinking their own goat's milk.

Mother Farrell would give them other treats, too, if they were good; she used to tell them not to go into the orchard and pick the apples as they ripened, but to knock on the kitchen door and she'd give them all they wanted. Still, it didn't seem fair that the Farrells should have so much when the O'Rourkes had so little. There were no children to play with in the Farrell family, only a grown-up son and two grown-up daughters, a bachelor and two spinsters. Jimmy and Gertie and Tony used to throw snowballs at them in winter, or sometimes even stones as they rode by on their bicycles, not to hit them but to see if they could be frightened into falling off. They never were, of course, and maybe they didn't even notice, because they never made a fuss about it; but Roger Farrell started a row when he caught the children jumping over the stone fences between his pastures.

They were ancient fences that had divided those pastures for no one knew how many hundreds of years, but they were easy to knock down. They were built in the typical style of rocky Connacht, the same as can be seen throughout the counties of Sligo and Mayo and Galway and parts of Clare, where the rocky fields were never much inhabited until Cromwell made the region a vast place of exile for the conquered Irish from the more fertile lands to the east and south. As the newcomers cleared the rocks from the thin soil that was to be theirs, they piled them up at the edges of their fields to mark the boundaries, but the fields had to be small because there was so little land for so many, and the fences were made narrow, only one stone wide.

To look at them, it seemed a marvel that they could stand at all, and it must have taken great skill to build them, for each stone was balanced on the one below, with support from before and behind but none on either side and no mortar to hold it in place. Some of the chinks between the stones were big enough for a child's arm to slip through, and a passerby on the road could look through them and see the cattle on the other side of the fence. The wind blew freely through the chinks, and perhaps that was why they were there, to keep the wind from blowing the fences down. But a child jumping over the fence could dislodge the stones with his foot if he didn't clear it;

and a small child clambering after could move a stone at the bottom and the whole structure would tumble down, leaving a gap for the cattle to wander through.

For any farmer this would be a burden, with the strays to catch and the fence to be carefully repaired; but to Roger Farrell it was a crime beyond all toleration or forgiveness. His cows were not only his life, as politics was life to Eoin O'Rourke; they were his god.

Roger never went to Mass anymore, since he'd had a falling out with Father O'Malley years ago. While his mother and sisters were in church he would be out in the fields counting his cows, opening the big gates from one field to another and numbering the animals one by one as they went through. It was his Sunday ritual, and perhaps as he had so many cows it was his best way of keeping track. The children coming home from Mass would sometimes see him still at it, and walk along behind to watch.

Roger didn't mind that, but when he saw them jumping his fences he chased after them with his blackthorn cane and followed them home to confront their mother.

"What devilment are you after doing?" she demanded, and the three of them stood silent while Roger, in his slow, mumbling way, explained. He was choking with anger, but there was not much he needed to say; Maire knew well what the problem was, and had warned Jimmy and Gertie about it before.

"They'll not be doing it again," she said. "Now into the house with you, children, and wait till I come." There were apologies to make, which did not come easily to Maire O'Rourke, and the children's caning when she was ready for it was more severe on that account.

There was no more racing in Roger Farrell's fields after that, but Jimmy couldn't stay out of them altogether. He still had a packet of fags he had sneaked from his father, and they were hidden in one of Roger's haycocks. It didn't seem right to just leave them there, and if Roger found them he might guess where they came from and make more trouble.

126

The next day, when it seemed that everything was forgotten and he would be safe, Jimmy vaulted the fence once more, taking care not to disturb so much as a flake of dust on a stone, and hared for the haycock on the other side. He found his fags and was about to run back when he heard a sound from behind the haycock, and stopped in alarm. Then he recognized the sound, for he had heard it before when he was playing in Roger's fields. He peered cautiously around the haycock, and what he saw made him giggle. There was Roger Farrell lying fast asleep, a half-finished bottle of poteen in his hand, and the sweet-sour smell of that strong Irish moonshine issuing from his open mouth as he snored.

Jimmy scrambled to his feet and tiptoed to the fence, choosing a low spot where he could get over it noiselessly, and then a thought struck him. Could Roger be seen from the lane, if one went a little farther along it and peered over the fence? From where he stood, Roger was hidden by the haycock, but if he just went a few yards up the hill? Jimmy tried it, not daring to look over the fence but peering through a chink when he thought he'd gone far enough. Yes, there he was, and still snoring. He'd be out for hours.

It wasn't a very nice thing to do, but Jimmy still smarted from his caning, and one bad turn deserved another. He ran to the house and found his mother in the kitchen, feeding Patrick a gruel of milk and mashed potatoes. She looked at him suspiciously.

"You been in Roger Farrell's field again?" she asked.

"No, Mom," Jimmy lied, "but I seen him."

"Seen him where?"

"Lying on the ground by his haycock. I seen him from over the fence by the lane."

"Lazy good-for-nothing, like all the Farrells. But you stay out of his fields, don't you go in there and make more trouble for me."

"He's been having a swig, Mummy. He's got a bottle of poteen with him and he's snoring his head off."

"Be off with you, I don't believe it."

"It's true. I seen him often doing it, with his bottle in his hand counting his cows. That's why he has to count them so often, he can't ever get the number straight."

"Don't you talk like that now, Jimmy. Roger Farrell's a good neighbor and you mustn't be saying such things."

"It's true, Mummy, it's really true. You can go and see him yourself."

Maire half rose from her chair and put the spoon down, but it looked to Jimmy as if she was reaching for the broom to whack him, so he ducked out the door and hid in the shed behind the stack of turf to peer out and watch what might happen next.

Maire sat down again and picked up the spoon to give Patrick some more of his gruel, while she thought about what Jimmy had told her. It couldn't be true, but if Jimmy was telling her stories like that she should make sure they weren't true before she punished him. And on the other hand—well, she'd better go and see.

Roger's position was unchanged when she reached the fence, just as Jimmy had described it, but as she let her hands fall in dismay they knocked a stone from the fence and Roger, hearing the noise, stirred and looked up at her, bottle still in hand, with a bleary look in his eye that Maire knew only too well—she'd seen it too often on Eoin to mistake it. She turned in horror, grabbing her skirts and running across the lane to get out of Roger's sight.

Jimmy, observing from behind the stack of turf, grinned in satisfaction.

Maire brooded about what she had seen, and wondered what to do about it. There was no use telling Eoin; he'd only take that terrible man's side and find some excuse for him. Eoin was a bad enough example for the children as it was, without having the same trouble from a neighbor. And the shame of yesterday's scene, when Roger Farrell had come to her to complain about her children's games; what harm was there in them, really?

Maire couldn't decide what to do. If only Father O'Malley were still alive; she'd talk to Father Lynch, of course, the new pastor, but it would do no good. And she'd write to her sister Eileen in Crossmolina; Eileen knew the Farrells, and might think of something.

It didn't occur to Maire that Eileen or Father Lynch might mention the story to someone else, with the best of intentions, or that Roger Farrell might not like it if the story spread around Ballycarrick that he took his bottle into his hayfields. As it turned out, everybody knew that already, and some were surprised that it had taken Maire so long to find out. If she thought he was a bad influence on her children, ·they said, let her keep them home.

But Roger was angry, and he told his solicitor to start a suit against Mrs. O'Rourke for slander. He claimed eight hundred pounds damages, an impossible sum, more than Eoin earned in a year, and more than the value of all he owned.

Eoin knew enough about the law to understand that Roger had no chance of collecting so much, but still it was a case that had to be taken seriously, and he had to hire a barrister to defend him in court. There were a lot of strange people coming to the house, and conferences in the sitting room with the door closed, and the children were kept out of the way so they wouldn't know what was going on; but Jimmy had to be told because he was to be a witness at the trial, and give evidence of what he had seen. That was something he hadn't thought of when he first told his mother the story, but Jimmy wasn't scared; whatever the judge and the barristers said to him, it couldn't be any worse than standing up before his father to recite his lessons in school or take his punishment at home.

When the day came it was a Saturday, and Joe McFeeny, the undertaker, offered to give them a lift into Sligo Town because he was going there anyway in his lorry to take a load of turf to market. There wasn't room for Jimmy in the front of the lorry with his mother and father and McFeeny, so he climbed up on top of the turf, eight or nine feet high, and rode like a king in his chariot surveying the world around him, wearing his shoes and the Sunday suit he'd never worn before except at Mass. It needed a powerful lot of brushing when they got there.

The judge was a kindly man who asked Jimmy only a few short questions in a gentle voice, and the two barristers did most of the talking. There was no denying that Mrs. O'Rourke had written the letter, and no denying that what she had said in it was true; no denying that it was a right unkind thing to say about a man, but didn't he deserve it and had it done him any harm? The judge pondered and gave his decision: damages to be paid in the amount of one pound.

There was a ripple of laughter among the spectators, and the judge pounded his gavel for order. Eoin thanked the court with a straight face but a twinkle in his eye, and found enough coins in his pocket to pay the damages on the spot. Maire bustled Jimmy out of the courtroom in front of her, lips together in a satisfied smile; Roger took his pound and stalked angrily past without giving them a look. After that there was no more begging milk from Mrs. Farrell when the cow was dry; they made do with the goat's milk, foul-tasting though it was.

10.

Childhood's
End

Jimmy was fifteen at the time of the slander suit, a schoolboy no longer, but not yet a man either. He had been treated
like a man when he gave his evidence; they'd asked him questions and he'd answered them, and gotten everything straight
and never had to say anything about the cigarettes he'd sneaked
from his dad and hidden in the haycock. He thought about
it on the way home, bouncing around in the back of McFeeny's
lorry, empty now that the turf was sold.

There must be more to life than playing in the fields like a
kid with your younger brother and sister, Jimmy decided,
though that was more fun than the work he did for Roger and
other farmers in the area. He was big enough already to handle
a scythe, harvesting the wheat and oats or cutting grass for hay,
to earn his pocket money. Most of the time it was pulling things
out of the ground, picking potatoes and snagging turnips for
half a crown a day. There was no future in it—he made more
money catching rabbits at night with his big battery-powered

lamp. He could stop a rabbit dead in his tracks by shining the spotlight on his run ahead of him, and the rabbit would turn aside and lose his way, and hop about until the old dog caught up with him and picked him up by the head. A good rabbit would fetch five, six, or even seven shillings; meat was scarce because of the war.

But it wasn't good enough. Jimmy didn't want to spend the rest of his life at Toberpatrick, and he'd never get away if he didn't learn a better trade than farming. His brother Joe knew that, and he'd gotten away—not just to the old aunt's place with Mary, but away from there too, selling provisions and hardware in a shop in Carrick-on-Shannon, and then he'd joined the Garda and gone away to Dublin to be trained, and then to a station in Galway. That would be the life, riding around in a great car with the blue light on top, wearing a uniform with silver buttons. Charlie wanted to join the Garda too, but he didn't know whether they'd take him; Charlie had never done anything but spade turf and dig potatoes, what did he know? Anyhow, Jimmy wasn't old enough for the Garda, so he'd have to think of something else.

It was McFeeny who solved Jimmy's problem, and without Jimmy even knowing it at the time. All the while Jimmy was pondering these things in the back of the lorry, McFeeny was talking about him to his mother and father in the front. Mc-Feeny wanted a good strong boy to help him in his undertaking business. A boy who would know how to behave himself in the graveyard, and could help lower the coffins without letting the rope slip through his hands; who could build the coffins out of pine boards, and pitch them inside and out and line them with clean linen cloths; who could pull his end of the big cross-cut saw when McFeeny was felling trees in the pine woods, and help trim off the branches and run the logs through the sawmill without cutting his arms off. Could Jimmy do those things?

"He can learn," his father said. "He's quick."

" 'Twould be good for him," said his mother. "Keep him out of devilment."

So Jimmy was apprenticed to McFeeny, the undertaker, a respectable and dignified profession that would assure him a high regard in the community, even if it did begin, like most professions, with mainly manual labor. If Charlie was accepted by the Garda, that would make three of Eoin's sons launched on their careers. Mick had so far shown no great desire to leave home, but that was just as well because his mother still needed him. They were very anxious about Tony because he was ill so often; he had been down with a fever for several months a few years before, and it had left him so weak he didn't seem fully recovered even yet. Matt would be all right; he would be trained for the priesthood, that had already been decided, and Aunt Doty in America was going to send the money for him to go to Saint Mary's College in Summerhill when he finished school next year. The rest were still young; time enough to think about them later.

Mary wasn't married yet, though she was already past the age at which her mother had married; Aunt Annie was to blame for that. Annie was getting old now, and set in her ways. She never went outside her own barnyard, except to Mass; all her days she sat by the fireside, smoking her long clay pipe. People said she'd get cancer from that, but Annie didn't believe it. She had a cricket that lived in the ashes of her fireplace, and she treated it like a pet, covering it with a domed pot lid when she went to bed, and scolding Mary when she cleaned out the ashes, for fear she'd disturb the cricket or throw him out with the ashes. It was company for her. It chirped when the house was still, and Annie thought it brought her luck. But it wasn't bringing Mary any luck.

Tom Finnegan's boy, Michael, had his eye on Mary, and as Eoin had done, when he was courting Mary's mother, Michael would come by the shop nearly every day to buy a pennyworth of boiled sweets on his way to the hillside pasture, where the Finnegans kept a dozen black cattle just above Aunt Annie's fields. Or he'd stop in to look at the flagstone just inside the door that was supposed to foretell the weather. It was a massive flat slab of gray limestone that looked too big for any man or men to have set in place; perhaps the fairies had a hand in it, or perhaps it had always been there and the house had been built around it. Nobody really knew the answer to that, but everybody knew that in a dry spell that stone would sometimes be damp when there was no damp anywhere else around, and then it would rain the next day, without fail.

If the stone wasn't damp there would be another day of fine, sunny weather, and Michael would tease Mary until she agreed to walk out with him in the evening, those long, bright June evenings when the fields were flower gardens of buttercups and daisies, mustard and cress, wild lupins and purple loosestrife, and the hawthorn was white in the hedges, and the brown bogland ablaze with golden gorse. They would sit on the hilltop and watch the sun go down over the broad sea beyond the bay, filling the sky with salmon pink and laying down a bright burnished copper-gold track on the water from half nine until nearly ten in the evening. Then the color would deepen in the sky, from pink to mauve to purple to darkening blue, and by eleven there would be stars overhead but still a pale halo of reddish light over the horizon to the west and north, to show where the sun was rolling around the pole just under the rim of the visible earth.

On such an evening it would be midnight or after before the young couple were down off the hill and walking along the road to Aunt Annie's house. One night the old aunt's patience was exhausted, and she laid down her clay pipe and strode forth into the road with her blackthorn cane, her heels beating an angry tap-tap on the road as she walked, and her long black skirt brushing the wild carrots and Queen Anne's lace that crowded the road on both sides.

She was upon the youngsters before they saw her, and laid the cane about their shoulders in her anger and suspicion. Mary broke away, crying, and ran home, the aunt chasing her with cane upraised, while Michael stood there in astonishment, not knowing what to do. He told his father of it in the morning, and his father told Mary's father, and Eoin went down to see Aunt Annie and nobody ever knew what was said between them, but there was a coolness between Maire and her aunt for a long time after that, and Aunt Annie never used her cane on Mary again.

The incident prompted Maire and Eoin to do some thinking about the second daughter, Gertie, who was fourteen that summer and finished with her father's school. It would be a fine thing for Mary to marry a farmer and join his acres to those she would inherit from Aunt Annie, but Gertie would have no such dowry, and would need to learn a suitable trade. There was a school of domestic science at Swinford, twenty miles away, where Gertie could be a boarder, looked after by the nuns. She'd go to Mass every day and be trained in the refinements of cultured living as well as the practical skills of housework and cookery. Aunt Doty, their rich relative in America, had earned all her money as a domestic servant; perhaps that wasn't as promising a career as it used to be, but there were jobs to be had in hotels that might be even better. And the fee for the Swinford school was not beyond Eoin's reach, for it was part of the nuns' work of charity, and supported by their foundation.

Gertie went off to Swinford and Matt to Summerhill, and then there were only six of Eoin's own children left in his school, and one more, three-year-old Patrick, still to come. Eoin was fifty-nine, and though he was coughing quite a bit, he didn't think it was very important. Of course he smoked too much, but he'd been doing that all his life, and was too old to give it up now. And he was drinking too much, but that was a habit too, and he held his liquor well. A man was entitled to his pleasures.

It was a long time since he'd had one of those blackouts that had bothered him after his election defeat. There had been some hard feelings over that, because when he split the Fianna Fáil vote, the other party, the Fine Gael, won a totally undeserved victory, the first in the history of the district. But that was over now, too; in the next election Eoin had taken no part, and the Fine Gael man had been thrown out. If Eoin's mistakes hadn't exactly been forgotten by his enemies, they were forgiven now by his friends. He missed the excitement of politics, but there was a new stability in his life. No new children on the way and no likelihood of another; they were all growing up now and needing his attention. The difficult times were over, and Eoin was beginning to mellow. The future looked good for him.

He was thinking of these things one wet day in March when it had been raining for a week and the lane was so deep in mud he could hardly force his bicycle through it on his way to school. His legs didn't seem to have the strength they used to when he pushed down on the pedals, and he had to rise a little from his seat to add weight to the stroke each time the wheels got mired. His coat was heavy with rain, a burden on his shoulders and an encumbrance around his legs. He muttered an angry curse on Roger Farrell, who had called him out the day before to measure a field he wanted to rent, when the rain was coming down in sheets, whipping him front and back as the gale winds from the sea blew in whirling gusts from every side.

"Surely not today," he had said to Roger. "We'd best wait until the weather clears a bit."

Roger had stared at him with the arrogance of the young countryman who feels himself stronger than the elements and doesn't yet know what their constant buffeting is doing to him. "You've got a coat, haven't you," he had snorted, and stamped out the door without waiting for an answer, leaving a trail of mud on the schoolroom floor. And Eoin, reflecting that the rain could go on for weeks, had gone out that evening with his surveyor's chain and done the work.

His coat was still wet when he put it on in the morning; it had hung by the chimney all night, but that had only made it smell of the smoldering turf, and warmed the water in it but dried none of it out. No matter; it was soaked again with cold water the moment he stepped out the door.

He was breathing heavily when he reached the school, but he didn't think anything of that. He was late, and the children already had the fire going, so he stood close by it to warm himself as he began the day's routine. The room was stuffy, with the sour smell of wet clothing and wet children. Eoin noticed angrily that the floor hadn't been properly swept; the mud left by Roger Farrell was still there by the door, big smears with the smaller prints of children's muddy boots all around and across them. He set two of the boys to clean it up while he opened his books.

It was toward the end of the morning that Eoin had another blackout, and this time he knew from the sudden stabbing pain in his chest that it was going to be worse than the others, far worse. The children mustn't know, especially his own children. But Rita was terrified when she saw him slump over the desk and then slide to the floor; it was her first year in school, and she'd never seen this happen to her daddy before. Tess, seven years older, remembered what it had been like the other times, and wasn't much afraid, but it had never been as bad as this. She hugged Rita in her arms to comfort her, while Willie, Peter, Christy, and Brigid gathered around their father, wondering what to do. John Kearin, who lived next to the Finnegans and had been Tess's favorite friend since she'd started going to school, saw the worried expression on her face and said to her, "I'm going for the doctor."

Nobody was supposed to leave the school without the teacher's permission, but this was different. John ran out into the rain, coatless and bareheaded, his long legs taking him down the muddy lane faster than the schoolmaster had gone on his bicycle, all the way down to the main road and up the hill to the slate-roofed house with the long wire leading into it from the telephone pole, where Dr. Hart lived and had his surgery. John ran up the path to the door and was reaching for it when it was opened by Mrs. Hart, who had seen him through the window, and he fell breathless against her, the rain from his long hair and dripping shirt making a wet stain on her apron. "God and his angels bless us," she said. "What's happened, child?"

"The schoolmaster," John panted. "He's fainted. He's—he looks—he might be—he's just lying there—"

"The Lord preserve him," said Mrs. Hart, and leaving the boy to get his breath she burst into the surgery, to come out a moment later followed by the doctor, with his greatcoat already on and his black bag in his hand.

"Ring for the ambulance, Molly," he said. "Come on, boy."

It was a heart attack this time, a severe one, and when Eoin came back from the nursing home several weeks later Dr. Hart insisted that his bed be brought downstairs, because he wouldn't be able to climb the stairs any longer. He would need complete rest for at least six months, before he could go back to teaching. And he'd have to give up the smoking and drink if he didn't want it to happen again. It was a cruel sentence, but there was no way around it.

The big bed was brought down to the sitting room by the front door, where the painting of the Sacred Heart hung over the fireplace, and for the next two years that was Eoin's room, and the children had to tiptoe past it when he was asleep, especially the older boys when they came in late at night. His strength came back slowly, and his cough got better, though he never lost the hankering for tobacco.

His temper got shorter as his damaged heart grew stronger, and he pestered the doctor until he was allowed to keep a clay pipe, like Aunt Annie's, and draw on it once or twice a day, but no more. Or that was what the doctor said; when Maire or the district nurse, who came every week to give him injections, found him breaking the rule they'd take the pipe away from him, and threaten to smash it if he didn't behave himself. Which only made his temper worse.

All this time he had to pay for a substitute teacher at the

school, a junior assistant whose wages took nearly half his salary though she knew little to teach the children and could do little more than keep order in the classroom. It rankled him, and it made it harder to pay Gertie's fees at Swinford and give Maire the money she needed for the household. So in September, before the six months were quite over, he was back at his desk in the school again, and sneaking an occasional Sweet Afton when nobody was looking, as Jimmy used to do behind his back.

He wasn't strong enough to ride his bicycle anymore, so he bought a donkey and trap, and every morning he'd ride to school in the trap, wearing his stiff white collar and neatly brushed trilby hat, with Rita sitting beside him and Willie leading the donkey, while the rest of the children ran on ahead, all but Patrick, who was too young for school. Eoin wasn't really strong enough to teach, or even fit to walk out of the house, the children thought, but no one dared tell him so. It wouldn't have done any good.

He got through that year all right, though there was a lot of snow in January and February, and when the snow was too heavy for the donkey to plod through he'd stay in bed, and Willie would trudge out to pass the word to the neighbors that the school would be closed until the snow melted. Nobody minded that, and perhaps it was these intervals of rest that helped Eoin through the winter.

In the spring Aunt Doty came over from America for a visit, and stayed through the summer. Joe came up from Galway on his holidays, and Eoin was glad to see him beginning to take a responsible interest in the family. Charlie passed his exams for the Garda, which weren't very difficult, but when it came to the physical they turned him down; his eyes weren't good enough.

Eoin was outraged at that, but he never told Charlie what had happened; he just said the answer was no. He was just as glad to have Charlie around the house, if it came to that; Charlie took care of the cow and the hens and the goat and the donkey, as well as the potatoes and cabbages and all the rest of it. Mick had too much to do in the house to attend to all the chores himself, and Tony wasn't strong enough.

Charlie, however, was beginning to worry, and so were the others. Their father's illness was more dangerous than he was willing to admit, that was clear. He had to go on working, he had no choice, and if he wasn't keeping strictly to his doctor's orders, they couldn't blame him for that. But how long could it go on?

Joe was the only one in the family earning his own living, and though he was starting to send his mother a few odd pounds every month, it wasn't much. Mick, Charlie, and Tony were only making pocket money from the work they did for neighboring farmers: half a crown a week and their lunch in the busy season. Jimmy was barely earning his keep from McFeeny; Gertie's fees had to be paid at Swinford; and while Aunt Doty was paying the main fees for Matt at Summerhill, he had other expenses that had to be met. And there were seven smaller ones at home, Tess about to finish school and Patrick about to begin. Charlie worried, but didn't know what to do about it.

Summer came at last, and Mary said yes to Michael Finnegan. There was nothing Aunt Annie could do, since Eoin and Maire approved. It was agreed that the young couple would live in Aunt Annie's house, so Mary could go on taking care of her. But Mary would rule the household now, and Aunt Annie's house and land would be hers and Michael's when she died.

They were married in Saint Columbanus's Church and afterward the two families and all the young men and girls of Ballycarrick gathered at the Imperial Hotel in Sligo Town for a reception that lasted all afternoon and well on into the golden evening. They danced Irish jigs and reels and German waltzes and the strange new jitterbug steps the American soldiers had introduced during the war, when they came across the border on leave from the naval base in County Derry.

Eoin was in good form and drank a little of the wine, and made a long elegant speech when he proposed the toast to the bride.

After the cake was cut and Tess had caught the bridal bouquet, Michael and his brother lifted Mary off her feet, and suddenly all the young men in the party were seizing her together, hoisting her over their heads and carrying her feet first out of the ballroom, while the rest of the crowd followed in procession to see her deposited safely in the hired car, with her husband beside her, to be driven off to the railway station. Eoin watched from the steps of the hotel and then went into the bar with Tom Finnegan, Michael's father, and for this occasion the doctor's orders were quite forgotten.

It took a long time to pry Eoin and Tom away from the bar, and on the way back to Toberpatrick Eoin was silent, thinking of his first-born daughter and how little he had known her in the years that she'd lived at Aunt Annie's, of how she had come home to help her mother when Rita and Patrick were born, and how she'd soon be having little ones of her own, his grandchildren.

The drink he'd taken made him feverish, and he could feel his face flush and the blood beating in his temples. As he fought down a wave of nausea he wondered if he would live to see his grandchildren. Tears began to flow down his cheeks, and Gertie, sitting beside him in Johnny Hogan's noisy old Ford, whispered to her mother, "What is Daddy crying for?" Her mother didn't answer, but she looked worried, and Gertie at sixteen was suddenly worried too.

That night Eoin had a choking fit as he was getting ready for bed, and Maire had to call Charlie to help her get his collar off. He sat slumped in his chair gasping for breath, while Charlie fumbled and tugged at the big clumsy stud, and finally ripped the collar and pulled it away. Then Eoin breathed a heavy sigh, and after a few minutes he came around and opened his eyes, and dismissed his son. He nearly went that time, Charlie thought.

But Eoin wasn't ready to go yet; there was something he had to do first. Willie wanted to be a priest, like Matt, and there was a chance he might be able to make it, because a new scholarship was being offered at Saint Mary's in Summerhill, which was worth almost as much as Aunt Doty was paying for Matt. Willie would need extra coaching, because it depended on winning a competitive examination. But he had one more year in his father's school before he would take the exam, and that would be time enough.

Even before the school opened that September, Eoin began helping Willie with the extra grammar, Latin, and history he would need. They would sit together at the kitchen table in the evenings, with candles to light their books as the summer passed and the evenings grew dark, and Rita and little Patrick used to think it great fun to sneak up on them from the shadows and blow out the candles.

By Christmastime Willie was making good progress, but Eoin was finding it hard to concentrate. He wasn't eating enough, and he'd lost so much weight that his big overcoat hung on him like an empty tent; there would have been room for two of him inside it. And in the spring he had another heart attack in the middle of the night, and the doctor came and then the ambulance, and this time there was to be no more getting up and going back to school to teach.

It was a long final illness, and lasted until summer, when Gertie came back from Swinford and Matt from Summerhill. They both went to see him in the nursing home, and Maire warned them not to be too frightened, for their father's face was so thin and his strong arms only skin and bones. Gertie put a white ribbon in her hair to please him, and he teased her as he always had. When she left she could hardly keep herself from crying.

He died on Midsummer's Day, the brightest day of the year, and was buried in Saint Columbanus's cemetery, in a coffin draped with the green, white, and orange Tricolour of the Irish Republic, and carried by his old comrades of the IRA. The list of mourners and messages of sympathy filled more than a column of the *Sligo Champion* the following week, coming from all over Ireland, England, and the United States, from politicians, teachers, priests, relatives, and former pupils in every walk of life.

As the *Champion* wrote in its appreciation, in his thirty-five years as school principal at Ballycarrick he had "proved himself a most beloved, efficient and zealous teacher, a tireless worker, ever ready to impart to his pupils the knowledge that was so profusely and exuberantly bestowed upon himself."

That was true, Maire thought as she read it; every word of it was true.

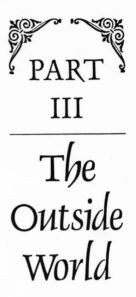

PART
III

The
Outside
World

II.

The
Barmaid,
the Navy,
and the
Bog

W hen Eoin O'Rourke died he left no will, for what did he have to leave? Eleven minor children for his widow to care for; three grown sons to care for her, and a married daughter. A two-story house with a slate roof, three acres, a cow, a goat, a donkey and trap, and a dozen or so hens. An old coat, a suit of clothes, a pair of boots, a trilby hat, a bicycle. For one year after his death his salary was paid to his widow, and there was a small pension from the teachers' union, but it was nothing much, barely enough for one, let alone the whole family. It was only in later years that government welfare payments made a difference. In 1948 it was up to the children to look after the mother.

There were times when they didn't have the price of a loaf of bread, and when the cow was dry and the hens weren't laying and the garden yielded little enough for growing children. Then Maire would go down to Johnny Hogan's little shop, and he'd give her something to go on with, and she would pay for it later when a little money arrived from one of the older boys, or her tiny pension. She hated to keep Johnny waiting, but it was better than taking charity from the neighbors.

Maire's one resource for fighting off her worries was the church. She went to Mass as often as she could, weekdays as well as Sundays, and in the evenings the family rosary grew longer and longer, as she added more "trimmings" at the end— the prayers for Eoin and other deceased relatives and friends; prayers for help in their need, and for whatever special purposes she had in mind each day; prayers for a happy death.

The sessions irritated Jimmy, and Gertie found them depressing; for the older boys it was a comforting routine. The four little ones accepted it as part of their daily lives, without question or particular interest, but for Matt and Willie, already committed to the priesthood, and twelve-year-old Peter, who was beginning to think about it, this nightly "school of prayer" had special meaning.

Willie had won the scholarship his father had coached him for, though the news had come too late for his father to hear it. He would soon be joining Matt at Summerhill, and Maire prayed silently that a way would be found for Peter to do the same. It would be a great thing to have three priests in the family, and there was no more promising career for country boys like hers. There were societies to pay for their education; they would lead comfortable lives as parish priests or perhaps even bishops, like her uncle in Kerry; with no children they would always be able to help the rest of the family. It would be a fitting reward, Maire thought, for her devotions.

Gertie was a more difficult problem. She had finished her domestic-science course at Swinford with no particular enthusiasm or distinction. "It was nice," she told her mother, "you got good training there. It taught me a lot about the home, and I learned to cook; I learned a lot about that. But there's no jobs here. Nancy O'Halloran's going to England, to work in a hotel. That's where I'm going, Mummy, England!"

Maire was horrified. England, Eoin had taught her, was the enemy, the place where Ireland's conquerors had come from, and now, thank God, had been driven back to. England was a Protestant country, where Gertie's Catholic faith would be endangered. England was where young Irish men and women went to look for jobs if they couldn't find work nearer home, and many of Maire's neighbors' children had done that, as she well knew. But please, God, not her own child; and most of all not Gertie, the rebellious one, who needed her mother's guidance more than any of the others, except perhaps Jimmy. Besides, Gertie was only seventeen, much too young to go far from home; it was not to be thought of.

Gertie paid no attention to all this. Seventeen didn't seem young to her; she was quite sure she could take care of herself, and went cheerfully into Sligo Town to register with an agency that had jobs in England and would pay her passage if she accepted one. All she had to do was get a passport, and that looked easy when Gertie studied the forms she had to fill out. There was only one difficulty: her mother had to sign the form to show she gave her permission, and Maire wouldn't do it.

When Joe came up from Galway for a visit, Maire talked to him about it. She was seeing more of Joe now than she had when he was a boy at Aunt Annie's, for although the Garda station where he served was so far off, he was doing his best to take his father's place.

"Why don't you send her to Gorman's, where I used to work?" he said. "Old Mrs. Gorman always had girls about Gertie's age doing their time with her. She takes good care of them."

Gorman's hardware and provisions shop in Carrick-on-Shannon was run on the family plan, like most such places, and since the Gormans didn't have enough grown-up children of their own they ran a kind of boarding house and training school for children of other families. For two or three years a respectable country girl like Gertie would be given her bed and board and occasional pocket money, more or less depending on how well she did what she was told and pleased the proprietress. She would be well looked after, and the proprietress would see that she didn't get into trouble.

Maire knew Mrs. Gorman only slightly, as a prosperous and successful woman who had inherited the shop from her first husband, and did well enough out of it to have a lodge near the strand in Ballycarrick, where she and her second husband went on weekends and holidays; the rest of the time they lived over their shop. Aunt Annie had made the arrangements for Joe to work for her, seven years before, so Maire went down to talk to Aunt Annie about it, and then went to see Mrs. Gorman. She seemed a kindly woman, rather heavy, with pale blue eyes and graying hair, but she had polite manners and a strong sense of discipline, and assured Maire that she was always strict about her girls' behavior.

"You need have no fear, Mrs. O'Rourke," she said. "She'll be like my own daughter to me."

Maire was pleased with this arrangement, but Gertie wasn't. "It's blooming hard work," she told her mother after the first week. "I really slave in that place. I work harder than the boy there. Weighing up them big bags of flour the lorries come for, and all the grain and everything, and sweep the floor and serve at the bar, all day long and in the evening, and then in the morning she gets me up to milk the cows."

"It won't hurt you." Her mother's voice was coldly disapproving. "We all work here just as hard. Mrs. Gorman is a good woman."

"She's so blooming fat, Mummy, she can't even stoop over to tie her own shoelaces. She'll call me out of the shop when she's in the kitchen to come and tie her shoelaces for her. Why do I have to do that? She's got a serving girl with her in the kitchen."

"Gertie, you must be kind to her. She's being very kind to you, and you must help her with her infirmities."

Gertie didn't think Mrs. Gorman was kind at all, and resented having to work so hard for no reward but an occasional ten-bob note, accompanied by a patronizing little lecture, when Mrs. Gorman thought she deserved it. And she didn't like Paddy O'Reilly, the barman, who was always telling her off for putting the glasses away on the wrong shelf or not washing them enough.

"You're just like my father," she said to him one day, looking at his broad shoulders and iron-gray hair and the square set of his jaw. "Nothing I do is ever good enough for you."

"Come now, Gertie," he said kindly, "you shouldn't say such things, and him only in the grave since June. He was a fine man and good to you. I'm only trying to teach you your job, as he would want me to."

Gertie turned her back and splashed the glasses furiously in the basin. She didn't want Paddy to be like her father, and what he said only made it worse. She wanted to leave all that behind now, and show herself she didn't need a father. She was nearly eighteen; she knew all the answers. She didn't want to be told.

One day when she saw Paddy go into the toilet she ran after him on a sudden impulse and locked the door from the outside. It was a piece of childish spite, and she meant to let him out after a while, but when she ran back to the bar she forgot, and it was an hour or more before she heard Mrs. Gorman looking for him, and suddenly remembered. If Paddy was angry, Mrs. Gorman was livid.

"One more prank like that and you'll be sent packing, young lady," she said. "You'll be out of here and home again before you know it."

Not that, Gertie said to herself, I'll mend my ways, I will. Better the hard work than go home in disgrace.

While Gertie was at Mrs. Gorman's, Jimmy decided that it was time for him to be off too. He had never earned much working for McFeeny, and after the day in the graveyard when he watched while other hands lowered his father's coffin into the ground, he couldn't face going on as an undertaker's boy.

He had never thought much about money before; if he went from Monday to Friday and didn't have a penny, it didn't make any difference, because he wasn't interested. But the last time he had seen his father, the day he borrowed a bike from someone and cycled into Sligo Town to the hospital, there had been talk about what would happen, and someone had said—was it his father, or had Jimmy said it himself, or just thought of the phrase?—"You'll have to beg, borrow, or steal." The words rang in his ears and he knew he'd have to do something to prevent it.

He looked for a job, but at nineteen Jimmy had no training for anything except farm chores like saving turf and digging potatoes, and there was no money in that. Suddenly he realized how he'd wasted the six years since he had finished school, and how much he'd lost by playing hooky in the years before that. He cycled all the way to Castlebar one day to see a man who had advertised for a young fellow without saying what he'd have to do, and it turned out to be a messenger boy's job, six shillings a week and no keep.

"I couldn't even pay for me digs on that," he told the man in disgust.

"This job's for a boy who can live at home," the man said. "Where do you live?"

"Ballycarrick."

"That would never do, 'tis too far. What's the matter with you, young fellow, you look old enough to do something better than running messages. How old are you?"

"Nineteen next month."

"You could join the army, or the navy. They'll teach you, and you get your keep and your uniforms and your pay as well. If you're ready to leave home, that's what I'd do, if I was you. There's a recruiting office open this week in Sligo, that's near where you are."

Jimmy thought about it as he pedaled the long miles back to Ballycarrick, and when he got there he stopped at Hogan's shop and walked around to the shed in the rear where he and young Billy Hogan liked to play cards and smoke Wild Woodbines when they had a few shillings to buy them. Billy was there, and Jimmy went in and said:

"Well, I'm joining up the navy, there's recruiting in Sligo. Will you ever come with me, Billy?"

"Join the navy? What for?"

"For a living, of course. You don't want to stay here all your life, do you?"

"Better here than those stinking old tubs you'll be in."

"Come on, Billy, you'll like the sea. You like it when we go out fishing in the bay, don't you?"

"Fishing's one thing, navy's another. It's all yes-sir, no-sir, aye-aye-sir spit-in-your-eye-sir, scrubbing the decks, and you won't see a girl for months at a time."

"Well, I'm going, Billy, I'm not staying here no longer."

"What'll your mother say?"

"Ooh, I'll not tell her, she'd black my eyes if she knew. Don't you say nothing about it to her, not till I'm gone. Don't tell her then, don't let her know I ever told you. I'll write to her when I know where they're sending me."

"She's not going to like it, Jimmy."

"I don't care. She's got Mick and Charlie to look after her, and Brigid and all the others. There's too many of us, Billy. She'll be better off without me around the house, really she will."

"Then why don't you tell her?"

"She wouldn't let Gertie go to England, would she? Then she won't let me go either if she can stop me. Once I'm in the navy there won't be nothing she can do about it. She'll get over it."

Jimmy went off to Sligo the next morning, without saying another word to anybody, without packing any gear, because he didn't have any, without taking even a toothbrush. All he took was a pair of shoes that belonged to Mick, because they were fairly good shoes, and Jimmy's were worn almost through. He put on Mick's shoes and left his own behind, and cleared out.

He had a few bob in his pocket from working for a farmer

the week before, and he rode to Sligo on the bus. The next
thing he knew a navy doctor was examining him, and telling
him to drop his pants. Jimmy got all upset, because he didn't
have any underwear—he never wore any, nor did the other
fellows around home, but that had never mattered before.

"Jesus!" he said. "What do you want me to do that for?"

"Holy Mother of God, what an innocent!" said the doctor.
"Have you never had a medical examination before?"

"Why should I? I never been to a doctor in my life."

The doctor laughed, but it wasn't an unkind laugh, and
Jimmy felt better. "Well, you're a healthy enough specimen.
Don't get any wrong ideas, this is just routine. Come on now,
drop the pants."

He passed the physical, and was told to go home and report
the next morning for shipment to the naval base on Haulbowline Island in Cork Harbour. "I'm not going home," Jimmy
said.

"Why not?" asked the doctor.

"Well, if I go home, I'll be copped on so," and Jimmy explained his predicament. There wasn't any navy regulation that
covered the situation, but the O'Rourke family was well known
in Sligo, and the doctor decided that under the circumstances
what Jimmy was doing was probably the best thing after all.
He'd taken a liking to Jimmy, and besides, the navy needed
him. It wasn't easy to get good healthy recruits; Jimmy was the
only one who'd come in that day.

As a new recruit Jimmy was entitled to a clothing allowance
of six pence a day until his uniform was issued to him, and
that wouldn't be for a few weeks, although he'd start eating
navy food the next day. With that and the few shillings of his
own, Jimmy was suddenly rich, and he had no difficulty finding
a cheap bed in a Legion of Mary shelter in Sligo that night.

When he got to Haulbowline Jimmy wrote home to his
mother, as he had promised, and was surprised to find that she
took the news quite well. In her reply she corrected his spelling

mistakes, which was to be expected, but she didn't scold or disapprove. He had signed up for six years, and that was something she couldn't change, so she accepted it, as she had accepted all the other surprises in her life. In any case, Jimmy was launched on a career now, and it was an honorable one and he might learn something.

Jimmy agreed, but he wasn't in any particular hurry about it. The first few months of training were mainly "squarebashing" —marching up and down the courtyard in the old naval base that Britain had built in the nineteenth century and turned over to Ireland as part of the treaty settlement of 1922. Jimmy was earning seventeen shillings and eight pence a week; not a lordly sum, but enough for him to have a few pints on Saturday nights. Stout was nine pence a pint on the island, ten pence on shore, and eleven pence in the lounge bars, and on Saturdays Jimmy and his friends would take the train into Cork City at the upper end of the harbor, where there was a greater variety of bars and more entertainment. One night they missed the last train back, and had to walk the whole fourteen miles along the railroad tracks, which took until dawn, but they didn't mind because they all had a skinful at the time.

Then one day one of the warrant officers called Jimmy in and told him his mother was in the hospital, and he'd better go home and see her.

"I can't," said Jimmy. "I don't have any money."

The warrant officer sighed, and looked at him with the unwinking patience of a man to whom nothing ever happens that hasn't happened a hundred times before. "I'll give you a voucher," he said. "We'll stop the money from your pay when you come back."

There was nothing Jimmy could do about it, but he was relieved to discover that servicemen could travel at a greatly reduced rate; he could take the train to Sligo and back for less than two weeks' pay.

Jimmy didn't see any point in telegraphing the news that he

was coming, but he wondered uneasily what kind of reception he'd get. His mother was grateful, but so ill that she could manage only a weak smile; the others seemed to Jimmy unnecessarily cool.

"What are you doing here?" he was asked when he stepped in the door, and Jimmy didn't know what to say to that. It was as though they were telling him he had no right to be there, because he hadn't been a good son to his mother; but Jimmy didn't think he'd done anything wrong. He still had that same old affection for her, and she was ill, so here he was.

Jimmy stood there in the door, smiling and saying nothing, and the moment of coolness passed. He was glad to be home, and he told Mick and Charlie and Tony all about life in the navy, and it was a good reunion.

Maire hated being ill, and it seemed to her that God must be punishing her for something, though she didn't know what. She had had a simple hernia operation, and it seemed to heal perfectly well, but she had grown impatient lying in bed, and felt impelled to be up and about and working as she had always worked. She must help the boys in the vegetable garden, and make sure they didn't let the weeds get ahead of them. She insisted on using the hoe herself, though they warned her not to, and suddenly she had a fall, and the stitches pulled and the hernia ruptured again.

They took her back to the hospital for another surgical repair and a stern lecture from the doctor, and this time she knew he was right. The wound was slow to heal, and for weeks after Maire went home, the district nurse came in to change the dressings and teach the children how to make their mother comfortable.

Brigid did it best, though she was barely twelve, and for years after that she was the one who looked after Maire when she was poorly. Like Gertie before her, Brigid missed a lot of school that way, because her mother never really got back her good health. But Brigid learned a lot about nursing, too, and as Father O'Malley would have reminded Maire, that was more than she would have learned in school.

When Jimmy went back to Haulbowline, Charlie did a lot of thinking about his own position in the family. Mick was now in charge as "the woman of the house," taking care of the younger children while Maire was ill. Jim and Gertie had left home, Matt and Willie were in college, Tess was engaged and would soon be married to John Kearin, and Peter was studying for a scholarship that he would probably win, and then he'd be away at school next year. It seemed to Charlie that he and Tony were the only ones still left at home with nothing important to contribute and no future. Charlie decided to do something about it.

Like Jimmy, he found there weren't any good jobs for a man who had left school at fourteen, and done nothing since but work in the fields with a spade, a hoe, and a scythe. He was twenty-two, and the most useful skills he had learned were digging spuds for the family table and turf for the family fire. When he heard that Bord na Mona needed men to open a vast peat bog in County Offaly for commercial turf production, he took the job to see what he could earn.

Saving turf at home was a fairly simple operation. Most of the bog was common land, and all the farmers of the neighborhood had the right to go into it each year to cut what they needed. It was family work, the women and children helping the men. The digging was done with a slane, a narrow spade about a foot long that turned up a sod, of convenient size for a small fireplace or stove, a little larger than a brick. The sods were cut as soon as the rain stopped in the spring, and laid out to dry; in a few days, if the weather was fair, they had to be turned over to dry on the other side, and later they would be stacked in little piles, angled to one another to leave passages for the drying wind, like the stone fences. As they got drier they were stacked into bigger piles, and finally hauled to the roadside in wheelbarrows, and taken home by donkey cart. By that time spring would have passed nearly into summer.

The turf-cutters take off the scraw first, the top layer where the heather grows, and the turf is fluffy and soft, and so wet it has no more body than the dough for a cake. If a bog isn't well drained, or a man is opening a new part of the bog to cut the first drain, he can sink to his knees in it if he doesn't mind his step.

Below that the turf is black stuff, a tightly packed accumulation of ancient forest material compressed for centuries under floods, glaciers, and the weight of the layers above it, airless and undisturbed since prehistoric times.

On the Sligo hillsides the bog lies like a blanket over the gravel, only two or three feet deep in places, some of it hardly worth cutting even by hand for the home fireplace. But in the flat bottomlands of Offaly, where it goes down six or eight feet or more, it is harvested by great machines like sophisticated bulldozers, which dig it up and dry it and mill it to a fine powder. The powder is burned like coal dust in electric power stations on the edge of the bog, or compressed into standard-size briquettes that are light and clean to handle, but burn like country turf in the fireplaces of city homes.

Charlie's job was to help get the bog ready for the machines, for they couldn't move on it until it was drained. He had never seen such a vast stretch of wild, empty bog, dull brown in the October mist, a flat wilderness without tree or hedge or fence that disappeared in the distance, with only the huge tower of the electric generating station squatting at the horizon like a great milk jug without a handle. He lived with a gang of strong-backed young men like himself in bare wooden barracks at the edge of the bog, and every morning they would ride out on a shaky narrow-gauge railroad, mile after mile of empty wilderness that made Charlie think he was in Siberia, to the place where they were digging.

They were given shovels to use that were wider than slanes,

because they weren't saving turf, they were digging ditches. The lines where they were to dig were marked, and they had to keep the ditches straight, so there would be no waste. The sides of the ditches had to slant, V-shaped, so that the banks wouldn't collapse, and they couldn't go too deep, because the bog had to drain slowly. As the water dribbled out, the surface of the bog would settle and the turf under it become more compact; then the men would come back another week and widen and deepen the ditches, so that the lower levels could drain and the surface settle further, till the bog was dry enough and compact enough to stand the weight of the machines.

It was back-breaking work, but a kind that Charlie was familiar with, and he enjoyed it. He was earning a little money, and could send his mother a few shillings every week. But he knew it wasn't enough. From time to time he would get a letter from his mother with official printed papers of some kind in it, which he would have to sign for her, though he didn't quite understand why. It had something to do with his father having left no will; there were debts to pay after his long illness, and the consent of all the heirs had to be given before she could sell any of the property, or even borrow on it.

That should be Joe's business, Charlie thought; Joe was head of the family now. But clearly their mother needed more money, and digging turf wouldn't provide it. Charlie resolved to go to Dublin to look for a better job, as soon as he had enough money put by to keep himself until he found it. That was going to take time, so Charlie bent to his work and went on digging.

In the spring Gertie got the sack. She wasn't particularly upset about that, because she didn't like working for Mrs. Gorman, but her mother was furious. It wasn't only the lost opportunity, it was the way it had happened that was so disgraceful.

For all her promises, Mrs. Gorman hadn't been keeping as watchful an eye on her charges as she pretended, and sometimes when she was off in Dublin or at her lodge in Ballycarrick, Gertie and the two other girls in the shop would go off together to the local dance hall in the evening. There was nothing wrong with that if they had asked Mrs. Gorman's permission, and come back at midnight as she always told them to. But to go out without permission and stay out later than they should—that was another matter.

Everybody knew what happened to girls who did things like that; there was an endlessly repeated story of a girl named Kathleen who had a baby, the most terrible thing that could happen to an unmarried girl. But Gertie and her friends didn't believe it, and one night Mrs. Gorman came home from Dublin to find that they had all gone to the dance hall without permission, and she went and found them and sacked all three on the spot.

The next day Gertie was home again, and told her mother that the whole trouble was because Mrs. Gorman hadn't been there when they went to the dance. She would surely have given them permission if she had, and anyway they had done nothing wrong and she was glad to be away from that horrible place. Her mother listened somewhat skeptically but didn't seem completely unsympathetic. Gertie, nursing her grievance, felt encouraged.

Then Mrs. Gorman arrived the following day in her car to give her side of the story. This was something Gertie hadn't expected, and as she watched her mother bring the visitor into the sitting room and close the door, she was filled with alarm. She went out to the shed where she had hidden so often as a child to postpone the inevitable beating when she had done something wrong. She could still feel the sores where that long thin broom handle had come down on her back the day she had been throwing stones with Jimmy and one of them had gone through the big glass window pane in that sitting room where her mother and Mrs. Gorman were talking now. She stayed in the shed until Mrs. Gorman had gone, and then, reflecting that she was a big girl now, she went back to the house to face her punishment.

As she walked she smoothed her dress down, as she'd been taught to do at Swinford, and tossed her head to settle her hair, which hung in shiny black waves to her shoulders as it had done since the day Jimmy cut it for her and her mother tidied the rough edges. A stray lock fell over her eye and she stopped to set it back in place, so that it would look nice against her ivory complexion. Her shapely legs moved in a long, smooth stride, her carriage was erect and her shoulders straight with more boldness than confidence, and the high June sun cast the shadows of her long black eyelashes on her cheeks. She was taller than her mother now, a startlingly beautiful girl of nineteen with a flash of high spirits in her eyes.

Her mother was standing in the kitchen, the broom in her hands, watching her with a tired, puzzled look, and Gertie thought with surprise that she looked more worried than angry.

"What am I going to do with you, Gertie," she said.

"Mother, I didn't—"

"Not a word! I'm not going to let you out of my sight from now on"—and she flung out the word *sight* as though it had the power to chain her daughter to her side—"you're not to be trusted. Here!" She thrust the broom into Gertie's hands. "Sweep the floor."

Gertie swallowed her astonishment and did as she was told. She was afraid to speak, and resolved in her heart never to speak to her mother again. For a long time she kept to that resolve, except for a dutiful "Yes, Mummy," or "No, Mummy," when she was addressed, and Maire thought her behavior much improved. But Gertie hated it.

She read the want ads in the *Sligo Champion* for barmaids and grocery-shop assistants, and wrote to a lot of them until she got an answer from a Mrs. Flynn in Ballina, County Mayo. It took her all morning to get there on her bicycle, and all evening to get back, but Mrs. Flynn hired her, to work in a bar and grocery in Westport for fifty shillings a week and her keep. It would mean freedom for her, the beginning of a life of her own. She'd be living in, as she had with Mrs. Gorman, but Mrs. Flynn was so much nicer—younger, with curly red hair and a lean, slim-hipped figure, more like an older sister than a mother. And if fifty shillings wasn't much, at least it would be hers, and she'd get it regularly. No more of those patronizing ten-bob notes for being a good girl!

There was only one problem for Gertie. Westport was a good few miles beyond Ballina, too far to go on her bike. She was to start in two weeks, and Gertie had said yes, she'd be ready. But she didn't have money for the bus, and she didn't want to ask Mrs. Flynn for it. She couldn't ask her mother, either, the way things were between them.

So Gertie sat down and wrote a letter to Jimmy, asking him to loan her the fare. Jimmy was good like that, Gertie knew; he wouldn't let her down. But a whole week went by without an answer, and Gertie couldn't imagine what had happened. When Matt came home for the weekend from Summerhill, she told him about it on Sunday as they were walking home from Mass.

"I don't know where I'm going to get the money from," she said. "I won't ask Mummy."

"You'll have to do that," said Matt. "She has your money. Jimmy sent it to you, and she's got it and the letter."

"And she never told me! Blow me down, that isn't right, Matt, it isn't. She'll never give it to me now, she's that hard on me."

"I think she will, Gertie. She knows why you need it. She's written to Mrs. Flynn and had an answer from her, and made inquiries, you know, from Aunt Eileen in Ballina. She knows Mrs. Flynn, and she told Mummy you'd be well cared for. What did you think she was going to do? Let you go off like Jimmy without saying a word to her? It's not natural now, is it, really?"

"Oh, Matt, you're always taking her side!" Gertie was disgusted; but all the same, things looked more hopeful. "Will you ask her to give me the money? She'll listen to you."

"You can do it," Matt said. "But I'll tell her you're going to, if you like."

"Oh, no!" Gertie wailed. "That will make it worse!" She broke away from him and ran toward the house, crying with frustration and doubly frustrated to be crying like a child, when here she was trying to prove to her mother that she could go off by herself with a real job to earn her own living. Suddenly she stopped, wiped her eyes, and turned around to wait for Matt to catch up with her.

"All right," she said. "We'll speak to her together. As soon as we get home."

Maire was behind them, walking more slowly with the smaller children, and when Matt and Gertie got to the house they waited for her on the doorstep. Seeing them there talking together, she guessed what was in the wind, and wasn't surprised when Matt asked her rather formally if she would join them in the sitting room. "There's something Gertie and I would like to talk to you about," he said.

Maire came in and shut the door, and suddenly Gertie was a frightened schoolgirl again. After the weeks of strained silence between her and her mother she didn't know what to say. Her mother waited, a faint smile on her tight lips and a rather anxious look in her gray-green eyes. Matt looked from one to the other, watching the color rise in Gertie's face as she fidgeted in her chair. There was nothing to do but break the silence himself.

"Gertie wants you to give her the two pounds that Jimmy sent," he said softly.

Gertie's mouth opened in surprise as she heard the sum; she never dreamed that Jimmy could spare so much. And once her mouth was open the words came, and she poured out all her excitement, her longing to get away from home and start a life of her own, her promises to behave herself and obey all the rules her mother or Mrs. Flynn might lay down, her gratitude to Jimmy for the money, her promise that out of her earnings she, too, would send money home to her mother.

"You don't need to do that, child," her mother said. "You'll be earning little enough. God be good to you. I hope it's the right thing for you, but if Matt thinks it is I'll let you go."

There was a twist of humiliation in that for Gertie, since Matt was a year younger and yet his advice was being taken in her affairs. But she didn't mind; after all, Matt was a boy, and he had more schooling than she and knew more of the world. He was studying to be a priest, and in Gertie's mind he was already "Father Matt," and what a fine priest he was going to be!

Gertie went off to Westport the next morning, and Matt and Willie went back to Summerhill, and in the autumn Peter went away to Ballinafad College, on a scholarship provided by the African Mission Society. Matt had helped in that, too, for he was already sponsored by the society and had agreed to go to Africa for them when he was ordained.

It sounded a long way off to Maire, but once the children left home it was all the same whether they were in Dublin, America, or wherever, and was Africa really any farther off than America? Toberpatrick wasn't so crowded anymore, and it would be easier to stretch the money.

Then came a letter from Charlie, who was working in Dublin now and had more money to spare for her. Why didn't Tony join him there, he wrote, there were good jobs to be had and he could share Charlie's digs. Why not, thought Maire, it would be good for Tony, who was twenty-one now, and able to care for himself in spite of his weak eyes and the fevers that sometimes came over him.

With Mick to help her in the house and garden, Christy nearly finished at school, and Brigid so clever at caring for her when she was poorly, they would be comfortable enough and well off. Rita and little Pat were no trouble now; Pat was nine, a sturdy boy who was already making himself useful. Maire smiled, and called Tony in from the potato field to tell him.

12.

Dublin
Bachelors

Charlie's first job in Dublin was driving a horse-drawn bread van, selling fresh-baked loaves, unsliced and unwrapped, on commission. Even in the Ireland of 1950, deep in a postwar depression and not yet fully acquainted with the Industrial Revolution, horses were not as common on city streets as they once had been, and good drivers were hard to find. Charlie was a raw young lad from the country who didn't know anything about selling bread, or selling anything, but he did understand horses, and that got him the job.

His route included a few shops and a lot of homes, which was the way a man started at the bottom in that business. There was more money to be made selling bread wholesale to retailers than delivering a loaf or two every morning to one family after another. He learned to be a pretty good salesman, and progressed after a while to an electric van, and added more shops to his route. It was pleasant work, not very demanding, and it kept him outdoors, which he enjoyed. He was earning better than five pounds a week, which was considered good pay, and he could send his mother a pound or so, pay for his digs and his meals, and save a little for himself. But the hours were long, and he never knew when his day would be finished.

In the evenings when he first arrived in Dublin, Charlie liked to ramble down O'Connell Street, as any other country fellow would do, to see what the place was like. There was nothing as grand in Sligo as that broad avenue with the line of trees and statues down the middle, and the hundreds of motorcars going by on each side. The Gresham Hotel was a palace compared to the Imperial in Sligo, where they'd had Mary's wedding reception, and the picture theaters were like palaces too, but when Charlie looked at the posters outside them he wondered if his mother would approve.

Halfway down the avenue he discovered the bronze plaque on the front of the General Post Office, recording the spot where Padhraic Pearse had proclaimed the Republic in 1916. Charlie stared at it in awe, and then looked around him remembering what his father had told him about the bloody fighting in those days. There was no sign of it now; the building had been restored, and in front of it massive columns rose from the street to form an arcade over the sidewalk, its stone ceiling higher than the chimney of Toberpatrick. Over that was a peaked roof with statues of people Charlie couldn't identify, however much he craned his neck. It was said that one could still see the bullet holes in the bronze figures on the monument to Daniel O'Connell at the lower end of the avenue, but Charlie couldn't find any. He marveled at the huge thinly draped women at the four corners of the monument, larger than life with their breasts half exposed and wings like angels, and thought it a very odd combination.

The post office was a favorite place for soapbox orators, perhaps because of its historic associations, or because the portico gave protection from the rain or sun, as the case might be. Charlie found himself there one evening in a crowd listening to a pair of Jehovah's Witnesses, who were talking in a style he'd never heard in Sligo, about a religious sect he'd never heard of either.

Pretty soon he noticed a young man beside him in the crowd who was laughing at some of the things the soapbox preacher was saying and seemed to understand what was going on. Suddenly the young man looked at Charlie.

"Fine lot of blather that fellow's talking, isn't it?" he said.

"That it is," Charlie answered, "that it is. I never heard the like."

"Ah, you'll hear a lot of it if you come round here often enough," said the stranger. "You've not been in Dublin long now, have you?"

"Not too long," said Charlie. " 'Tis a big place. I'm after coming from Sligo, a little place there, and even in Sligo Town I've never seen anything like this. If my mother found me here she'd have me by the ears, 'twould be, 'Down on your knees, my boy, and ask God's forgiveness for listening to that blasphemer.' "

The stranger laughed in a friendly way, as though he knew what Charlie meant. "Well, there's better things to do in Dublin than stand around on a cold streetcorner like this," he said. "I wonder now, if you're from Sligo, did you know anyone there in the Legion of Mary?"

Charlie didn't; the name was new to him, but easy to recognize. Anything to do with Mary had to mean the Virgin Mother of God, to whom his own mother had taught him to pray the rosary, and suddenly Dublin didn't seem such a strange place to him anymore. Here was a real Dubliner, talking to him about something called a Legion of Mary. It was worth looking into.

This was the beginning of a lasting friendship between Charlie and Bill O'Hara, who was an insurance salesman, though Charlie didn't know that until years later when he went into the insurance business too. Charlie found him a most genuine man, kind, sincere, and honest, and for the next few years the legion became the center of Charlie's social life. They had weekly meetings—always beginning with the familiar rosary—and assignments of "apostolic work" to do, visiting the sick, feeding the poor, and going out on the streets to find lonely youngsters who needed help, as Bill had found Charlie.

For a while Charlie tried this "street work" too, but his heart wasn't in it; he had a better time supervising a group of young boys whose job was to sell Catholic newspapers and deliver them to the subscribers' homes. Then there were Legion of Mary dances, Saturday night "hops" with recorded music, which kept Charlie and his friends out of the pubs and dance halls, and helped him avoid getting too involved with girls before he was ready to marry and settle down.

He had made some unconscious decisions during the years of his father's last illness, and while he didn't think about them much in those early years in Dublin, he didn't depart from them either. One was to stay out of pubs, not so much in reaction against his father's example but because his mother had carried on about it so. Charlie had experimented briefly with drink as a teen-ager, especially when he went off with his brothers to football matches. There had been one occasion at Ballina when the boys had a beer or two, and when it got back to their mother there was hell to pay for it. She was terribly mad, and Charlie never forgot it.

The other decision was to avoid getting married until he was in a position to keep a wife in reasonable comfort. There were, of course, men who married on a bread-van salesman's earnings, but for Charlie that wasn't enough. Dublin wasn't Sligo, and Charlie judged that on five or ten pounds a week marriage would only make life miserable for himself and his wife. So he became a "mixer," which had its frustrations but he enjoyed it. He'd go to a hop and meet some nice girl, and he might bloody well care for her. He'd take her out, and then when he'd feel he was getting involved, he'd break it off.

The Legion of Mary helped, and so did the cycle club he joined, and the football league he played in. There was never much time to do these things; he'd go around all day with a basket on his arm, six days a week selling bread, go to a hop Saturday night, cycle out to the country or play football all day Sunday after Mass, and be back at work before dawn on Monday. In his early twenties it was child's play—he had a healthy life and no worries.

Charlie lived in digs in Upper Gardiner Street, a downtown neighborhood of three-story terrace houses, side by side with partition walls and a common front of grimy brick. You could tell they were separate houses because under the grime the bricks had been painted different colors, and up on the roof each house had its own row of chimney pots. The doorways were a Victorian imitation of the more elegant homes in Fitzwilliam Square and Harcourt Street—tall and broad with ornamental wooden pillars on each side, but machine-cut instead of hand-carved, and the curved fanlights above were undecorated and a little too squashed to be semicircles.

They had once been handsome homes, and the ceilings were high over the two lower floors, and the windows tall and wide, with the ragged remains of old lace curtains against the glass, and faded threadbare draperies to pull together behind them. The big dining room and drawing room in the house where Charlie lived had been partitioned into two rooms each, and meals were served in what used to be the small sitting room on the ground floor; the kitchen was still in the basement.

Mrs. Roche, Charlie's landlady, was an elderly woman with sagging shoulders and a crooked back, but she kept the place clean and served Charlie his breakfast and his tea in the evening, and would have provided lunch for him as well as she did for the other boarders. But Charlie was always too far away from Gardiner Street at lunchtime, so he made arrangements to stop in at another boarding house on his route for the main meal of the day. Mrs. Roche allowed him a few shillings a week off his rent for that, and it worked out very well. The other boarders were friendly enough, young men up from the country like Charlie, but it wasn't like being at home with his brothers. So he wrote to Tony, and wrote to his mother so she'd understand, and told them Tony could share his room.

Tony came and got a job in a pub, as a general factotum and handyman around the place, behind the bar and in the bottle shop, but he wasn't too keen on it and didn't stay long. One of the girls Charlie knew worked in a building-contractor's office, and one day Charlie called in to have a chat with her and see if there might be anything doing for Tony in the building setup.

"Well now, your brother is it?" she said to him, "We're starting a new job in Palmerstown presently, and I know they'll need some new men. Come back in a week or so and I'll talk to the fellows upstairs meanwhile. We'll fix him up."

So Tony worked as a laborer carrying bricks and beams instead of bottles, and shoveling gravel and sand and concrete to build a hospital. He didn't like that any better, so he took a post-office exam and passed it, and from then on he worked nights sorting letters and parcels.

At first it seemed a good idea for one of the boys to be working days and the other nights, for the little back room they shared was hardly big enough for the two of them when they were both there in the daytime. But trying to sleep in it at different times was even worse. One of them was always waking the other up. So Tony found digs of his own around the corner and moved out, taking his file of de Valera pictures and Sinn Fein pamphlets with him, and after that they met only on Sundays, and went to the odd show together, or a concert in Saint Francis Xavier Hall, for Sunday was the only day their times off coincided.

In the spring Mick wrote to say that he was coming to town, and Charlie left Mrs. Roche for a larger place where he and

Mick could be together in the same house but have separate rooms. He went to his boss at the bakery to see if there was anything he could do for Mick that would be better than the building trade or the post office. Mick was put on the maintenance crew, cleaning the ovens and oiling the slicing machines. It wasn't much, but it was a start.

Mick was nearly twenty-six, but this was the first time he'd been on his own away from home, and the first time he'd made any money, except for the odd shilling or two as a farm boy. He was an expert at housekeeping and bringing up children, and he'd left home only because the youngest of the fifteen O'Rourkes was now nine years old and the mother didn't need him anymore. Mick was fond of children, like his father; he'd never minded changing their nappies or giving them their bottles, and he'd enjoyed it when they climbed in his lap and played their little games with him. He wasn't exactly lost without them now, but he was shy among strangers, and he didn't know exactly what he wanted to do with himself. He'd never had a chance to develop any particular ambition.

He was good company for Charlie, and he was happy. He didn't mind the unexciting work he was given to do; cleaning was a job he understood and was good at. Charlie urged him to try for a selling job, and learn to drive one of the electric vans, but Mick wasn't interested. He went with Charlie to the Legion of Mary meetings and joined in the Saturday night hops, and he soon acquired Charlie's outgoing ways with the girls, though after a couple of years he seemed to be finding it a disappointing, frustrating experience. He liked to sing, and had a good voice, a rich tenor that was as popular in the pubs as in the legion meetings.

Mick enjoyed the pubs, but Charlie by this time had taken the Pioneers' pledge, and wouldn't go there with him, so gradually the brothers drifted apart. Mick's shyness disappeared after a pint or two, and he was popular at the bars because he was always ready to stand a round for the lads as long as his money lasted. It was a rather limiting way to spend your time, Charlie thought; Mick never met the lads outside the pubs, and they'd be no friends to him if he weren't so ready with his money. But that was Mick's way, and he was like his father; you couldn't change him.

Charlie was ambitious and wanted to make something of himself, but he didn't know quite what. He had thought about becoming a schoolteacher like his father, but it was too late for that. If he'd gone on to secondary education after he left the national school he could have gotten a scholarship for teacher training, but he'd missed out on that. He would have loved to go to the university and get a degree in agriculture or something like that, but he'd have to pay for it himself, and he couldn't get into the university until he had his secondary education.

When he'd been working the bread route about four years, he had enough money to pay tuition at night school, and he decided to try it. After a few months he realized that there were too many classes, the hours were too long, and he didn't have time to do the reading, although he had dropped out of the Legion of Mary and cut down on his Saturday-night hops and Sunday sports. He found a private tutor who would take him through the courses more gradually—English, Irish, mathematics, geography, and Latin. It took him six years to complete, and he had to take the Latin and mathematics exams twice, but he finally made it, and at the age of thirty-three he entered Dublin University. One year of that was enough; he learned a little economics and history, though he failed the exams at the end of the year, and he never had time to do the reading in Irish and English literature.

It wasn't exactly the kind of education that qualifies a man for a highly paid profession, but it was more than Charlie had ever had before. He found that he loved studying and reading. Among other things, he discovered what a rich language Irish was—rich in poetic expression, in subtlety and flexibility, in shades of meaning and vivid imagery, in a literature that stemmed mainly from centuries long ago, but was making up in the twentieth century what it had missed in the eighteenth and nineteenth.

Irish was not the family language of the O'Rourkes, though it was spoken often enough in Sligo, and it was taught in school. Charlie had never thought of it in those days as anything other than a chore, like his other lessons, but now in Dublin he was finding the language a pleasure to read, perhaps because it reminded him of home. The English-language newspapers and magazines regularly contained features in Irish, and Charlie found a frankness and sincerity in them, an openness and realism that was often missing from the articles written in English.

Irish was, after all, a kind of in-group, almost esoteric language. It was no longer confined to an oppressed peasantry, speaking it in defiance of law and without benefit of schooling, as in the eighteenth century, nor a hobby of folklorists and a sentimental passion of romantics, as it had become in the nineteenth. It was a living language shared by the well educated and the remote country folk, and largely ignored by others. If that made it rather clubby and vulnerable to snobs, it also made Irish a language in which one could write with a certain freedom of privacy and friendship. There was less risk of offending people who didn't agree with you, because if they didn't understand the language they wouldn't read your piece.

It didn't seem paradoxical to Charlie that along with a better understanding of the Irish language and literature he also learned to take a more objective view of the English people and what England had done to Ireland over the centuries. In school he had learned to hate England and blame the English for Ireland's troubles, as nearly all Irish children did in those days, and many still do. Eoin O'Rourke wasn't the only schoolmaster to teach history that way; it was the usual thing in the national schools.

In his year at the university Charlie was introduced to a broader view of these things, and began to question the bias in what he had been taught before, and read up on the subject himself. He came to the same conclusion many others in Ireland were coming to—what had happened was a tragedy, but it had happened and must be accepted.

Ireland had to learn to live with England, and it could be done in peace because Ireland was at least a Republic, at least in the twenty-six counties, and even England had recognized that fact since 1949. The two nations could deal with each other on more equal terms, and there was no sense quarreling about the six counties of the North that were still in England's hands, because it would be a long time before the Republic could do anything about that.

These were new insights for Charlie, but they didn't add a penny to his earnings and they didn't make any impression on his brothers. Mick wasn't interested in such things; Tony was as keen on politics as ever, but he stuck to his father's viewpoint, and Charlie saw no point in arguing with him. He wasn't seeing much of Tony anymore, and he talked about that with Jimmy one day when the navy was visiting Dublin and Jimmy had shore leave.

Jimmy went to see Tony, and found him in a gloomy basement room, the walls streaked with damp, a gas fire that wasn't working, rickety chairs, and nothing on the stone floor but a filthy rag of carpeting so thin that it slipped and rumpled when Jimmy walked on it and nearly tripped him up.

"Jesus," said Jimmy as he walked in. "What are you doing in a place like this, Tony?"

"It's okay," said Tony. "I like it." He looked thin and he had a cough, and Jimmy wanted to know what was going on, but there were a couple of strangers sitting at the table drinking, ugly fellows with mean looks that didn't appeal to Jimmy at all.

"Who's the bucko?" one of them said to Tony.

"My brother," said Tony. "He's all right." But he didn't introduce them, and he didn't invite Jimmy to sit down.

"Well, I've got twenty-four hours' leave," said Jimmy awkwardly. "Will you come out with me tonight for a few jars and show me the town?"

"Sure, Jimmy, sure," said Tony. "But not now. I'll be with you at Mooney's at half six. On the corner." He seemed relieved, and went with Jimmy to the door to show him out.

When they were outside Jimmy turned to him and said, "What's the drill, Tony?" The only answer he got was: "Ah, you'll find out one day."

Tony showed up that evening at Mooney's as he had promised, but he only had time for a couple of pints because he was on duty at the post office at eight, and they talked all the time about the navy because Tony wouldn't say anything about what he was doing. Jimmy concluded that it had something to do with the IRA, because Tony had always been hot on that. The IRA wasn't doing much in those days, as far as Jimmy knew, so he didn't think there was any reason why Tony shouldn't be with them when he wanted to, but Jimmy thought it was rather odd that he wouldn't talk about it to his own brother. And he didn't like the way Tony looked.

Charlie and Mick didn't like it either, but there wasn't anything they could do. They knew Tony had seen a doctor for his cough, because it was the same doctor they went to when they were ill, and the doctor had told Mick that Tony should be watched. But Tony wasn't the kind of man who would stand watching.

The next time Tony went to the doctor his cough was clearly more than just a reaction to the damp in his digs. It was tuberculosis, and Tony was sent to the sanitarium at Crooksling, in the Wicklow Mountains. It was nearly two years before he could go home to Sligo to be nursed back to health by his mother.

While Tony was at Crooksling, Willie came to Dublin, to study not for the priesthood but for a teaching career like his father's. He hadn't given up on a priestly vocation, but it was a serious matter, not to be decided on the basis of his childhood games. He didn't want to be an African missionary, like Peter and Matt, and it would be hard on their mother if all three of them went so far away; if he went into teaching, the training wouldn't take so long, and the time when he could start helping to support his mother would come much sooner.

Besides, he could get a scholarship for teacher training, and no one yet had offered him one for the seminary. He'd be studying many of the same things he'd have to learn to be a priest, so the time wouldn't be wasted if he changed his mind later. A seminary would give him credit for what he had learned in teacher training.

So Willie was enrolled at Saint Patrick's in Drumcondra, not far from where Charlie was living at the time, and Charlie helped him find digs and saw a good deal of him while he was there. They used to cycle all over Dublin together, down to Sandymount Strand when the weather was fine, and sometimes as far as Joyce's Tower and the Forty Foot Bathing Place in Dun Laoghaire. One day in June when Willie had taken his last exam and there was nothing left but the conferring of certificates and the final dress dance to celebrate, the two of them cycled all the way out to the sanitarium at Crooksling under the high sun and clear sky, twenty miles up and down hills, but mainly up. They found Tony in good form, walking about and talking of going home, envying them the strength for the long bicycle trip.

They cycled home again in the evening and freshened up for the dance, which was Charlie's first experience of evening dress, though he was twenty-nine by now, a tall, handsome man with the dark hair and square-cut features of the O'Rourkes, and a ready smile to belie his serious habits. Dawn was breaking as the dancing ended, and Charlie felt a strange elation, a new confidence that his days of selling bread by day and slaving over his books by night would be ending soon, and there would be better things in store. He would miss Willie when he went off to Longford to his first teaching post, but he needn't live alone all his life. For the first time the idea of marriage began to appeal to Charlie—he wouldn't say who, for there had been too many lovely girls he'd met that night. But it was something to think about, to look forward to.

13.

Discovering England

Jimmy's six years in the navy were nearly over when he visited his brothers in Dublin, and he had no intention of signing on for another hitch. He had an able seaman's rating and he'd learned gunnery and been on one foreign cruise to France and Spain, where he'd seen little but the bars and the girls on the waterfront, because he'd never had any money. In the beginning that hadn't bothered him—whatever he had, he'd spend it, and never worry about the next day. This attitude had changed a little in the last two years, when he was coxswain of the CO's launch and spent all his time in Cork Harbour. He met a girl in Cobh named Audrey McCarthy, a plump, smiling girl with a heart-shaped face like his mother's, but blue eyes and golden hair that made her look entirely different. He'd been doing a line with her ever since he got back from the foreign cruise, and he didn't think the navy life would be much for a married man.

When his enlistment ran out, the CO called him into his office and said, "There's a promotion coming up for you if you'll sign on again."

"Sorry, my lad," said Jimmy, with a sudden sense of freedom that he hadn't known the last six years, "I'm away now." And he took the train to Dublin to see if Charlie could get him a job. But there were no jobs to be had, except laborer's work in some timber place, and the wages were poor so Jimmy turned it down. The only thing to do was go to London and try his luck there, but first he decided to go home to Toberpatrick for a few weeks, to see how his mother was getting on.

The place seemed empty now that all the older ones had left. Christy, Brigid, and Rita were teen-agers, and Patrick was twelve; they had all been children when Jimmy joined the navy. But there was no one around to do the heavy work—the stone fence was falling down; the lane was full of potholes, an old beech tree was dying and looked ready to fall. The henhouse needed mending and the garden was choked with weeds. Jimmy got to work putting the place in shape, and put a little money into tools and timber for the henhouse, thinking it was the least he could do for his mother when he'd been away so long. But she was suspicious; this wasn't the Jimmy she remembered, and when he told her about Audrey she thought she understood.

"What do you intend doing?" she asked him. "I hope you're not going to bring the one here and take over this place on me."

"Audrey? She'd not come here. She likes Cobh too much. Anyhow, it's to London I want to take her, if she'll come." But he was offended, and two days after that he packed his bag and cleared out. He'd write to Audrey from London, when he was settled, and see what happened. He would look in on Gertie first; she was already there, an outpost of the O'Rourke family in London as Charlie was in Dublin.

Gertie had loved her year in Westport with Mrs. Flynn, where there weren't so many sacks of flour to lift, and more of the business was done in the bar than in the grocery shop. She had made herself at home, going off to dances with the other girls, and joining a Gaelic Games club to play camogie, the girls' less lethal version of hurling, the traditional Irish brand of field hockey. But fifty shillings a week didn't go far, and when she had an offer to go to the American Hotel in Galway as a barmaid, for nearly twice as much, she didn't hesitate. Her friend Nancy O'Halloran was there, back from a trip to England with her brother. He had found work there but Nancy hadn't, or anyhow nothing that she wanted, and she didn't want to be living off her brother. But he was there and would help them get settled if they went together, and if they'd had experience at a big place like the American Hotel in Galway, they'd have no trouble getting jobs.

Gertie thought about it as she waited on the tourists and the snobs in the hotel's elegant lounge bar, where chatting with the guests was discouraged and nobody said a friendly word to her. She felt lost there, and hated the place, and would have gone with Nancy at once if she hadn't known how much it was against her mother's wishes. They argued about it a lot, because Nancy didn't want to go alone, and didn't want to wait.

"Why do you worry?" said Nancy. "You're over twenty-one now, the old one can't stop you."

"She'd never forgive me, she wouldn't."

"But you can't stay here all your life. She let you come this far, didn't she? What's the difference, Galway or England?"

"It's England she's afraid of," Gertie said. "You know what it is, her religious upbringing, she's always banging religion into us morning and night. She says the girls that go to England, no sooner they're off the boat than they're going with Protestant boys, and to hear her talk she'd as soon you'd go with the devil."

"You'd never do a thing like that, would you?" Nancy was half shocked, half laughing; it seemed so incredible.

"Oh, it's all the same to me," said Gertie. "Only I don't have to tell my mother that."

"No, you don't, do you. Let's go then. I'll write to Jack and tell him we're coming."

They took the train together to Dun Laoghaire, and the boat from there to Holyhead, without even stopping in Dublin to see Charlie, because Gertie was sure her mother would have written to him to stop her from going. Gertie didn't know how he could do that, but she wasn't taking any chances and didn't want to argue about it.

It was three hours of seasick misery on the boat that night, the howling wind tossing spray in their faces when they went on deck, the saloon hot and stuffy and crowded with drunks, the beer bottles rolling back and forth across the floor and down the stairs when the ship heaved and pitched in the heavy sea, and rolled so steeply that the girls thought it would turn over. When they got on the train at Holyhead at one o'clock in the morning, they had only the straight-backed benches of a third-class carriage to rest on, their worn-out stuffings as hard as the wood beneath, but the girls were too exhausted to care, and slept sitting up through the long night ride to London.

Jack met them at the station and took them along to his digs to tidy up and get a little rest before going on to Margate, where the manager of the Imperial Hotel had told him he'd give the girls a try.

"Margate?" said Gertie. "Where's that?"

"It's a seaside resort, a lovely place," said Jack. "It's not far, just about the closest place to London for people to go. You'll like it, it's sunny there, and there's a lovely strand, everybody goes there. The Imperial's a fine place, too, right on the Marine Parade. It's beautiful."

Gertie was dubious. For the first time it dawned on her what a big step she'd taken, coming from the sheltered life she'd always led to land over here among these busy people with their loud voices and strange way of talking. But it was too late to go back now.

When she got to Margate she found that Jack was right—it

was a lovely place, and she'd never seen such crowds of people in all her life.

"Where do they come from?" she asked Nancy. "I didn't know there were so many people in the whole world."

"Wait till Bank Holiday, there'll be more," said Nancy. "What do we care? Have you seen the tips they leave? Boy, do you pick up money waiting on tables! There's nothing like that in Galway, is there? Blimey, we'll be making a bundle here."

The good times lasted all summer, but when the days grew shorter in September and the crowds stopped coming, the Imperial closed for the winter, and the girls were lucky to get jobs in a pub in Lewisham, the White Horse. Gertie didn't like it there, and had that rebellious feeling that she was being given too much to do and not getting enough for it—the generous tips of the holiday makers had vanished. Blow this, she said to herself, if they don't get more staff here I'm going to leave. The manager wouldn't believe her when she told him, nor would Nancy, but Gertie found a better job in North London at the Nag's Head, where there were three other barmaids. Gertie, with her tall, statuesque figure and her glossy black hair and ivory skin, was more conspicuous among them than she realized.

She had a bit of a tongue that the customers liked, too, a devil-may-care sauciness and a quick retort for any fresh lad who tried putting her on. It was easy. A barmaid with ten brothers and four sisters was something new in North London, and nobody had ever heard of an Irish navy until she told them about Jimmy. When she said she had a brother studying to be a priest they wouldn't believe her, but they did when she took three days off to go to Matt's ordination, and came back with pictures. She got more respect from the crowd after that, but while her admirers kept their distance, the number of them grew.

Gertie went through a lonely time in her first years at the Nag's Head, in spite of the nightly ~¹ offering over the bar. She didn't want to go out with any of the English boys, and without her old friend Nancy to keep her company she was homesick. Talking about her brothers didn't really help, and one day she came to work looking so pale and red-eyed that Betty, the head barmaid, asked her what was wrong. Betty was only a few years older than Gertie, a rather plain girl with too long a nose and pale brown eyes, but she was a kind person with motherly ways, and Gertie was fond of her.

"I dunno, Betty," she said. "Maybe I'm just tired. It was a heavy night last night."

Betty looked at Gertie's red-rimmed eyes and shook her head. "You've been crying, ducks, that's not just from being tired."

"Crying my blooming eyeballs off, if you want to know," said Gertie with sudden force. "London can be a blooming lonely place, oh-boy-oh-boy it can."

"Lonely for a girl like you? You're not giving yourself a chance, that's why. The boys would be falling over you if you'd let them."

"I don't want them big louts falling all over me. That's just what they'd do, wouldn't they!"

"Oh, go on, Gertie, these London boys aren't all as bad as that. What's the matter with you? Come on over with me to the dance hall after closing tonight, there's a nice English fellow that goes there I want you to meet. You know the one I mean, he comes into the pub here and drinks cherry brandy, but he's never tried to flirt with you, I've watched him."

"Cherry brandy?" said Gertie. "The one with the lean face and fair hair, and that slow way of talking as though he wants to be sure of what he's saying before he says it?"

Betty chuckled. "You've noticed him, I see. Well, he's had his eye on you for I don't know how long."

"I thought he came in here to see you," Gertie said in a soft, wondering voice, almost a whisper.

"Blimey, he never did! And it's not the fine flavor of cherry brandy he's wanting, either!"

Gertie laughed, and there was color in her cheeks again, and Betty went off to the kitchen. That evening when the fair-haired Englishman came in for his cherry brandy, Gertie watched from the other end of the bar as Betty served him. She didn't say anything, but she tried to imagine going out with an Englishman, and it wasn't easy. At least, she thought, he looked harmless enough. She decided to chance it.

By the time Jimmy arrived in London, Gertie was having such a good time she hardly noticed that it was her brother coming to see her. She was doing a strong line now with John Greenly, the fair-haired Englishman with the slow way of talking, and he had established himself as her first real boyfriend.

That first night she went to the dance hall, John had been as bashful as Gertie, and didn't even ask if he could take her home. They'd made another date for "the next time," but Gertie hadn't committed herself to when the next time might be. It just happened that there was a photographer in the dance hall, and when he saw the raven-haired Irish beauty sitting with a perfectly ordinary English workingman, she in a white dress with her hair curled in formal ringlets in the old-fashioned way, and he looking a little strained with a huge silk tie knotted tightly under his starched collar and Sunday-best suit, the photographer knew he'd found a customer. He took their picture before they saw what he was doing, and a day or two later he showed the print to John and made a sale.

Gertie was still trying to make up her mind whether to go to the dance hall again when the picture arrived in the post, out of the blue as far as she was concerned. She blushed when she looked at it, for there was no mistaking that wide grin on her face or the gleam in Johnny's eye. There didn't seem any point in refusing to see him after he'd sent her such a nice present.

She was in the dance hall that same evening, and many evenings after that they walked out together after closing time, which the girls at the Nag's Head weren't supposed to do, but everybody liked John and it was easy to see he was good for Gertie, so nobody objected.

John was a little nervous when Jimmy showed up, and wondered if he had been sent over by the family to give him the once-over. Gertie knew better; Jimmy was the last person his mother would choose for a mission of that kind, and anyhow he'd be on her side whatever happened.

"Have you found work, yet, Jimmy?" she asked, knowing what he was really after.

"I'm looking around," he said, "but no luck so far. Anything doing at the Nag's Head?"

"Ah, you'd never do here," said Gertie. "You belong on the other side of the bar, you do."

"Not for long if I don't have a job. London's as bad as Dublin from what I've seen."

"Have you tried the London Transport?" John asked him. "There're always looking for men for the buses and the Underground."

"That'll do me for a starter. Where do I go?"

John told him where to go and who to see, and Jimmy found himself part of London's great underground railway system, where the heat and noise and stuffy air was worse than a navy engine room when he was assigned to the deep tubes in the central city, but not as bad on the open-air platforms of the suburban stations.

He started as an ordinary porter, but after a while there was an opening for a ticket collector. It was light work, but it had its pitfalls; he had to know the price of a ticket from each station to everywhere else in the system, because sometimes there would be cash fares to handle. In the rush hours a tardy commuter would often slip through the barriers to get on the train without a ticket, and then he'd have to pay when he got off at the other end. He'd name the station he'd come from and the fare, if he knew it; if he didn't, the ticket collector was supposed to know it, or look it up in his book, but there usually wasn't time for that.

It was a kind of honor system as far as the passengers were concerned, and everyone assumed the English passengers were honest. Anyway, it would have cost the London Passenger Transport Board a lot of money and public opposition to install a more foolproof system. Jimmy soon discovered that the ticket collectors had their own little hobble. When they took in a cash fare this way, they were supposed to write it down, the amount of the fare and the station the passenger said he had come from, to account for the money. For the first few days that was what Jimmy did.

"Don't be an idiot," one of the more experienced collectors said to him. "If he gives you five shillings and says he's come from Margate or whatever it is, put down two-and-six in your book and say it's from East Ham. That way you get something for yourself."

"No," said Jimmy, "I couldn't do that."

"Oh, go on! We're all at it, you might as well be at it too."

"Well, I'm not here for a vacation, am I. The wages are not all that good."

"That's right, mate. You'll see."

It was easy enough for a five-shilling fare, and even easier to make a shilling off smaller fares, because Jimmy knew all the nearby stations and the fares to them. But when a man gave him ten shillings one morning, Jimmy couldn't remember offhand a station he might have come from to reach that platform on a five-shilling fare. So he just put down five shillings on his card and left a blank where the station name should have been, until he could get time to look it up when the rush was over.

He was just ready to do that when a plainclothes inspector came up and asked for his card. The inspector looked at his watch and said, "Twenty-five minutes ago there was a fare paid here of ten bob. It's only marked down here as five, and the place isn't entered."

"Haven't put that one down yet," Jimmy said without blinking. "Been too busy. That five shillings is another fare. Went by so fast I didn't hear what he was saying about where he'd come from. What's the difference? He could have been lying. How do I know he come from where he said he did?"

"Our English passengers are generally reliable," the inspector said haughtily. "They are honest about their fares. We expect our Irish employees to be the same." He handed back the card and walked off, rather stiffly, Jimmy thought. He wasn't going to lose his job over it, because there was nothing the inspector could do; but he'd have to enter that ten-shilling fare now, and instead of making five bob on it he'd lose five of his own, because he'd have to turn in the fare already entered.

At Christmas Jimmy wanted to go back to Cobh to see Audrey for a week or two, but the London Transport wouldn't give him the time off, so he gave them a week's notice. The same inspector called him in to the office and said, "What do you want to leave us for?"

"There's nothing for me here," said Jimmy.

"We'd like you to stay," said the inspector. "We might even give you a better position. There's a future for you here."

Jimmy had been going through the training course, along with other young ticket collectors, and among other things his voice had been tested, for announcing train departures at the major stations over the public-address system. "Your voice is very good on this recording machine," the inspector said.

That was a surprise to Jimmy, whose accent by now was a mixture of Sligo, Cork, Cockney, and plain seaman, and who larded his conversation with Irish and English workingmen's slang without giving much thought to what he was saying. He didn't know whether the proposal was a bad joke or just one of those irrational things the London Transport sometimes seemed to do, like other railways, to confuse passengers. Anyway, he turned it down, and when he came back to London after his holiday with Audrey, he was out of a job again.

He went to the Labour Exchange, the government employment agency, and when they asked him why he'd left his previous job he said, "Well, I was unsuited."

"What?" The man behind the counter couldn't believe his ears; if an unskilled Irishman wanted to be "suited" in a job, there must be something radically wrong with him.

"I was unsuited," Jimmy repeated.

"Would you fancy the building industry? They're looking for roofers at an estate in Camden Town."

"Not interested. There are other things I can do better." Jimmy walked out in disgust and around the corner to the nearest pub, where he soon learned of an opening at the Wonderloaf Bakery, all-night work at the ovens, but there was great money in it because he'd go in at ten o'clock and finish at half eight, which was a couple of hours overtime a night. And it was warm, which was good in winter, but when spring came, it got to be too much.

It was Audrey's uncle, a supervisor at a Ford plant in Essex, who got Jimmy fixed up. The job was a "handy number," in Jimmy's phrase; he worked in an air-conditioned foundry, making sand cores for engine castings. The money was good, the hours were regular, he found a comfortable flat not too far from the plant, and the following year he and Audrey were married and she came back to England with him. It looked for a while as if that would be a saving—he wouldn't be spending all his cash going over to Cobh on holiday weekends to see her.

Gertie and John were married the same year, but without the same support from the bride's family. John was, as Gertie's mother had feared, a Protestant; he belonged to the Church of England, which he maintained was as good as being a Catholic, and Gertie didn't mind, as long as he agreed to let her keep on going to Mass and bring up the children as Catholics. But it bothered her conscience, and she didn't dare tell anyone in the family about it. She talked it over instead with her parish priest in Holloway Road. He had seen hundreds of Irish girls come to London and marry English Protestants, and after he had questioned her awhile, he told her there was nothing to be afraid of as long as she kept her own faith.

"You haven't lost it yet," he said, "or you wouldn't be coming to me. Bring your young man around and let me see him, so I can judge whether he's fit for you or not."

John thought that was a good idea; he wanted to meet the priest who would be having such an influence on his wife. They hit it off quite well together, but before giving his permission for the marriage, the priest wrote to Father Lynch at Saint Columbanus's to see what he would say about it.

Father Lynch went to see Gertie's mother, expecting her to be brokenhearted at the news. But there was more anger than sorrow in her reaction; it wasn't as though she hadn't expected something of the sort from the beginning. Once again Maire wished Father O'Malley were alive to help her; all she could do now was pray for her stubborn daughter. Father Lynch approved of that, and when his report reached London, Gertie received permission for a Catholic marriage.

Maire didn't want to turn her back on her own daughter, but she couldn't give the wedding, she couldn't even go to the wedding, and for the time being she didn't even want to meet her daughter's Protestant husband-to-be. It wasn't that Maire was intolerant of Protestants as such; there were a few Protestant families in Ballycarrick, and Eoin had taught their children in his school. Maire thought them pleasant people in spite of their beliefs, and they never made any trouble. One of her close friends when she was a child had been a Protestant, and nobody minded that—except for the trouble Maire had when her friend got married.

She had married a Protestant boy, which was right and proper, and Maire had been invited to the wedding. It didn't occur to her that there would be any harm in going, and Aunt Annie didn't object, so Maire went without giving the matter any thought. Only when she was in the church, and discovered how different the ceremony was from a nuptial Mass at Saint Columbanus's, did Maire begin to wonder. She mentioned it in her confession that Saturday—not to Father O'Malley, it was before his time, but to the pastor who was there. Maire never could remember his name. He had been so shocked that he refused to give her absolution, and Maire had gone home to Aunt Annie in tears, not knowing what to do.

"Don't carry on so, child," Aunt Annie had said. "That old billy goat doesn't know it's time to come in from the hedges. 'Tis no sin nowadays to watch your friend say her vows, even if she doesn't do it in the true Church. 'Twould be different if it was you up there being married to a Protestant, but you'll never do that and he's a fool for frightening you. Go back to the church now and stay away from the old one. Find Father O'Brien, the curate, and say your confession to him."

The curate did what the pastor wouldn't do, and though her penance was a full five decades of the rosary, Maire didn't mind that. She never went into a Protestant church again for the rest of her life, not even when she visited Dublin and Charlie wanted to show her the magnificent old cathedrals, Saint Patrick's and Christ Church, which had been built and consecrated to the Catholic Church so many centuries ago, and only stolen by the Protestant invaders. They were defiled now, Maire thought, and she wouldn't go inside.

Nor did she ever get over the horror of Aunt Annie's suggestion that she, or any good Catholic girl, much less a daughter of her own, might marry a Protestant. When Gertie did it, Maire couldn't stop her and didn't try, but she didn't meet Gertie's husband until a year or two later, when they brought over their first baby, Stephen, to show her.

"She didn't get up and dance when I came to the house," John remembered later. "I don't think any of them liked me, anyway. Father Peter was there, and she took us all down to that big hotel in Sligo and bought us a meal."

It was an experience that Gertie didn't remember so clearly, and in the years after it she hadn't seen her mother often. After Stephen came Mary and Janet, and it was too expensive to take them all to Ireland on holidays. But Gertie was true to her mother's teaching, and faithful in attendance at Mass and seeing that her children were too. It was easier for John to go with them than to go off by himself to the Church of England, and gradually he became interested and began to take instruction.

John met all three of Gertie's priestly brothers and liked them, perhaps because they accepted him as he was, without any complaints about their sister marrying a Protestant. Matt came to see them on his way to Ireland for his first home leave after three years in Nigeria, and arrived just in time to baptize Stephen. Willie stayed with them for quite a long time before he was ordained, when he was going through a difficult period and not sure he would ever make it as a priest. He had given up teaching and joined a cloistered order of the Sacred Heart, but this was too great a wrench away from the world he had always lived in, and he had to give it up.

He was full of uncertainty then, and had to get away from Ireland, from the Church, from teaching, from everything he had done before, so that he could think it over and sort out his ideas. He got a clerical job with an English trade union, and stayed for months with Gertie and John in their flat in Tottenham. John got to know him quite well, and a few years later, when Willie had resolved his uncertainties and completed his seminary studies, John went with Gertie to his ordination in Dublin. By that time Peter had been ordained, too, and like Matt had stopped in England on his way to Africa, and baptized Janet.

Eventually John was baptized in the Catholic Church too, not by any of the O'Rourkes but by the priest in Holloway Road who had married him to Gertie. It didn't happen until after Maire died, but, as Peter said, it must have been a happy day for her.

14.

Cross-
Channel
Traffic

Maire never went to England, although most of her children did at one time or another. It was the first place to go if you lived in Ireland and went anywhere at all; not as far away as America, not as expensive to get to, and easier to come home from if you didn't like it. Nothing in England seemed particularly strange or foreign; the Irish had been dealing with the English for centuries and knew them pretty well. They weren't afraid of them, except when there was some special reason for concern, as Maire had been concerned about Gertie when she was seventeen.

People in Ireland spoke of the sea that divided them from Britain as "the channel," and referred to Britain as "the mainland." British money still circulated in Ireland, even after the Republic replaced the "free state" in 1949 and Ireland's political independence became complete, except for the six counties of the North. To people like Maire, that was just politics, and she hardly noticed the change. British coins still fit in Irish telephone boxes, and when British prices and unemployment went up, so did the Irish. Like it or not, Ireland was still tied to the British economy, and if an Irishman wanted a good job and high wages, England was where he went. From Sligo to Lancashire or Yorkshire was a little farther than to County Cork or Kerry, but not much; you could write home for the same amount of postage, and the letter would get there almost as soon.

Maire wasn't particularly distressed when Gertie's sister Tess began talking of going to England a few years after Gertie left; Tess was twenty-two by then, and already married. She had never given Maire any trouble; she had grown up a quiet one, playing with Willie more than the others because he was the closest to her in age, and never involved in Gertie's mischief because Gertie was almost three years older. Matt was between them, and Peter was next after Willie, so Tess had grown up with the three future priests.

Not that she thought it much fun to play Willie's game of going to Mass all the time, any more than Gertie did; and when Gertie ran off to jump the fences with Tony and Jimmy, Tess would go down the lane to play with Johnny Kearin, a stocky little boy with flaming red hair who had a dog that could do tricks. She was never around the house as much as Jimmy and Gert, and didn't suffer so many "flakings"; the worst Maire ever found to punish her for was answering back when she lost her temper. But Tess thought her elder sister was "more favored" than she was; she had to wear Gertie's hand-me-down clothes, and it made her feel funny when Johnny Kearin recognized them.

Tess was not yet fourteen when she caught the bouquet at Mary's wedding, and maybe it was only luck; but she and Johnny had been each other's favorites all through school, and it was he who had known what to do on that terrible day a few months before when her father had collapsed in the classroom. He seemed like one of the family already, and it was taken for granted that the pair would marry when they were old enough.

They waited only until Johnny was eighteen and Tess seventeen, and Tess's father had been buried a little over two years. Johnny was working on his family's farm, which wasn't a big one but it was big enough, and there was room to spare in the house. Johnny's mother had died, and so had his younger brother; his elder sister Margaret had gone to Yorkshire, in England, where she was a hospital nurse, and all the other young Kearins except Johnny and his brother Tom were in Dublin.

It was a quiet wedding, with none of the celebration that had cost Eoin so dearly when Mary was married; and afterward Tess moved into Johnny's home, to be the woman of the house for her brother-in-law and father-in-law as well as her husband. She and Johnny were content with that for a while, and they had no other place to go. But neither of them was particularly keen on farming, and when the father died a few years later, it was John's brother who inherited the land. John and Tess decided it was time to look for a better way of life.

John was fond of his sister Margaret, though she was a good deal older, and in the spring he and Tess crossed the channel to Yorkshire to pay her a visit. They liked her place—high in the hills between Ilkley Moor and the Yorkshire dales, with views of rolling pasture land and hedgerows of hawthorn and wild roses not very different from Sligo, if less spectacular without the sea. John found he could get work in Leeds, not far away, as a painter and paperhanger, and it paid well enough to keep them and their two little children, Mary and Tom, in more comfort than they'd known in Sligo.

Mary was three and Tom was two when the Kearins settled in Leeds, and for a while they didn't have any more children. The streets weren't exactly paved with gold in England, and Tess wondered sometimes if they would do better in America, but there was no way of getting there. As soon as Mary was old enough to be left alone with Tom, with a neighbor to look in on them every so often, Tess began doing part-time work at the hospital as a nursing auxiliary, and that helped. There would have been no way of doing that in Sligo, but there were plenty of Irish families in Leeds doing the same thing, and it seemed only natural. The work had to be interrupted for a while when Carmel and Stephen were born, but they were spaced out, so that by the time Stephen arrived Mary was already eleven.

Tess and John were too busy to be homesick for Ireland, though John talked about it a lot. They went home every few years for a holiday or a special occasion—Peter's ordination in 1962, Chris's wedding in 1966, and other years when they had the money and the time. They would have stayed in Ireland if John had found a better job there, one that would be worth pulling up stakes and moving the whole household. But as each year passed and their little two-story council house on the hillside outside Leeds became more comfortable, more filled with their own things that they had worked so hard to get, it became more unlikely. They were settled in, and could barely tell the difference between themselves and the English people they lived among and worked with. And it was the same with their Irish neighbors.

In later years, when the troubles got bad in Northern Ireland, it was a little different. A flood of refugees from Belfast and Derry and South Armagh came to Yorkshire and neighboring Lancashire to get away from the shooting, and suddenly there was a lot of anti-Irish feeling in England. The refugees had to be provided with homes and jobs and social services, and that put them ahead of some of the English who had been on the waiting list for years for a better home—the refugees were "jumping the queue," and the locals didn't like it. The refugees were British subjects, because Northern Ireland was part of Britain, not Ireland, in all but geography; but that made no difference. The British regarded them as Irish, not English, and for a time all the Irish in Britain suffered from their unpopularity. And when the IRA—also mainly British subjects from Northern Ireland—started exploding bombs in England, that only made matters worse.

But anti-Irish feelings in Britain didn't bother Tess and

John; the quarrel was an old and familiar one, and they were used to it. Their sympathies were with the refugees, British subjects though they were; who would want to live in Belfast or Derry now, could you imagine bringing up children there? And what might happen to Joe and Chris when they were on border duty, would they be shot? When the fighting spilled over the border, and bombs went off in Dublin and Galway and Dundalk, what a sad thing it was, and for no good; was anybody they knew getting hurt? It was a nagging anxiety, but there was nothing they could do about it, just as there was nothing Joe or Chris or the other O'Rourkes in Ireland could do about it.

In time one gets used to such things, and even when the fighting in Northern Ireland was at its height, it wasn't as big a problem in Yorkshire as the invasion of other British subjects from other parts of the world—the coloreds from Africa and Asia. Bradford, a few miles from Leeds, became known as "little Pakistan" because so many settled there; London suffered race riots, and queue jumping by the British from Africa and Asia made the refugees from Ireland seem few by comparison.

Meanwhile, John talked a lot about wanting to go back to Ireland and stay, but he never did. He told Tess he wanted to be buried there when he died, but she only laughed at him. "You'll be buried where you die," she said, "never mind being buried in Ireland." And John said no more about it.

When Tess and John settled in Yorkshire, Brigid wanted to go with them, for she was as interested in nursing as were Tess and her sister-in-law Margaret, and there was no way for her to be trained while she stayed at Toberpatrick. But she was getting a lot of practical nursing experience there, and couldn't leave it yet.

That was the year Matt was ordained and left to take up his missionary work in Nigeria, while Gertie was doing a line with John Greenly in London, and Jimmy was working in the London underground. Brigid, at eighteen, was nursing her mother, who was feeling poorly a lot of the time, without knowing why. Rita was at Mary's house caring for her three children while Mary was in the hospital with her fourth—the first time she hadn't had her baby at home, but she was having a hard time of it, and the hospital service was much improved by now. Chris had gone to Dublin for a job in the post office, which he would soon leave to join the Garda like his brother Joe. Patrick was still in school, so the garden was being neglected again, but Joe had come up from Galway in the spring to do the plowing and plant the potatoes and cabbages and onions, and they still had their cow, though they'd gotten rid of the hens. It was 1956.

The boys always came home for Christmas, except Jimmy, who had never done that since he joined the navy, and this year Matt wouldn't be able to come. Maire understood that, but it was a shock to learn that Tony wouldn't be there either. Nobody had told her he was so ill; she thought he was still working at the post office with Chris. Charlie and Willie had never expected his illness to last so long; they had thought he'd go home that summer, and when he took a turn for the worse they still hoped he'd be out by Chrismas. But one of his lungs had been collapsed to save the other, and now there was no way of keeping the bad news from Maire any longer.

Nobody knew how to tell her, until one evening when they were sitting around the fire listening to the radio and Tony's name was mentioned on a request program, "For Tony O'Rourke in Crooksling Sanitarium, hoping you'll soon be well and home again, with love from your mother and your brothers and sisters"—with all fourteen names—"in Sligo and London and Leeds and Nigeria." Willie had sent in the request, thinking it would give Tony pleasure and provide a way out of what was becoming an impossible situation.

"Sweet Jesus, have mercy!" Maire exclaimed. "What's the meaning of this?" And Charlie tried to explain how Tony had neglected himself in that damp apartment, how the doctor had given them a warning that they hadn't understood, how Tony was in Crooksling and they had been to see him and he seemed to be getting on so well, and how he had taken a turn for the worse.

Maire was indignant. "Heaven help us, why didn't you tell me!" she exploded.

"What could you have done, Mother? You're not that well yourself."

"Well, you're not going to leave him in that dreadful place all alone. You'll send him home to me so I can take care of him."

"Mother, that's just why we didn't tell you. You know we can't do that. They're giving him the best of care; it's a fine modern place with all the latest machines, and the finest doctors in the country. There's nothing more you can do."

"I can go and see him, that's what I can do." Maire sniffed loudly, anger and disapproval covering her anxiety. She started out of her chair, but there was a sudden cramp in her stomach, and she sat down again. "Brigid, dear, my pills," she said, and Brigid fetched them.

It was a bad start to an awkward Christmas, and if it hadn't been for the holiday and the presence of so many of her family all arguing against it, Maire would have gone to Crooksling at once. Instead she went back to Dublin with Charlie, Mick, and Christy after the holiday was over, and journeyed out to Crooksling to make her own inspection of her son, and talk to the doctors. Tony couldn't be moved just yet, they said, but he could go home in the spring if he continued to mend.

He came in May, the scar on one lung healed, the other lung permanently out of use. He was under strict orders to take it easy, get plenty of rest, and do nothing strenuous; with only one lung he couldn't do all the things he used to do. He was to stay off his bicycle for six months at least, and after that to go carefully, never strain himself, never get out of breath.

Tony obeyed orders for a little while, but nothing could keep him to a regimen like that for long, neither his doctor's orders nor his mother's anxiety. Coming home after being cooped up so long was like a return to boyhood, and Tony loved it. He was back in the sweet green meadows of Toberpatrick, where the wind dashed the sea spray high on the rocky shore, and the clouds scudded by in the blue dome of heaven overhead, ringing the peak of Ben Bulben with a white fluffy crown. When the rain spread in dark masses from the west and dropped cool and fresh on his face, there would as often as not be sunshine on the gold-green slopes of Slieve Gamh, and a great arching rainbow brilliant against the towering darkness over the sea.

He got out his old cycle, thinking it wouldn't do any harm if he took it easy, and at first he was content to coast downhill and pedal lightly on the way back, getting off to walk where the steep slopes began. He loved to ride along the narrow lanes between the low stone fences, carefully balanced gray stones daubed with splashes of white lichen, as though some child had run by painting them carelessly here and there from a dripping pail of whitewash. The black cows would turn and stare at him as he went by, big eyes in silent, solemn faces, wondering what strange creature this might be that had come to disturb them.

Tony didn't keep to his good resolutions long; in a day or two he was back to his old habits, cycling like a maniac. He was a very devil on his bicycle all over the hills of Sligo. And his sight wasn't good; he had always had difficulty with his eyes, and the medication he was taking seemed to make it worse. One day when he was charging downhill toward Mary's house he passed so close to a horse and cart that the pedal of his bike came off on the side of the cart.

Brigid tried to reason with him when she gave him his eyedrops, and sometimes he'd be coughing and choking, and when she got him calmed down she'd swab out the back of his throat. He was a big man, like his father and his brothers, big-boned, strong, and tough in his own way. He had a tremendous will to live, but he fought his illness the wrong way, trying to do things that were beyond his capacity.

Gradually he had to slow down, and when he went into Sligo

Hospital for a checkup the doctor suspected there was more to his trouble than the scar on his lung and the failing eyesight. He was losing the strength of his legs, and having trouble with his kidneys. So they did some more tests and discovered the cause. He had multiple sclerosis, and as it developed it would take a ravaging, devastating form.

As Tony's condition grew worse, his mother seemed to gain strength. She had to go into the hospital for a hysterectomy, but she made light of it, and Brigid didn't find out until years later that she'd had cancer of the womb, and should have gone on with radiation treatments after leaving the hospital. The treatments were painful and she didn't think she needed them; like her son and husband, she obeyed doctors' orders only when she chose to. Maire had more faith in her prayers to Saint Anthony. Besides, she felt much better after the operation, and began to take more of the burden of nursing Tony, which relieved Brigid.

Christy had joined the Garda by this time, and Peter had completed his novitiate and two years at the University College in Cork, and was in Dromantine Seminary. Willie had been sent to Rome by the Sacred Heart Fathers. Patrick was at the vocational school in Easkey, cycling twenty-five miles or more there and back every day in the autumn and spring, riding the bus in the winter. He was learning carpentry, woodworking, mechanical drawing, and some metalworking, and what interested him most was the class in agriculture.

At fifteen he was old enough to do his own digging in the family garden, and he restored it to the beauty and fruitfulness it had known in his father's day, fine healthy vegetables growing in straight rows with not a weed to be seen between them. There was plenty to eat that year, and Patrick won first prize in the school garden competition. The next year he won a scholarship from the County Agricultural Committee, which gave him a year in a boarding school with the Franciscan

Brothers, for classroom and practical training in agriculture and horticulture.

Rita was eighteen, and back at Toberpatrick because Mary didn't need her anymore. Mary had seven children now, four boys and three girls, and she had made a decision, which there was no need to tell her mother about, or anybody else, but she'd made it. Seven children were enough. Her house was full, and the older ones were all the help she'd need with the younger ones, if there wouldn't be any more.

When Rita went home to care for her mother and help her with Tony, Brigid was free to go to England at last. Maire raised no objections; if Tess was safe in England, Brigid would be too. Besides, she knew of Brigid's longing to be trained as a nurse, and thought it would suit her very well. There was no hope of such training in Sligo.

For four months Brigid trained at Whittington Hospital in North London, not far from Gertie's home, and was much too busy and excited to be homesick. But she wasn't well. She tired easily, and there was a nasty swelling on her neck; at first she thought it was the long hours of work and the foggy English winter, with its choking fogs, yellow and smelling of soot, so different from the clean sea mists of Sligo, and never a breeze to blow them away.

It wasn't the fog, it was goiter, and Brigid had to have a thyroid operation, which meant a long convalescence, and ultimately she had to drop out of her class. It was a miserable disappointment, and she might have gone home in despair if Jimmy and Audrey hadn't persuaded her to stay with them instead. They had a flat in Sevenoaks, near the Ford plant on the eastern fringe of London, and Audrey was even more homesick than Brigid, though she'd been in London nearly two years.

Audrey's mother was forever writing to her to come back to Cobh, and Audrey was forever urging Jimmy to do it, and talking of the good jobs she was sure he could get there. But

Jimmy didn't want to leave. He was making good money at Ford, more than he could hope for in Cobh or anywhere else in Ireland. He'd even joined the Ilford Club, in the next town, and used to play a bit of golf, more for the pleasure of getting out in the fresh air than for becoming proficient at the game. Now that Brigid was with them she could baby-sit with Patricia, and Audrey could go around the golf course with him, and they'd have lunch and a couple of beers, and Audrey began to feel a bit better.

Brigid felt better too, and when she thought of what it would mean to go back to Ireland—serving her time as Gertie had done, years of hard work before you made any money, and some old lady telling you what to do and what not to do as if she were your mother—there didn't seem any sense in being homesick. If her health wasn't good enough for full-time nurse's training, at least she could be a part-time nursing assistant, like Tess in Leeds, and it was better to be on her own.

She had lost weight during her illness, and discovered that her new slim figure was a great improvement over the old chubby farm-girl look. There was a touch of red in her dark brown hair that made it glow when she undid the tight bun she'd worn as a nursing student and let it flow in waves around her heart-shaped face. She was nearly as tall as Gertie, with more delicate features and the same impish grin, and as she regained her strength and the color came back to her cheeks, she decided that life in London could be fun.

She found a flat in a rather attractive Victorian terrace house in Ilford, where a girl from Tipperary was looking for a roommate, and had a brother living in the other flat on the same floor. They had a lot of friends in the neighborhood, and it wasn't long before Brigid was going out with a Tipperary boy named Michael McSweeney, who worked at the same Ford plant as Jimmy.

Brigid didn't see as much of Jimmy and Audrey after that, and when she started talking about her friend Michael they knew why.

"Why don't you bring him with you and spend the evening together here?" Audrey asked one day when Brigid was making excuses not to baby-sit. "We wouldn't mind, and Patricia will be asleep. You can give him tea if you like—and there's chops in the fridge."

There wasn't any way of saying no to that, but Brigid was nervous about what Jimmy might think of Michael. Just because they worked in the same plant didn't mean they'd like each other, and so far she'd never even mentioned her brother to her boyfriend. He knew she had one in England, of course, and nine more in Ireland or wherever, but that was it.

She needn't have worried. "My God," said Jimmy when Brigid brought Michael to the door that evening, "so this is who you've been talking about!" One look at Michael's broad, freckled face and the two of them were doubled up with laughter.

"We've been pals since I first came to Ford," Jimmy went on. "Haven't we, Mick? I've been telling you about my sister all along and you said you were doing a line with someone else!"

"I never knew you were talking about *her*," said Michael. "Trouble with you is, you don't know what a fine lass your own sister is!"

"Well, I hadn't seen her since she was a kid, until she blew in last year. You've grown up a bit since I joined the navy, haven't you, Brigid?"

She blushed, and would have slapped his face if she could have reached, but Michael was in the way and she gave a contented chuckle instead. It was a good feeling, really. If Michael was an old friend of Jimmy's, what was there to worry about?

In the summer Audrey's father and mother came over for a visit, and while they were there Audrey gave an engagement party for Brigid and Michael. If it wasn't quite like being back at Toberpatrick it was the next best thing, and all the guests were Irish even if they were living in England. Mummy would like that, Brigid thought. She told Michael they'd be married by Father Lynch at Saint Columbanus's, and he didn't object. Audrey cried a little, and so did her mother. They'd been talking again about going back to Cobh, and Jimmy was finding it harder and harder to resist the pressure.

"There's a house going in Canon Street," Audrey's mother said. "It's just around the corner from the shop. It will need a little fixing, but you're handy at that kind of thing, Jimmy. And you needn't worry about putting a little money into it, we can see to it if it comes to that. It's a nice place, really, all it needs is a bit of paper on the walls, do you know? Same as we had to do when we first moved into our place. But it's a real house, Audrey, not just a flat like you're living in now, and it will be lovely when you've fixed it up."

"Mummy's right, Jimmy," said Audrey, "you'll be able to do whatever needs doing."

"Course, I can do it, whatever it is. But I'll need a job too, don't forget."

"You'll have no trouble, Jimmy. Look at all the things you can do. In the navy and all, and in the London Transport and the factory here. There's plenty of shipping in Cork Harbour that could use a good navy man, and the steelworks and the shipyards and all kinds of things. After all the jobs you've had, you won't mind starting another."

"Besides, Jimmy," Audrey's mother started again, "you'll be on to moving out of this little flat soon whatever you do; you've two little ones now and there'll be more, this place will never be big enough. And if you have to move, why not come home where you belong?"

It wasn't what Jimmy wanted, but he knew Audrey had never been really settled in England, and maybe never would be. What was the use of making good money in England when he was spending it all taking Audrey and the kids back to Ireland twice a year or more? Every time they went they had to dress the kids and doll them all up in new clothes, and the fares home kept going up. Jimmy could live anywhere, he knew that, but Audrey couldn't. That was the difference, she wanted to go home.

"Okay, we'll do it," he said. "We'll make up our minds to go home."

Brigid had always known that Audrey would take Jimmy back to Ireland sooner or later, but the news was a blow. Audrey had never put down roots, she decided, that was the trouble; and for that matter Jimmy wasn't a man to put down roots anywhere. But Michael wanted roots, and so did Brigid, and that meant having a house to live in as soon as they could, instead of a little flat like Jimmy and Audrey's. They couldn't do it right way, but it was something to work for.

Brigid liked the house she was in, a three-story Victorian brick with a bay window on the ground floor, nice high ceilings on the floor above, and two spacious bedrooms on the top floor. Like thousands of others of its kind, it was wide enough for only two rooms on each floor, one in front and one in back, with a staircase and narrow passage on the side. There was a tiny garden in the rear between high walls, and a little paved yard in front where they might someday park a car.

The owner wanted to sell, and though Michael and Brigid had nowhere near enough money to buy it, he was asking so high a price that she didn't think anyone else would either. Meanwhile he was letting the rooms, and not doing too well at it. The brother and sister from Tipperary had gone back home, and so had the first-floor tenants, who were from Donegal. The whole upstairs, all four rooms, were empty except for Brigid; the owner and his wife lived on the ground floor. Those top four rooms would make a lovely flat for us when we're married, Brigid thought, and with a little persuasion she got the owner to agree.

In September the two youngest O'Rourkes, Rita and Patrick, turned up on Gertie's doorstep in Tottenham, and she barely recognized them. Patrick had been seven and Rita nine when Gertie left home to work for Mrs. Flynn in Westport; now Rita was a long-limbed, slim-hipped lady of twenty-one, with curly chestnut hair and a farm girl's fresh complexion, and Patrick was as tall as Jimmy, with the same broad shoulders and wide-set eyes, and the strong, tough-skinned hands of a young man who worked in the soil.

"Blow me down," said Gertie, "what brings you two here? When I got your letter that you were coming, I couldn't believe it. How's Mamma?"

"Mummy's in good form," said Rita. "She's looking after Tony, you know, she won't let anyone else near him. Tony's been real bad these last few years, but he's better now. And Mary comes up sometimes to help. Her kids are big enough to look after themselves now, so she can get out and help Mummy."

"And that's how she let you out to come here, is it?" Gertie looked at her younger sister appraisingly "Well, it's time you had a better chance in life, isn't it. How do you like London?"

"I don't know, really. So many people, all in such a rush, and all the cars and buses! I don't know how you put up with it."

Gertie grinned. "You'll get used to it, Rita. It's not Tober-patrick, but it can be nice. Sit down now and I'll make a cup of tea."

It had been Pat's idea to come to London; when Rita heard he was going, she went with him. Pat had spent the last two years in the National Botanic Gardens in Glasnevin, on the north side of Dublin, in a work-and-learn scholarship he'd won by a competitive examination, after his year in the Franciscan Brothers' school. It was training in scientific horticulture, which could lead to a job with a County Agriculture Committee. That would be a start on his chosen career, but it didn't satisfy Pat's ambitions.

The first year at Glasnevin he had lived at a hostel attached to the gardens, run by a matron who saw that her seventeen-year-old charges got proper lunches and went to bed on time each night; the second year he moved in with Charlie and Mick in their digs at Drumcondra, only a mile or two away. Like Charlie, Pat was a serious-minded young man, who had no time for the pubs where Mick spent his evenings. His ambition was to get into a university, and for that he needed more education than the vocational training he'd had so far. He went to night school, and in the two years he was in Dublin he qualified in five subjects, which was enough to get him into the university if he'd had the money. But he didn't.

There were very few scholarships available at the time, and none of them offered enough to pay all his expenses. He had no way of borrowing the money, and nobody in the family had enough to give him what he needed. Charlie was committed to helping support Peter while he studied for the priesthood, Joe was their mother's main support, Mick was always generous but didn't have the resources, nor did any of the others.

Pat thought it over while he was home on vacation that summer, and decided the best place to earn the money he needed was London. There were Irish building contractors there who would pay him twenty-two pounds a week for common labor, digging ditches and hauling bricks, and that was more than he could earn any other way. It would be heavy manual labor for a boy of nineteen, but he was very fit and athletic, and didn't think that would be any problem. Rita encouraged him; he ought to see what the outside world was like, she said, and not spend all his life digging in Irish gardens. She wanted to see the world too, and it would be a fine thing if they went together.

As it turned out, they didn't see much of the world, and what they saw wasn't particularly rewarding. Rita got a job in a factory, working a bookbinding machine, and found it noisy, monotonous, tiresome work, which kept her constantly on the go with never a moment to rest, and made more money for her employers than for her. She enjoyed living with Gertie, but helping with her two little children in a rather crowded flat was no improvement over caring for Mary's children in the comfortable house in Sligo. By Christmas she was ready to give it up and go home, but she discovered that Pat was already thinking along the same lines, and decided she'd wait until he went too.

Pat was in a cheap boarding house in East London near his work, living a Spartan existence with very little social life because he had neither the money nor the energy for it at the end of his exhausting days. Digging in the hard clay of a London building site was a more back-breaking job than turning over the soft topsoil in the Botanic Gardens at Glasnevin. He was developing new muscles and putting new strength in his arms and shoulders, but there was no pleasure in it and nothing to be learned, except the disappointing discovery that the little money he was saving would never be enough to put him through four years at a university. He'd have to settle for the diploma they'd given him at Glasnevin, he decided, and see what kind of job it could get him.

He started writing letters to Ireland, and got a reply from the Horticultural and Agricultural Research Institute, a new organization funded by the Irish government that also had some American money. They were opening a new research center in County Wexford, and experimenting with freeze drying foods, which was a new development in Ireland in the early 1960s. This looked to Pat like a career with a future, and after some more correspondence he was invited to Dublin for an interview. It was spring by then, and when he went back to Ireland Rita was only too glad to go with him.

Brigid's wedding to Michael McSweeney that summer became the biggest O'Rourke family reunion since the father had died. They were married in Saint Columbanus's Church, with a reception afterward at the Imperial Hotel in Sligo, just like Mary and Michael. Gertie and Tess couldn't come, because they were both expecting, but Tess's daughter Carmel came to represent her mother and be a bridesmaid, along with Mary's Anne and Jimmy's Patricia. Matt was in Nigeria, and could only send his blessings by telegraph; Tony couldn't go to the church or the reception, because he'd taken a turn for the worse, and could hardly walk or get out of his chair anymore without help. He should have been in a nursing home, but Maire wouldn't let him go, at least until after the wedding.

It was a shock to Rita to see how Tony had failed while she was in England, and even more so to Jimmy, who had been the closest to him when they were boys together, and who hadn't seen him since that day in Dublin eight years before, when his illness was just beginning and he had refused to talk about his mysterious friends in the IRA.

All the rest were there, and Tony joked with each of them from his place by the fire in the sitting room, chattering in a feverishly excited way as though to pretend, as he had always pretended, that his illness was nothing to worry about, he'd soon be all right. Yet he must have known, as they all knew, that it was an agony from which no real recovery could be expected. He was battling his illness with all his strength, as he had always done, and each day that he was still alive was a victory. Brigid, with her nursing experience, knew better than any of them what it was costing him.

Patrick came up from his new job in Wexford, where he was doing research on diseases in black-currant bushes; Joe came from Galway with his wife, Breda, whom he had married with less ceremony the year before; Jimmy came with Audrey and their two children; Mary and Michael were there with their seven; Rita was maid of honor; Mick and Charlie came from Dublin and Chris from his Garda station in Mullingar, all three of them still bachelors; and Peter, newly ordained a priest, was there with Willie, who had at last decided that the priesthood was his vocation too.

Willie, after his year of indecision in London, had accepted an offer from the Diocese of Bridgeport, Connecticut, to finance his seminary training on the condition that he accept appointment to a Connecticut parish when he was ordained. Connecticut was a long way from Sligo, but Willie didn't mind;

this was his opportunity, and the only way he could find to realize the ambition he had had since it first occurred to him at Father O'Malley's funeral when he was seven years old. He had hesitated a long time, and tried to make his way in the secular world, but he found himself even less at home in it than he had been in the cloistered order of the Sacred Heart Fathers. Pastoral work would be right for him, he was sure, even in America; as his brother Joe said, if ever a man had a true vocation for the priesthood, it was Willie, after what he'd been through.

Their mother agreed, and after the worrying and praying she'd done in the years of Willie's uncertainty, she felt his decision now must be a special grace from heaven. As Maire bustled about among her children and grandchildren, ruling the little ones as she had always done, and getting more obedience from them than their parents had given her at that age, she had a sense of fulfillment such as she hadn't known since Eoin died. Brigid had chosen a fine man for her husband; Joe and Jim had married well too, and so had Tess. All her children were good to her, though she still couldn't accept Gertie's husband, but that couldn't be helped; all of them were doing well for themselves and in good health, thanks be to God, except Tony, and that couldn't be helped either.

She was a proud mother to count three priests among her sons, and especially proud that day, for Peter, the youngest of the three, was to perform the marriage ceremony for his sister, and offer the nuptial Mass. It was the first time one of her children would do such a service for another, and in Maire's heart it helped to heal the wound left by the absent Gertie.

15.

Decisions

Peter was a very earnest young priest, with an almost mystical attitude toward his faith and his work that rather surprised his brothers and sisters, and awed his mother. They hadn't seen much of him since he had gone away to Ballinafad College thirteen years before, and he had grown lean and tall as a string bean, with lofty ideas that made Joe think he had his head in the clouds. Like Willie, he had his father's gift for teaching, and the summer of Brigid's wedding he was getting an advanced degree in education from the African Mission Society in Cork, before following Matt to Nigeria.

Peter dated his interest in the priesthood from the year his father died, when he was twelve. Of all the children he was the closest to the father in the long months of his final illness, the one who sat by his bed reading to him while the others were out working or playing, and who helped him get dressed and undressed when he was able to get about a bit, and did the intimate personal things for him that he wouldn't let Maire do.

Peter knew his father was dying, as everyone did, and he thought about it a lot, with a twelve-year-old kind of intellectual detachment that helped him mask his feelings.

For the first time he was sorting out in his mind his impressions of his father as a schoolmaster and his feelings about him as a father and a man. The schoolmaster had been the dominant impression as long as he could remember, for his father's habits had always been as didactic and dictatorial at home as in the schoolroom. Peter felt that he was learning only too late how different it was to be a son instead of a pupil, and how much better to love than merely to obey.

He had been taught to look forward to his own death not with fear but with hope, and wondered if his father was doing the same. Either way it made little difference to Peter's sense of loss, and he turned to thoughts of mortality itself, as a common experience facing everyone, a spiritual thing that was not just the end of a life but part of life, a thing to be reckoned with all through life.

It had a bearing on what Peter wanted to do with his own life after his father died, and this was a question very much in his mind, as it was in the minds of his elder brothers and sisters. He didn't want to be a schoolteacher; he thought that that must be a suffocating, stultifying kind of life, a famine of the spirit for his father, whose learning was so far beyond the little children he taught and the unlettered farmers who came to him for help as surveyor, peace commissioner, and politician. In the Church, Peter thought, he could escape all that. He would learn the real meaning of death and what it had to do with life; he would be dealing with such things in his work, and he would know all about them.

When Matt went to Summerhill and discovered that the African Mission Society was looking for recruits and had scholarships to offer, Peter decided that that was just the opportunity he needed. He was at the top of his class in school in everything but mathematics, and winning the scholarship was no problem. It paid his tuition at Ballinafad College, and

Charlie, who had just started his bread-van route in Dublin, promised to help with his personal expenses. At that point Charlie would rather have been a priest than a bread salesman himself, and helping Peter was the next best thing.

The schooling Peter received at Ballinafad was not greatly different from that offered at most other secondary schools in Ireland in those years, for apart from vocational schools they were all run by religious orders. Peter's time of testing came when he finished Ballinafad and at the age of nineteen entered a monastery at Kilcolgan for the nine months of his "novitiate."

This was a period of prayer and meditation, combined with such menial tasks as scrubbing floors and washing dishes, useful and necessary work performed as a spiritual exercise in humility, service, and self-denial. It was a Spartan life consistent with the monastic tradition of subduing the passions of the flesh, and for a boy in late adolescence it was a physical as well as a spiritual trial.

But for Peter it was a kind of honeymoon, a time of great calm and consolation, of constant meditation and examination of conscience, in which he was spared the traumatic emotional experiences of a more worldly adolescence. These were to come to him later, in a different context, when he could face them with more maturity. At Kilcolgan he had the feeling expressed by Saint Peter at the Transfiguration; "Lord, it is good for us to be here."

There was a kind of hothouse spirituality about this experience of religious conversion, in a cloister protected from the cold winds of the outside world and warmed by centuries of Christian mysticism. But Peter found in it the strength and assurance he was looking for. He felt that Kilcolgan was brilliant with the light of faith, which he would be carrying to other people in the darkness of the outer world. He resolved, in the words of one of the saints whose meditations he was studying, "never to deny in the darkness what I have seen in the light."

When he emerged from Kilcolgan his first taste of the outer world had no darkness in it, but a different kind of light—the rational view taught at University College, Cork. He discovered intellectual qualities in himself that he didn't know he had, and the love of reading he had acquired from his father developed into a fascination for literature and history. He read Synge and Yeats with a new and quite worldly understanding, for the primitive, passionate Ireland of the west with its Gaelic traditions that they wrote about was the land he had grown up in. It was like going home again, for the poetry and drama of it were in his blood.

He read Plato and Aristotle and Machiavelli and Burke, and was amazed that Ireland could produce a university that would teach such a balanced view of human experience. It was as refreshing a change from Christian doctrine as that had been from Irish Republicanism, and Peter was glad to be allowed at last to find his own way through what he studied. It was the kind of teaching his brother Charlie had longed for but never received. Peter read authors he'd never heard of before, people like T. S. Eliot and D. H. Lawrence, and found himself running riot with ideas about life and people and the world. It was as different from his meditations in the monastery as anything could be, and he found it profoundly exciting.

Peter's class was one of the first to experience a secular university before their seminary training, and when he arrived at Dromantine College to begin his theology studies the change was a shock. After so much intellectual freedom he felt imprisoned by the rigidities of pre-Vatican II theology, and found the teaching stereotyped and unconvincing. For a typical assignment he would be given a thesis to demonstrate—"God is merciful," or "Christ is true God and true man"—and would be required to cite quotations from Scripture, all in Latin and taken out of context, to prove the point, as though it were no more complex than a theorem in Euclid's geometry. Everything had to be neatly tied up, but in Peter's view of life nothing real or true could be tied up that way.

Peter was doubly unhappy because theology was not, after

all, what interested him then. He had done so well in history at the university that his professor had urged him to stay on there and take a master's degree. But the African Mission Society was paying his tuition to be a missionary priest, not a historian, and they wouldn't let him do it. This was Peter's first occasion of conflict and frustration with the society and the Church, and suddenly the "darkness" he had worried about in Kilcolgan was upon him.

Did going on to the priesthood mean denying every personal ambition that seemed real to him? Peter began to recognize for the first time the inescapable tension of the priestly life, the struggle of being both a priest and a man at the same time. To be a priest must he be so God-like as to unman himself in this way? And in other more intimate ways, too; the burdens of celibacy were so much more difficult for him now at twenty-three than they had seemed in Kilcolgan at nineteen. It took him a long time to understand what these things meant; at first he resented them.

Dromantine College was at Newry in County Down, one of the six counties of British Northern Ireland—although Peter didn't worry about such details as a student in 1960. There were no political upheavals at the time, and what mattered to the young seminarian was the beautiful and lonely wilderness of the Mourne Mountains nearby, and the rocky shore of the Irish Sea beyond. He spent many hours on long solitary walks while he pondered his problems of faith and conscience. His only company was the cattle grazing on the upland meadows, and they reminded him of a text from one of the minor prophets: "How can a man become wise whose discourse is with the sons of bulls?"

In his distress he wrote to a cousin of his father's, Mary Bridget, who was a nun. He had never met her, but he had heard his father speak of her, and when she answered his letter she showed such understanding and strength of faith that Peter drew courage from her, and the correspondence developed into a lifelong friendship. She reminded Peter of what he had learned about suffering as a child, that for all its painfulness it can give insights that can be gained in no other way.

Peter's first reaction, like that of any young man of his age starting any career, was that the system was wrong—in his case, the seminary system. The stereotyped teaching in Latin, the narrow, faulty thinking, the inflexible rigidity of the teachers and their doctrines, all offended him. But he got on fairly well with the authorities; there was the odd clash on occasion, but no earthquakes.

After a while he realized that he was more at war with himself than with the system, and if God was all that He was supposed to be, He wouldn't expect Peter to throw aside all that he had learned before. He offered God this, that he would suffer the burdens of the system he found so confining, yet without denying anything within himself that he knew to be true. In darkness he would not deny what he had seen in the light.

Peter was ordained on December 21, 1962, and he found special meaning in the day because it was the shortest of the year, when darkness covered Ireland for all but a few hours at midday. The light was in him now, and his doubts were gone. He left Dromantine for Cork again, not the university this time but the African Missionary Society's headquarters, to earn a higher diploma in education and prepare for his missionary work in Nigeria.

After Peter's ordination Charlie didn't have to contribute to his support any longer, and he put the money in his savings account instead. He'd managed to save a little already, but after twelve years on his bread van he was only earning thirteen pounds a week, and it didn't look as if he'd ever do much better. He was thirty-five, and his one disappointing year at the university in Dublin had convinced him he had all the education he was likely to get. If he was ever going to branch out and make something of himself, now seemed to be the time.

When he went home to Toberpatrick in June for Brigid's

wedding he talked about it to one of his old friends, Tom O'Malley, who was making a very good living selling insurance. "That's something you could do, Charlie," O'Malley said. "You ought to buy a book yourself."

"Buy a book?" said Charlie.

"That's it, buy a life-insurance book. You buy it on the open market, and it has existing business on it. Someone has been selling insurance, let's say, and he has so many people paying him so much a week for the insurance, and he passes the money on to the company and keeps some of it himself for his commission. It's all commission, there's no salary, but the commissions can mount up if you have enough customers. Okay, so you find a man who's been doing this and he's had enough, he wants to retire, or he's got a chance to go into an agency or go into some other line of business, and he can't handle his book anymore. You buy his book from him, it will cost you two or three hundred pounds, or maybe a thousand, depending on how much business he has in it. And you've got the names and addresses of all these people, and how much they're paying, and it gives you a start. From there on you build up; you go out and collect from them, you talk them into maybe buying more insurance, you look for new business of your own, use your contacts. It's all a matter of personal contacts."

"But I haven't got a thousand pounds," said Charlie.

"You don't need a thousand, you'd want a smaller book than that to start with. But your business will be worth a thousand after you've been doing it awhile, if you build it up. It's all your own, you see, there's nothing to hold you back and nothing else to buy. You make your calls every week, and the more calls you make the more money you make. Naturally you use your acquaintances, they all need more insurance—everybody needs more insurance these days, it's a growing thing. And then you go out and canvass, you go out cold, knocking on doors, canvassing new areas. You can get another agent from the office to go out with you, a man with experience, to show you how it's done when you're first beginning. You split the new business at the end of the day, you come to an arrangement with him, and pretty soon you can go out on your own, do it all yourself and keep it all."

It was an idea worth thinking about, and it didn't take Charlie long to decide it looked at lot better than what he was doing. Charlie had a lot of friends and acquaintances to start with, and he'd been knocking on doors with his baskets of bread for years, there was nothing new in that. And he believed in insurance; he understood the value of it after what had happened on his father's death, though he wouldn't need to talk about that when he was selling.

It was very small business he'd start with, what was known in the old days as "burial insurance," just enough to give a man a decent funeral. But it would grow; as people got more money they'd want more insurance, and then there were other kinds—fire, burglary, accident, and so on—which he could branch into as he learned more about it.

When he came right down to it, Charlie didn't have much choice. This was the one business he knew about that he could get into without special training. And he had friends to advise him, to help him find a book he could afford, one that would be worth what he paid for it.

The next year or two Charlie worked harder than he had ever done before in his life. Initially he was earning less than he had from the bread van, and for every new customer there were others who simply said no, or, what was worse, kept him wondering for days and weeks while they thought about it and then decided against it, or bought so little that it hardly seemed worth the time and trouble he'd put into it.

Even the old accounts he had bought with the book didn't all stay with him; some died, or moved away, or had to drop their policies. There were days when if he'd been a salaried employee of a company, he would have gone to his boss and said, "Here's your book, I'm not interested in your job, I'm going after something else." But he couldn't do that; the book was his own, he'd paid his own money for it, hard cash, and it struck him that he'd better get on, make it go. If he sold the book and got out he wouldn't get his money back, because there weren't even as many accounts left in it as there had been when he bought it.

The pressure was on Charlie, and he knew it. It helped to discover that his old friend from the Legion of Mary, Bill O'Hara, was an insurance agent too, and he learned a lot from him about how to get and keep good customers. And it helped to look back on what he'd done in night school and the university, the long years of studying things that had meant nothing to him at the time, but were important and had to be learned anyhow; the exams he'd studied for and taken and flunked, and had to do over again until he passed them. He felt matured by those experiences, and he told himself that if he had survived that ordeal, he could manage this one.

By this time the idea of marriage, which had occurred to Charlie that night at Willie's graduation dance, was becoming more insistent. Not that he had much time for such things, with his new business, but he was still going to Saturday-night hops and "dress dances," and he began to look at the girls more carefully. He was beginning to shop around. He met a girl at a dance in the Silver Slipper in Sligo when he was home for Christmas holidays in 1963, the year he bought the insurance book, and she made a big enough impression to bring him back to Sligo a few times after that, but he wasn't ready yet. She was somebody to think about back home, while he struggled to get his business going.

Then one day in Dublin he stopped in at a shop on North Brunswick Street, across from the Richmond Hospital, to collect some business from Mrs. Sweeney, who ran the shop.

"You know there's a big dance coming up this week for the nurses at the hospital," Mrs. Sweeney remarked.

"Is there, now?" said Charlie. "I didn't know that."

"Yes, there is, it's for the girls who are finishing their training. I thought maybe you might be planning on going, if you know any of them. They're a fine lot of young ladies, they are, and you're not married yet, are you?"

"That's true, Mrs. Sweeney, I'm not. But there are plenty of girls back home in Sligo, you know."

"Sligo, is it? Now isn't that a funny thing. There was one of the nurses in here just now, she's after telling me she's looking for a nice young man to be her partner for the dance, and she's from some place in Sligo too. Coolaney, I think it was. Maybe you'd know her?"

"Coolaney, no. That's over the mountain from where we lived. I'd never go there on my bicycle when I was home. 'Tis too far."

"Well, you're in Dublin now, and you don't need to be riding your bicycle when you come to the Richmond Hospital to take a nice girl dancing, that you don't. Can I tell her you'll be there, though you come from over the mountain?"

"There's no harm in it, I'm sure. I'm quite willing to go." There would be no strings attached, he reflected; he didn't know how things were with the girl in Sligo, but he'd made no promise to her. Still, he felt obliged to caution Mrs. Sweeney. "Don't you go making plans for me," he said, "with a girl I've never met."

That was how Charlie met Una O'Kelly, who, it turned out, had a friend who was also looking for a partner for the dance, so Charlie brought along his friend Paddy McGuinness, and it was a double blind date. They all got along fine, and afterward Una said there was another dress dance coming up, and Charlie promised to take her.

In a little while, as such things happen, Charlie's romance with the girl in Sligo went on the rocks, and they forgot about each other. Charlie was following his usual routine, dancing with any girl he liked whenever he had a chance, but never seeing them away from the dance floor. The day came when he decided this wasn't enough, he'd have to ring up Una at the hospital.

From there on it developed. Charle discovered that Una's brother Roger was an old friend who had shared digs with him when Charlie was at the university. Roger was a dozen years younger than Charlie, and had done his secondary school in the years when Charlie was learning about Dublin life from the Legion of Mary. He had a good job now with the Agricultural Institute, and it was at his suburban home in Killiney that Charlie was introduced to Una's mother, who had come to Dublin for a checkup at Richmond Hospital.

Una's mother reminded Charlie of his own, in her piety and stubborn strength. She, too, was a widow and had led a hard life since the day her husband fell off a haycock and damaged his spine, about the same year Charlie's father had his first heart attack. Una's eldest brother was running the farm, while the others had gone off to Dublin as soon as they were old enough, like Charlie and his brothers and sisters, to find their own ways.

After they were married Una couldn't go back to her job at the hospital, for married women weren't allowed to do that in Ireland in the 1960s. She took a course in electrocardiogram techniques, and worked part time at the hospital for the first two years of their marriage, until Cathal was on the way.

Meanwhile, Charlie bought a neat brick-and-stucco bunga-low with a bit of a garden in a modern housing estate on the north side of Dublin, up on the hills overlooking the city, on the very edge where the open fields begin. It wasn't as big as his father's house, but then he didn't plan on having as many children, and it was a nice piece of property in a neighborhood of families like his own. He built an addition on the side after a while, to enlarge the kitchen, and put in central heating, and hung a picture of the Sacred Heart over the mantelpiece, just like the one that hung in the room where his father had died. It was a good home, better than he had ever had before.

When Jimmy and Audrey arrived in Cobh a few months before Brigid's wedding and had their first look at the house Audrey's mother had bought for them, they had a pretty good idea what to expect. Canon Street was up the hill from the cathedral, a broad, quiet residential street leading away from the narrow road where the shops were, and up to the school and playing fields above. On each side was a line of narrow two-story homes joined together with a common plaster front, their front doors opening onto the pavement, the little gardens behind them invisible from the street.

They were at least a hundred years old, but solidly built of local stone with slate roofs, each with a kitchen and sitting room on the ground floor and three bedrooms above, two in front and one behind. The rear bedroom wasn't bigger than the others; the rest of the space was taken up by the staircase, which reversed direction a few steps below the top, and came down to the entrance hall outside the sitting room, leaving a little passage alongside it that led back to the kitchen. Comfortable enough for a family with only two children and a third on the way.

"Let's go in," said Audrey, and as soon as Jimmy opened the door she wished she hadn't. It wasn't just "the bit of paper" that the house needed; there were cracks in the ceilings and holes in the walls, ugly brown smears to show where the roof leaked, and broken floorboards in the sitting room. The only plumbing was an outside toilet and one cold tap over the galvanized iron sink in the kitchen. There was an old stable attached to the rear of the house, its dirt floor littered with horse collars and old bits of horseshoes. Audrey stood in the old kitchen, with its bare wooden floor, and nearly cried.

"Christ!" said Jimmy. "It's going to take years to fix this up."

"Oh, Jimmy, what will we do?" Audrey wailed. "I wish I'd never listened to Mother. We should have stayed where we were."

"Well, it's not that bad now, is it? No worse than she had when you first came here; I remember your father telling me it had rats infesting it and everything, and look at it now. This place is run down, but the house is okay, well built and all, and while I'm fixing it we can make a few improvements. We'll turn that old stable into a back kitchen, and I'll build you a nice big

222

bathroom over it off the back landing, and we can put central heating in it and fix those ceilings and put up some nice yellow wallpaper. I know how to do these things. I've a few pounds saved, and I can work on it full time while I'm waiting for a good job to turn up. We can live at your mother's until I've got the place comfortable like."

Jimmy had never been very enthusiastic about this kind of work, but he'd done odd jobs of plumbing and plastering and putting on roofing slates, and what he didn't know he could learn. He had to pull down the ceilings after he'd patched the roof, and when he tackled the sitting-room floor he had to take it all up and put in new supports, because the foundations had sagged and the floor had pulled away from the wall. By the end of three weeks they were able to move in, though the wallpapering wasn't finished and he hadn't begun on the new bathroom or the stable that was to become a kitchen.

There was an old-fashioned range in the stable, and Audrey decided to light a fire in it on wet days in the winter to dry her laundry. "There's a funny smell in that old place," she told Jimmy the first time she tried it.

"It's those old horse collars," said Jimmy. "It won't hurt anything."

"No, Jimmy, it's worse than that, it's awful. I don't know what it is."

"You've got a fierce nose, that's what," said Jimmy. But he went to have a look, and Audrey was right, it was an awful smell.

There was a big flagstone just beyond the door, and some smaller ones beside it that looked dark and slimy.

"It's probably off the old flags there," Jimmy said. "Why don't you clean them up."

Audrey went to work with scrubbing brushes and disinfectants, and if the smell didn't disappear at least it was masked.

Jimmy cleaned out the accumulation of old leather harnesses and broken furniture that littered the stable, and started digging up the dirt floor to put down a proper foundation for the new kitchen. The flagstones had to go, and when he pulled up the big one he saw where the smell was coming from.

"Christ, it's a bloody sewer pipe!" he shouted. "The whole top of it is open."

"Then cover it up," Audrey called from inside the house. "I'm not going out there to look at it!"

Jimmy dropped the flagstone back in place and went out to find the plumber who was helping him and had done odd jobs in the house for its previous owner. He was having a pint in Jones's pub on the waterfront when Jimmy walked in and came straight to the point.

"Johnny," he said, "did you ever do any jobs with the sewer up in our place?"

Johnny knew at once what he was referring to. "Oh!" he said. "You've found that flag in the stable. Well, to tell you the truth, I left the flag on that because the sewer used to get blocked up a lot, the reason being that we could put the rods in there to clean it out."

"Jesus God," said Jimmy. "That's disgraceful to leave a place like that."

"Well, the old one, she was so damn mean she wouldn't buy toilet paper, you see; they were using newspaper and the whole sewer used to get blocked up."

"That's a good one all right, they might as well not have a toilet nor a sewer at all."

"They were from the country like, they were living rough."

"Well, that's not for us, I'll be honest with you. Get me a length of sewer pipe and let's get it fixed tonight."

The job didn't take long, but by the time Jimmy had his new kitchen finished and the new bathroom over it, nearly three years had gone by since they first moved into the house. His savings were gone, and the best job he'd been able to get was on the ferry from Cobh to Spike Island. He was back where he'd started more than ten years before, a job no better than coxswain of the CO's launch in the navy, and less than half the pay he'd been earning in London.

He started doing "foxers" then, odd jobs for other people in the spare time he'd used before to work on his house, but the hours were long and the pay was low. He had no car, and it was nearly a mile to walk down the steep hill to the waterfront, carrying his brush and bucket, and maybe a trowel, with plaster to mend a wall or rolls of paper to hang on it. With all that gear it was no joke to take a job any distance from his home, and the farther he had to walk, the less time he had to do the work.

He'd have an occasional pint with his father-in-law at John Jones's, on the square at the bottom of the hill almost directly beneath the opulent neo-Gothic Cathedral of Saint Colgan, with its huge flying buttresses and granite spire towering over the city and harbor. The most they'd ever have would be three pints, the father-in-law buying first, then Jimmy, then the father-in-law would buy a third, but Jimmy couldn't afford to even the score. They talked about what Jimmy ought to do to make more money, and one day a seaman came into the bar who knew Jimmy and told him the Celtic Line was buying a new oil tanker from Germany, and looking for a crew.

It meant leaving home for the first time since he had gotten married, but the pay was good and Jimmy was glad to be back on the sea. He had to miss Willie's ordination, because it was on that day that he flew to Hamburg with the rest of the crew to join the new ship, but after that it was mostly coastal trips, from the refinery at Cork to Waterford or New Ross, or up to Dublin, and he wasn't away from home more than a night or two at a time. Then the ship was in dry dock in Penzance for three months, and when he got home his baby daughter Hilary didn't know him at all.

The line went broke and Jimmy was out of work again, subsisting on the odd jobs he used to do in his spare time when he worked on the Spike Island ferry.

"What are you going to do?" asked Audrey. "We can't live like this."

"It's only for a little while," said Jimmy. "One of them big oil companies is buying up the ships, and they're going to run

them on the river here, from Whitegate up to Cork, the refinery to the tank farms. The men that used to be on them will
get called first. You'll see."

By the time summer was over Jimmy was on his ship again,
and it was the best job he'd ever had. Short runs, up and back
the same day, normally working from eight in the morning to
half four in the afternoon, and anything earlier or later than
that was overtime. No overnight trips, not even a cook on
board, and the men were practically their own bosses. Jimmy
was making fifty-five pounds a week plus overtime, double the
best he'd earned in London. Not bad money for an unqualified
man, he told Audrey. And she agreed.

16.

Arrival
in
America

T*he* first time Willie ever thought about going to America was when he was in Rome with the Sacred Heart Fathers, early in his training for the priesthood. He met a lot of American priests there, including Irish-Americans and Irish priests from American parishes, who had come to Rome as so many did for further studies, or on vacations, or leading groups of American pilgrims. Willie heard from them how difficult it was for American dioceses to find enough priests for their needs, how there weren't enough vocations among American boys, and how an Irish seminarian could get financial help from an American diocese if he would commit himself to going there when he was ordained.

Willie didn't think much of it at the time, because he thought his future had been determined when he joined the Sacred Heart Fathers. But he remembered it, and when he found that he had to give up the cloistered life, it was one of the things on his mind while he was living with Gertie and

John in North London, and working for a trade union. He wrote a lot of letters to America in that period, and one of the answers he received was from a monsignor in Bridgeport, Connecticut, who expressed surprise at what Willie was doing in England and wondered why he hadn't gone back to teaching in Ireland.

That seemed a good idea, and there was an opening for a teacher in Longford, not far from Sligo, which would give Willie a chance to be near home and see his mother again. He was in Longford the following year, when the Bridgeport monsignor came to Ireland on a recruiting tour, and by that time Willie knew what he wanted to do.

He didn't know how he would get along in America, but the monsignor was willing to take a chance. Willie's fees would be paid for a year at the seminary in Carlow, and after that he would go to Bridgeport for the summer as a deacon, and they would see. If Willie was successful, he would be sent back to Carlow to complete his training, and return to Bridgeport as an assistant pastor after his ordination. If it didn't work out—well, Willie would make sure it did.

Willie entered Carlow about the same time that Patrick started researching black-currant diseases at the horticultural station in County Wexford, which was only a few miles away. The idea of going to America had already occurred to Pat, since it was American money that funded the project he was working on, and when he heard of Willie's experience he wondered if something similar couldn't be done in the horticultural line.

"There's no question I'm frustrated," Pat told his elder brother. "There isn't any future in this thing I'm doing, it's just insecticide spraying and prunings and maintenance and that kind of stuff. I know I could do better, but I'm not academically qualified. If I had the degree from the university, I could probably walk into a job that paid me minimum three times more. Quite honestly, from the point of view of brain power, I know I have it, I can grasp things easily and pass any exam if I cram for it, and get top grades. It's frustrating, no question about it."

"You could pass the exams," said Willie, "but where will you get the money?"

"That's the thing, I haven't got it, and I'm not going to get it here. You know what it is, Willie, when other people in your group are getting ahead because they have the degree, and you're on a treadmill, you're just not going anywhere."

"I know what it is," said Willie.

"And the idea of working indefinitely in a research center, maybe with no real advancement, no progression up the ladder, what's the future? Where do I go? Well, I'm just going to try to make a big break. If you can go to America, so can I."

There were plenty of jobs in America advertised in the horticultural trade papers in Ireland, though it wasn't until Patrick got to America that he found out why. There was no shortage of young Americans able to do the work; it was just that newcomers from Ireland were willing to do it for less pay. Patrick answered a few of the ads, and when he was offered a job in a nursery in Connecticut for $110 a week to start, that seemed like a lot of money in 1964 in County Wexford. He wrote to Mick in Dublin and borrowed the money for the air ticket, packed his suitcase, and took off.

It was May when Pat arrived in Connecticut, and the dogwoods and lilacs and apple trees were in bloom, and he thought America was as beautiful as Wexford, though he wasn't used to such vast stretches of woodland, and he missed the views of the sea in his native Sligo. The nursery where he was to work was in a clearing in the woods on a two-lane highway; they grew azaleas and rhododendrons and dogwoods and little bushes of yew and juniper, so much smaller than the Irish varieties, and sold them to new homeowners in the mushrooming exurbia of Fairfield County. Pat had never imagined a place where so many people had so much money.

In the greenhouse there were masses of seedling petunias and alyssum and marigolds and the bright red poppies that grew wild in Ireland but commanded a good price in Connecticut; and young tomato plants and peppers and lettuces, which would have been sown in the open at home, but here it seemed the spring arrived late and a lot of things needed coddling before they were ready to be planted outdoors. There was a lot to learn.

The nursery was a family affair, owned by a lean Yankee in his sixties with a leathery face and long, bony-fingered hands. He was troubled with arthritis, and wanted a young man with plenty of vigor to do the stooping and lifting and digging for him, and maybe if he was smart and ambitious enough he'd be able to run the show himself in a few years, and the old man could sit at the cash register and take in the money without doing the heavy work.

The only other hired help was a fat Pole with a round head and drooping mustache, named Steve, who was as strong as a horse but getting old as well, and talking about retiring as soon as he could get his Social Security. Pat enjoyed the work, but he didn't want to be stuck with doing it all himself, and he didn't think there would ever be much profit in the place.

It was busy enough in early May and June, when the ex-urbanites came in their station wagons and loaded up with bushes and trays of seedlings and potted geraniums and bags of fertilizer and lime and peat moss; but when the hot, dry weather of summer came, the plants wilted in spite of constant watering, and the customers neglected their gardens and went swimming.

The weekends were busy times for selling, and all through the week there was always work to do. Even on Pat's days off the old man wanted him to come by and do a little watering. "It's no work, standing there with a hose," he'd say. "It won't take you long, just a couple of hours in the morning and again in the evening." But Pat didn't like it.

"He's a nice guy, but he's going to use me," he said to Steve. "Is it always like this?"

"You bet your life," said Steve. "He doesn't care. He'll have you working all the time if you let him."

"Maybe I'm suspicious," said Pat, "but I think he's getting more work out of you and me than he's paying for."

"They all do that if you let them," said Steve. "But let me tell you something, kid, you don't have to let him get away with it. You're smart, you can use your head, you speak good English. You can go anywhere in this country. Me, I didn't know anything when I first came here. I was young like you, but I couldn't speak nothing but Polish, I didn't have no place to go. So I got stuck in lousy jobs like this and never could do no better. You don't have to do that, you can make something of yourself. You ought to get out of here first chance you get."

"Soon as I get a few dollars in my back pocket," said Pat.

By Labor Day the season was over and he had saved enough to strike out on his own. He headed for New York, and went to work for an Italian in Brooklyn who had a small business mowing lawns and taking care of the gardens around some of the old homes near the ocean, where people were rich enough to have a gardener come once a week, to rake leaves in the fall and bundle the shrubs and mulch the rose bushes for the winter. By Thanksgiving that was all over, and Pat was out of work. Clearly, America wasn't like Ireland, where a gardener worked all year round, and in a mild winter the roses would still be blooming in January.

Meanwhile Pat went to night school to get his high-school-equivalency diploma, because that would look better on his job applications than trying to explain the Irish system of education. He wrapped it up in a couple of months, and went on a campaign for jobs that weren't as seasonal and unpromising as horticultural work. Early in the new year he got a job with an airline, in the reservations department. He was right in the heart of Manhattan, talking to people on the phone eight hours a day, booking flights.

It was a tremendous feeling for Pat to walk in off the street, with what seemed like zero qualifications for the job he was after, and talk himself into being hired. He knew nothing of American geography, which he quickly found was the most important requirement for efficiency; if a customer said he wanted to go to Albuquerque, New Mexico, Pat not only didn't know whether his airline went there, he didn't know where the place was or how to spell it. But he had the natural Irish friendliness, the spontaneous instinct to be kind to strangers and listen to their problems, the patience to go after the answer and find it, no matter how long it took. It never occurred to him to shrug off a customer's problems or simply pass the buck; he always took the trouble to find the answer, and that way he learned quickly.

Before he got the airline job he had to do something about his draft status, which was 1-A. Pat didn't know what that meant at first; registering for the draft was just something he had to do when he was admitted as a permanent resident in May 1964, and he hadn't thought much about it. Six months later, when he was starting to look for a permanent job in New York, he heard for the first time about a place called Vietnam, and ran into the same kind of dialogue wherever he applied for a job.

"We'd like to hire you," the interviewer would say, "you're a nice, clean-cut guy, and we could use you, but you've got a 1-A there, you're just twenty-one, you'd be with us maybe six or eight months and then the army would get you, and whatever training we'd given you would be lost. If you can get that taken care of, come back and see us." And Pat would walk out knowing that his application was going straight into the wastebasket.

The only people he knew in New York who might know how to get a thing like that taken care of were a family named O'Brien, who were related to some friends he'd made in Wexford. Gerry O'Brien was a few years older than Pat and had been born in Brooklyn, so he'd been through the draft mill before the Vietnam War began.

"Do what I did," Gerry said. "Join the National Guard."

"What's that?"

"It's a kind of part-time soldiering. You do your six months' active duty, then you're back in your job, which they have to keep for you, and then you go to camp for two weeks every year for more training."

"How long do you have to keep that up?"

"It's six years altogether. You're kind of in the reserves all that time. You might be called up, but only if there's a real big war or something. Then you have these drills, between times, weekends or evenings a couple of times a month. It's a bore, really, and it takes a lot of time, but they're pretty flexible about it, they don't interfere with your private life any more than they can help."

"Six years of that is better than two in the army full-time, I'd say. I didn't come to this country to give up two years of my life to the military."

"If you don't do something," said Gerry, "they'll be sending you a subway token any day now."

"What for?"

"That's what they do when you get your greetings—send you a subway token so you can get to the enlistment station. From there you get a trip all the way to Vietnam at Uncle Sam's expense. Big-hearted of them, isn't it."

"Not me," said Pat, and from then on between job interviews he spent his time calling on National Guard armories. He learned the subway system like the back of his hand. But everywhere he went there was a waiting list; although the Vietnam War was still only a small-scale affair in America, there were thousands of young men who had heard of it before Pat, and had made their preparations.

Last of all, because it seemed so unlikely, Pat tried the Seventh Regiment Armory at Park Avenue and Sixty-eighth Street, in the heart of what he'd learned to call the "silk-stocking district," though the name hardly applied anymore. There he found a tubby redheaded sergeant who looked as though he hadn't marched under a pack in twenty years and wouldn't last five minutes if he tried it now. But his name was Gilooley, and his father had come from County Sligo, and when he heard Pat's story he said, "Okay, fill in the papers and we'll see what we can do." By the end of the month Pat was in the regiment, and had his airline job too.

Pat had no particular feelings about military life or the Vietnam War, and he had never fired a gun before or even seen one, except a rifle that Jimmy had brought home from the navy once, to his mother's consternation. His training that summer at Fort Dix was an interesting change from answering the telephone in a midtown Manhattan office building all day, and on the whole he enjoyed it.

He was older than most of the draftees, and they made him feel like a man of experience, who had been around and seen Galway and London and Wexford, and made his own way, while they were still at school. Pat wasn't leaving home for the first time, and he wasn't leaving any sweetheart or even particularly close friends in New York. Above all, he wasn't going to Nam and he wasn't in for two solid years; in six months or less he'd be back at his job, and he was in no hurry. It was a new experience for him to watch other boys, nearly his own age, so depressed and homesick. Nothing quite like it had ever happened to him before.

Still, it was a lift to his spirits one day when he was pulled out of the ranks during close-order drill and summoned to headquarters, wondering if he was in for some kind of punishment, to find instead that he had a visitor—his brother Willie.

"Holy Mother of God," said Pat, "how did you get here?"

"Came down with some friends from Bridgeport," said Willie. "I'd never know you in that uniform, Pat, you look like you've been in America all your life."

"Beginning to feel that way, too," said Pat. "Stand out there in that hot sun drilling for a few hours and so would you. How do you like it here, Willie?"

"Oh, it's grand! I don't mind the sun at all, I love it. But this is just a trial visit. I've got another year to do at Carlow, and I don't know whether they'll want me to come back or not."

"You don't need to worry about that, Bill," said one of his companions, a chunky young priest with a sallow complexion and close-cropped hair. "You're doing fine. Why don't you introduce us to your brother?"

"I'm sorry, Father. Pat, this is Father Orsini, and the bearded Irishman with him is Father Kelly. They've taken it in their heads to give me a guided tour of America, or at least this part of it, show me how Americans live."

"They've given you an American name, too, I notice. It's Bill you are now, is it?"

"Well, I don't mind what the name is, as long as they'll keep me here!"

"Just don't lose your brogue," said Father Kelly, in the accent of a fourth-generation American clowning at a Saint Patrick's Day dinner. " 'Tis what your Hibernian parishioners will love you for."

"So they tell me," said Bill. "But to be honest with you, I don't think I can do much about that. I'm a Sligo man, and you won't catch me talking Kerry or Cork."

Bill was feeling ill at ease, not so much with the strangeness of America as with his own position as a "late vocation," still in a seminary and not yet ordained though he was past thirty years old. His young friends, still in their twenties, were already priests serving as assistants to his pastor, hardly a high rank but still a position of responsibility with a certain amount of independence. Bill had known that kind of freedom when he was a schoolteacher; now he was back in school as a pupil, no longer earning his own way, feeling like a nonentity. In Carlow, he was treated as a schoolboy, his work organized for him by his teachers, with assignments of books to read and papers to write, and examinations at the end of it.

This visit to America was a welcome change, but still he wasn't out of school yet. He was going through something of the resentment of the system that Peter had felt in Dromantine, though it didn't disturb him quite as deeply. That was one advantage of being older when he entered the seminary; he had already been through his years of uncertainty and indecision. Difficult though it was just now, Bill had made up his mind about his future in the Church; it was something he wouldn't question again. If it had its frustrations, he could stand them.

When Bill returned to Bridgeport the following year as a priest, he threw himself into his work as eagerly as the youngsters, and the first couple of years were the busiest of his life. He was instructing converts two or three times a week, doing three or four weddings each Saturday and as many funerals during the week, taking his turn at daily and Sunday Masses in the new liturgy that had just come into use, acting as chaplain for the Ladies Auxiliary of the Ancient Order of Hibernians, and attending occasional meetings of the men's AOH as well.

At first he wasn't allowed to forget that he was Irish, because the Bridgeport Irish-Americans made such a fuss over him, kidding about his brogue and telling stories about their ancestors. He had never before thought much about the hardships of the early Irish immigrants in America, the coffin ships of the famine years, the epidemics, the slums, the back-breaking labor of building the railroads and canals, the loneliness of coming to a strange land where none of your family had been before.

No wonder they banded together to help one another and created such a profusion of Irish-American organizations that had no parallel in Ireland. It was so different from the idea he'd always had of Irish-Americans as rich relatives, because they sent so much money home and seemed to be such a political power in America. And it was so different from his own experience, coming to a secure job in a position of high respect in the community, coming not just to Irish-America but to the Catholics of America.

Irish-Americans were not the whole of his parish, nor even

the majority; and many of them had no real interest in Ireland beyond the knowledge that a parent or grandparent or some ancestor even further back had come from there. Gradually Bill forgot about being Irish himself; he got caught up in the swing of parish life and that was it.

Getting used to America was mainly a matter of small practical problems. Bill had never had a checkbook before, and never heard of credit cards, until the other assistant, Jack Martin, said to him, "You've got to do it, Bill. You can't be carrying money around in your pockets here the way you do in Ireland."

He'd never driven a car before, and never dreamed of owning one, but he couldn't do his pastoral work without one. It was going to cost him twenty-two hundred dollars, and all he had was six hundred, but his pastor solved the problem.

Father Flanagan was in his late seventies, a frail man with only a few wisps of white hair left on the fringe of his shiny pate, but his mother had come from Tipperary, and he took a liking to the new young Irish priest. He had been pastor for forty years, under the old system by which the pastor got the entire Christmas collection for his own needs, to share as much with his assistants as he thought they deserved, and pay for the groceries and the housekeeper. Under that system there was often a good deal left at the end of the year, and in forty years it mounted up.

When Bill told him what the car was going to cost, Father Flanagan took a shoe box out of his closet and said, "How much do you need?"

It never occurred to Bill that a pastor could have such resources. "You're lending me parish money, Father?" he asked.

"No, no, it's my own, just what I keep here for emergencies; the rest is in the bank."

Bill got his car, a green Valiant, and paid off the loan in twelve months, but he was so terrified at driving on the right side of the road instead of the left that he didn't dare take it outside the familiar streets where his parishioners lived. It took him all winter to gain enough confidence to venture out on the Connecticut Turnpike.

The first day he tried it was Memorial Day, a holiday he'd never heard of before. But he had the day off, and it seemed a good time to go down to New York to see Pat again, and maybe go to the beach for a swim. The streets of residential Bridgeport were quiet enough when he set out, and he didn't realize what was happening until he'd found his way up the ramp and onto the turnpike, and then there was no way of backing out.

Long before he reached New York he was telling himself that if all the cars in Ireland tried to get into O'Connell Street at once, it wouldn't be as big a traffic jam as he was in right now. After that Bill had no more fear of driving on American superhighways; he'd seen the worst and survived it.

The day Pat came back to work after his National Guard training at Fort Dix was the day of the big blackout, when a sudden power failure darkened all New York and New England from Niagara Falls to the Atlantic Ocean. He was on his way home to Brooklyn in the IRT subway when the train ground to a halt outside the Fourteenth Street station, and all the lights went out and people started screaming. "I should have stayed in the army and gone for two," he said gloomily.

He followed the crowd through the cars to the rear end of the train, and stumbled along the tracks in the flickering glow from somebody's flashlight. They came to an iron staircase after a while that led up to a manhole cover in the middle of the avenue, and the lights from the cars blinded him but nothing seemed to be moving. Nobody knew what the trouble was or how far it had spread, but Pat concluded that the best way to get home was to walk, though it would take hours. The streets were alive with people, all talking to one another and laughing at the strangeness of it all, and suddenly New York City seemed friendlier than ever before. But what a way to go on your first day back on the job!

Pat liked his work at the airline, and moved gradually from reservations agent to chief agent to supervisor, and got into the management-training program. There were a couple of weeks in a company school in Florida to begin with, then two or three months in each of the departments, executive office, tour division, group department, ticketing, even a little work at the airport. Pat felt he was getting a great groundwork in the entire airline industry.

The company was in the midst of a sales-boosting campaign, with competition and prizes and pep meetings and a convention in the Bahamas that turned out to be one big bash of a weekend, with the best of food and wine, and a kind of cabaret show in which all the jokes were about the company. Pat decided that the airline business was the best in the world and he was lucky to be in it.

He didn't have much time for talking shop that weekend because his mind was on a willowy blonde with bright blue eyes who danced like a dream and had a bathing-suit figure that was the envy of the whole reservations office. Her name was Lynn Brucker, and Pat had known her slightly in New York, but only as one of the dozens of efficient, neatly groomed girls his own age with blue eyes and blonde hair and turned-up noses, who smiled at customers from behind their counters or ushered them on and off the planes and served their meals during flights. Lynn's job had something to do with statistics, and she used to come into Pat's area every morning to get the numbers she wanted from his records of the previous day's work, but it wasn't until they were on the beach together in Nassau that something happened, and Pat discovered there was more to life than selling seats on airplanes.

It was a romance that might have lasted no more than that one glorious weekend, if it hadn't been for the peculiar hours they worked in New York. The office had to be staffed from 7:00 A.M. until midnight, and everybody changed shifts every two weeks, but not always in the same rotation. Sometimes Pat and Lynn would be on the morning shift together, and Lynn would bring in coffee and her own homemade cookies, and they got to know each other pretty well. When they got off work at the same time they would spend long afternoons together going to the park and then out for cocktails and dinner, and when they were on the later shift they would dance until one or two in the morning and plan to sleep late the next day. But Pat was the kind of person who liked to be up and about in the morning, and it was pretty fatiguing sometimes.

It made a long day when they were on different shifts. Sometimes they could switch their days off and get four or five days off together at the same time, and take a minivacation together, touring the country on company planes at virtually no cost. Pat learned his geography, and before he'd given the matter much thought he and Lynn were talking about getting married.

There was only one problem, and it was the same one Gertie had faced almost ten years before—Lynn wasn't Catholic, she was Lutheran.

"I don't mind that," said Pat. "I've lived in America long enough to know that you don't have to be Catholic to be a good Christian. Do you mind my being Catholic?"

"It doesn't bother me," said Lynn, "but what about your mother?"

"It won't sit too well with her, to be honest with you. We've already gone through that once, when my sister was married in London. God, that was a bad experience! But it was different with Gertie. It's very shocking for a woman who's lived all her life in rural Ireland and one of her daughters does the proverbial thing, runs off to London and marries a Protestant. But she got over that, and I don't think this will affect her the same way. Sons are different."

"Maybe if we go over together, so I can meet her and—"

"I'd love to do that, I would. I want her to know you, and maybe that would help her get used to the idea. But she's not well now, and she's been taking care of my brother, who's been ill for years. I don't know, maybe it would upset her too much just now. I'll talk to Bill about it."

"Bill?"

"He's another brother, the one over here. He's a priest, in Bridgeport, and he's really closer to Mum than I am. I tell you what, Lynn, let's ask Bill to marry us!"

"Can he do that?"

"Of course he can, if he will. I don't know what he'll think about me marrying a Protestant, either. Bill's a good fellow, he's pretty liberal all right, ecumenical and all that, I don't think he'd mind."

"My God, do I have to have your brother's approval too? Of course it's right for your mother, but all those brothers and sisters, I don't want everybody in your family sitting in judgment on me!"

"Don't worry, Bill's going to love you. The others don't matter, they've got nothing to do with it. But Bill's the only brother I have in America, and I don't want to create a family problem here. What would I do if he refused to marry us? I'm not just going to City Hall, we've got to have a Catholic marriage."

"What if *he* refused to marry us! You mean what if *I* refused to marry you," said Lynn with sudden anger. "You've got your priorities wrong, Pat."

"Aw, don't be like that. You want a church wedding, don't you?"

"Of course I want a church wedding, but it doesn't have to be a Catholic church, I'd rather have it Lutheran. And it doesn't have to be your brother. If he doesn't like it you can find some other priest who does, if you insist on it being Catholic, and I suppose you have to do that."

"Let me talk to him, Lynn. He'll do it."

Lynn flushed and bit her lip. Was she making a mistake, she wondered, marrying into this crazy big Irish family? There was a strained silence after that, while both of them pursued their own worried thoughts.

17.

The
Missionary

When Father Peter O'Rourke went to Nigeria in the autumn of 1964, while Pat was looking for a permanent job in New York and Willie was studying for his assignment in Bridgeport, it was in some ways less of an adjustment for him than for his brothers in America. It was a mainly Irish community of priests that Peter went to join, and although Nigeria was hotter than Ireland in the dry season, and the rain was heavier in the wet, there were a lot of things about the people's way of life that reminded him of home.

Nature was kind to the Nigerians, he found, as God was kind to the Irish. Most of the people lived by subsistence farming, as many still did in Ireland. All they had to do was put down a few seeds and the rain would come and the sun would shine, and the crops would grow. It took very little labor and their methods were primitive, a little hoe to scratch the soil; they didn't have to dig very deep to put the seeds down. It was like the potato growers in Ireland before the famine, except that the Nigerians grew rice instead of potatoes, simple grain crops that they would turn ito all sorts of little stews and porridges.

The Nigerians had the same love of large families as the Irish, though they expressed it in very different ways. They buried their dead in their own homes, under the earthen floor, to keep them close and look after them; there were very few cemeteries outside the larger towns until the missionaries insisted on them. And before a man chose his wife, he tested her fertility, and married her only after she became pregnant. This horrified Peter at first; not only was it forbidden by the Church, but in the Ireland he'd grown up in it would have been the most awful, frightening thing a girl could do. In Nigeria it would have been more frightening not to do it, and Peter found that he had to start rethinking some of his ideas.

He admired the Nigerians' love of dancing, which seemed to have something in common with the traditions of Irish life in the happier, lustier days before the Great Famine, when the Irish were more earthy and natural, and in Peter's view seemed to have had more joy in their lives. The Nigerians still found it natural to "dance with joy to God, or in thanksgiving to Him," as Peter described it in one of his letters home.

"We are stiff and wooden compared to them," he wrote. "They're like rubber dolls. They have a tremendous sense of rhythm, even the young children. The Pentecostal movement really speaks to them. They will literally dance through the night, in the moonlight, with the drums beating—it is very very colorful."

The Church was inclined to frown on this sort of thing, but Peter decided that was only a Western viewpoint. The idea of the body being involved in worship was natural to the Nigerians, and Peter decided that they had the better of it. Westerners, he thought, were too intellectual, dividing the body from the spirit; with the Nigerians the intellect seemed to be at the tip of the senses. They saw it as all one whole—body, mind, and spirit—and by contrast the Western idea seemed atomized and meaningless. To the Nigerians it would have been meaningless to conceive of a mental act without a bodily act to express it with.

All this was an exciting new world to Peter, totally different from anything he had imagined. He had a sense of freedom as he absorbed these new experiences and pursued his own thoughts about the doctrines he was teaching these extraordinary people. While he was in Nigeria, the council known as Vatican II was meeting in Rome, to take a new look at Catholic theology and rituals, and the new ideas and new liturgies it came up with were a breath of fresh air to Peter.

He was isolated from the hurly burly the council's work stirred up in the cathedrals and seminaries of Ireland, and all around the conservative Catholic world, but he followed the stories in *Time* magazine, and he knew what the issues were, because he had been discussing them and reading about them for years in Cork and Dromantine.

Peter had taken his own books with him to Nigeria, and he was lucky enough to be stationed near a university with a fine library, stocked by British and American missionaries and their governments. He even found books there he hadn't been able to get in University College, Cork, for many of the works of liberal theologians had been kept out of Ireland in the years before Vatican II. He kept up his theological studies in this new atmosphere of free inquiry, while he worked out his own problems of conscience and faith in his daily work with the Nigerians.

First he had to learn to listen to the people he was trying to teach, not just talk to them. He had already been taught that listening was part of a priest's job, but in Nigeria he began to realize that it was more than that—it was the best thing possible for a priest, to really listen to a situation before trying to impose his own ideas on the people who wanted his help. He began to realize that if the Church wasn't listening, it couldn't effectively teach.

As he listened, he found that the Nigerians were as interested in learning about the white man's world as he was in theirs. In the remote bush country of northern Nigeria where Peter was first stationed, the people looked on the white man with awe and wonder, and he found it a rather humbling experience. "They want to know what makes us tick," he wrote to his mother. "All the basics—the way you laugh, the color of your eyes, whether you are short or long or how it would be. Very simple, basic things. Are we really human beings like themselves? I've never thought of it quite that way."

He listened to them talk about sex and marriage and why the Catholic teaching on these points was so hard for them to accept. He understood their desire for large families, for that was an Irish tradition too, and his widowed mother's only security. But sex before marriage? The Nigerians answered that a man wouldn't buy land without making sure it was fertile, and it was no different for a wife. Besides, if a man had no children it would be a disgrace to him, a slur on his manhood. Indeed, as Peter found out when one of his converts accepted the Catholic teaching on this point and then had no children, it was a horrific cross to bear—he was as ashamed as an unwed mother in Ireland.

The Nigerians were polygamous too, if they could afford it. Infant mortality was high, and a man needed a lot of babies. Besides, they said, when a woman is nursing a baby she won't have relations with her husband, and he must take himself somewhere else; another wife is better than a mistress. And they saw nothing immoral in prostitution; the man was doing the woman a service, keeping her trade going.

Peter tried arguing some of these points, but it got him nowhere. Adultery, yes, the Nigerians agreed that that was wrong, but they couldn't see any sense in the rest of the Church laws on sex and marriage. Peter came to the conclusion that it just couldn't be expected to work in Nigeria. So what was he to do about it?

His first reaction was to put a different question to himself—

were the Nigerians ready for Christianity? Peter had come to bring the good news of Jesus Christ to these people struggling with small crops, small farms, crowded houses; what message did he have for them? Surely it was something more than a new code of sex-and-marriage laws. The law of the Church was there, and Peter was not setting out to break it, but what would Christ himself have done? As the question is asked in the Acts of the Apostles, can you forbid these people to be baptized?

Peter decided he could not; and he took comfort in the discovery that most of the other mission priests felt the same way. He had no qualms of conscience, but it gave him severe intellectual problems. He came to the conclusion that a lot of the laws of the Church did not have deep enough roots in human experience; they were up there in the minds of academics, a long, long way from reality.

Most disturbing to the Irish missionary was the discovery that some of the pagan superstitions from which he was trying to free the Nigerians weren't so far removed from certain aspects of Irish Catholic life. Indeed, they had something important in common. The Nigerians believed in what Peter called a "god of the gaps"—where there was a gap in their understanding of what went on in their lives, whether it was the death of a child or the loss of a crop or a storm that swept away their houses, whatever it might be, they assumed the thing was done by a god of some kind, and they sought to placate the god that had such power. Was this any different from what Peter's mother had taught him? He had often felt the same way about things, without seeing anything wrong in it, and he puzzled over what made the difference.

It seemed to lie in the Nigerian view that theirs was a "god of retribution," a powerful and dangerous figure who could do harm to people if he wanted to, and was perhaps even capricious in doing it. There was a lot of that, too, Peter decided, in the tradition of Irish Catholicism. He felt as if he were seeing himself in a mirror, finding elements of paganism in his own habits of thought that he'd never recognized before.

They needed to be exorcised, and Peter went about it in his intellectual way, going back to his theology books and comparing what they told him with what he saw around him in black Africa. It was lonely work, but he felt himself in tune with the new spirit of the times. Indeed, when he came back to Ireland in 1967 and caught up with what had happened at Vatican II, he found he had been working out for himself some of the very issues discussed at Rome, and arriving at much the same conclusions. Certainly God had plugged a gap in his understanding, he reflected, but this was not "retribution"—it was a gift, and he was grateful.

When Peter left Nigeria he thought he was going home for a few months' leave, and he took only a few clothes with him, leaving his books and personal belongings behind. There they remained, to be used by someone else, for the Church had other plans for Peter. When he realized what they involved he was flabbergasted.

As a seminarian at Dromantine a few years earlier, he had rebelled against the stuffy rigidities of the teaching system and the narrow limitations of the doctrines he was taught. Now after three years in Nigeria his outlook was even more liberal, and he was impatient with old-fashioned doctrines. But the new winds of Vatican II were being felt by the Irish hierarchy, and Peter's liberal ideas were suddenly not only more acceptable, but positively welcomed. His record in Nigeria had been good; he had spent a lot of time teaching in a training school for native teachers, and shown a considerable talent for it. Now, at thirty-two, he was experienced enough to train Irish missionaries for service in Nigeria, and young enough to handle the new ideas.

His assignment was to develop new teaching methods to fit the new theology, and he was to go as a teacher back to Dromantine itself. He would have a year to prepare himself at Ireland's leading seminary in Maynooth, just outside Dublin, and get his degree of licentiate in theology.

This was good news to take with him on his summer vacation at Toberpatrick, but the elation vanished when he got there and saw what had happened in his absence. Tony was in Saint John's nursing home in Sligo now, too weak to get out of bed, incontinent, and hardly able to eat solid food. His mother had been heartbroken when he had to go, but the burden of nursing him had become too much for her own failing health, and there was no way out of it. All she could do was conceal her feelings in her letters to Peter, and let him think it was only a small thing, a temporary thing, and Tony would soon be home again. He was thirty-six when the ambulance took him away.

Rita had married the year after she came home from England, and Maire was now alone in the house where she had reared fifteen children. She didn't want to go live with any of her married sons or daughters; too many women in one house would never work, she said. She didn't believe in that; she'd stick to one corner as long as she could. She got on well with her in-laws, but she wanted her own home, as she'd always had it, even if it meant staying on her own.

Rita would come over to see her every few days, on her bicycle or pushing the baby carriage after Belinda was born, to bake her mother's soda bread and see to it that she had plenty of water. It was a long walk to the well at the end of the lane, and Maire could never have fetched the water herself because it meant climbing the slippery steps over the stone wall that guarded the well.

If Maire was lonely with all her children gone, she wouldn't admit it. But she showed it in little ways, like keeping a light in every room of the house after dark, so it wouldn't seem so empty.

For more than two years after Tony was taken to the nursing home, Maire, in her late sixties, made the long journey two or three times a week from Toberpatrick to Sligo to see him, bringing him little delicacies she had made, sitting and talking with him on his good days, grieving when his pain was too great and he couldn't talk. She would walk the three long miles from her house to the main road to catch the morning bus, and then another mile or two from the bus stop in town up the hill to the nursing home, then back the same way in the gathering twilight of summer evenings, or in the darkness and cold, the windy rains of winter, the blustering gales from the Atlantic and the freezing January sleet.

Maire was a strong women, physically and emotionally, and she needed that strength now, as she had needed it in all the nearly twenty years since her husband had died. She was a handsome woman still, her black hair now gray under the straw pudding-basin hat she always wore, her finely chiseled features a little stronger now, her face still shining with the clear complexion of an Irish country girl who had never in her life touched makeup. She had grown a little more plump in later years, but never really heavy, and when she strode down the lane in her black cloth coat on her long walks to the bus stop, she walked almost with the stride of a man.

When Peter went with her to visit Tony that summer he was amazed at her endurance, though he worried a little because she seemed to get out of breath so easily. She said it was nothing serious, and would tell him nothing more; as always she kept her troubles locked in. But by December the pain in her chest couldn't be denied, and she had to go to Sligo Hospital.

Rita went with her, to make sure she was comfortable, and Maire said, "What am I doing here? There's nothing wrong with me at all."

"Sure, you'll be home for Christmas," Rita answered, and at the time she believed that would be the end of it.

Maire was home for Christmas, but still in pain. Peter was there too, worried about her, but the doctor didn't yet have a full report on the diagnostic tests. It was on New Year's Day that the doctor gave Peter the news: it was cancer of the lung, and he could not expect his mother to live more than another six months.

Peter sat down and wrote to his two brothers in the priesthood, Willie in Connecticut and Matt, who had been transferred from Nigeria to Australia, and told them what had happened. But he didn't tell the rest of the family; he didn't want to upset them.

Peter didn't think his mother knew, and he didn't tell her. She was well enough after a little while to visit her married sons, Joe and Charlie and Jimmy and Chris, and stay a little while with each in turn, and when she got tired of one place she'd go to another. Then Peter got her admitted to Peamount Hospital in Newcastle, County Dublin, not far from the seminary at Maynooth where he was studying. He began to feel that it was providential he had not been sent back to Nigeria—now at least he could be near his mother as she was dying. The hospital was only a few miles from Maynooth, and he used to drive out and see her every day, and sometimes spend the whole evening with her.

Peter kept up a cheerful mood, as though death were far away, and thought he was fooling his mother. But one day in April she said to him, "What will you do for the summer?" and he answered, "I'll go home, of course."

Then she said, "You know well I won't be going home. I won't ever be leaving here. I know."

Peter laughed a little, as though he didn't believe it, and made no comment. But he watched her carefully for the next few days, and then he knew what he had to do. He telephoned all his brothers and sisters, seven in Ireland, three in England, two in America and one in Australia, and told them the end was near.

Matt got his phone call at seven o'clock in the morning on first Friday in May, Australian time; he had Masses to say at eight and nine, then grabbed a valise and caught the next plane, and was in Dublin in thirty-six hours. Willie, who had always been very close to his mother, found the news hard to believe; he had been bombarding Peter with letters insisting that there must be something that could be done. But he came, arriving just before Matt. Peter drove to the airport as each of the overseas brothers arrived, and brought them to their mother in the hospital and said simply, "There she is."

It was on the Sunday before Maire died that they were all finally together, all except Tony in his nursing-home bed in Sligo. Maire knew what was coming, and accepted it. She chatted with her children in a very peaceful, happy way, with a kind of grand mellowness, and Peter thought back to those prayers for a happy death that had been part of the "trimmings" of the rosary every night when he was growing up.

For the last day or two she was unconscious, but they took turns staying at her bedside. Peter fed her her last meal; he and Willie and Christy were with her when she died in the early hours of Saturday morning. Matt had gone home with Charlie a little while before to rest.

None of them, except perhaps Peter and Maire herself, had expected it to happen so soon. Rita couldn't believe it; for years afterward she found it hard to remember that her mother wouldn't be dropping in for tea on Sunday as she always used to, and that it would be no use going to Toberpatrick when she took the children out for an airing. Rita took over her mother's visits to Tony in Sligo, but with the farm work and her two babies—Padraig was not yet two, and Belinda barely three—she couldn't go as often. And Tony, perhaps, was taking his mother's death hardest of all. He was failing rapidly, the strength and toughness gone, the big bones painfully visible beneath his pale skin. He lived only six months longer, and died that same year at the end of November.

Tony died alone, and it was a long time before Rita could forgive herself for that. She had seen him the week before, and he had seemed a little stronger, so eager to talk to her that he wouldn't let her go. She had to catch the bus back to her home and children, and he kept saying, "Won't you wait another little while, can't you stay?"

She had stayed as long as she could, but then she had to go, she had to hurry. And the next week, the Saturday morning when she was getting ready to go back and see him again, word came that he had died. Then she remembered how he had wanted her to stay the week before, and she hadn't understood the warning. It haunted her for a long time after.

PART
IV

New
Views

18.

The Changing Church

The family reunion broke up rather quickly after Maire was buried, as is the way with such things; Brigid had to hurry back to London, where her baby boy was ill, and Gertie and Tess went with her; Jimmy had to get back to his ship, and Pat flew home to New York, relieved that he had decided not to tell his mother about the Protestant girl he was soon to marry. Bill had made no objections, as Pat expected, and would perform the ceremony a few months later in the church in Bridgeport where he was assistant pastor.

Matt went to the African Mission Society headquarters in Cork and persuaded them to let him go back to Nigeria instead of Australia, which he didn't like as well; before leaving he visited a while with Chris and Kay in Roscommon, and Charlie and Una in Dublin, for both of them had married since his last home leave. Mick, on the wagon now on doctor's orders after an operation for stomach ulcers, went back to his lonely digs in Dublin and his maintenance work at the bakery.

The house called Toberpatrick and the three acres around it were left in Maire's will to Joe, as eldest son and head of the family. She had told him about that, some years before, and explained that she wanted him to keep it as a home for the three priests, a place where they could come on holidays and see the others. It would be a burden for him, but not a very big one; he would use it himself for a few weeks every summer, and so would his brothers and sisters. Rita would cook for the priests when they came, and keep the key; though the house would be empty each winter it would be a means of bringing the family together in the summers.

None of the family wanted to live there year round; Rita and Mary had homes of their own, and the rest had no desire to return to Sligo. Even Tess, whose husband had been born within a mile of Toberpatrick and who often dreamed of returning to the home place, could see no way of doing it. They were settled in Yorkshire now with three children, and there was no work for them in Sligo; John had no desire to go back to farming, even if there had been land enough or money to buy it.

Peter and Matt had missed Bill's ordination, for Peter had been in Nigeria and Matt in Australia when it took place, and they celebrated a Mass for him at Saint Columbanus's and took him to dinner in the Imperial Hotel at Sligo before Bill flew back to Connecticut and Matt to Nigeria. Then Peter returned to Maynooth to finish his studies, and a few months later began his new career as a teacher of theology at Dromantine College, where he had been a student only five years before.

It was the summer of 1968 when Peter returned to Dromantine, and he had barely arrived before the fact that this Catholic seminary was in Protestant-ruled Northern Ireland took on sudden new significance. The border that divided Ireland was a political matter that had always been ignored by the Catholic Church, as it was by the Protestant Church of Ireland, the Irish trade unions, sports leagues, and other bodies that weren't bound by political arrangements. After forty-six years even the politicians on both sides were learning to live with the border, and the agitation to remove it seemed at last to be dying away. The idea of reuniting Ireland and driving the British and Protestants from the North was ceasing to dominate the politics of the Republic, and the Protestant rulers of the North were beginning to feel more secure.

Noting these developments, the Catholic minority in the North began to feel it was time to demand fair treatment— equal voting rights and a proportionate share of the homes and jobs available to working people. If they were to accept Protestant rule and give up the idea of union with the Irish Republic, it seemed only natural to want equal rights and a share of power in the government of their own little British province. To the Protestants it seemed equally natural to refuse such a demand, and to reject the notion that the Catholics might have had a change of heart about Irish nationalism.

A series of public demonstrations organized that summer of 1968 by the Northern Ireland Civil Rights Association were peaceful enough to begin with, but they soon ran into riotous attacks from the Protestant majority, with the police sometimes turning a blind eye and sometimes joining in actively on the Protestant side. The police and the government were, after all, Protestant. The Minister for Home Affairs, William Craig, was so violent in his denunciation of the Catholics that he had to be dismissed from office, but the violence continued.

On New Year's Day, 1969, the savage fighting at Burntollet Bridge, outside Derry, produced a kind of hysteria that swept through all Ireland and drew the world's attention. Suddenly the idea that Catholics in the North might accept Protestant rule died, and demands were heard again for crossing the border, destroying the Northern Ireland province, driving the Brits and the Prods into the sea, reuniting Ireland under the Republic. A period of progress toward reconciliation was over, and the fighting was on again, in a new phase.

These things were going on all around Peter, but they seemed to him to be happening in a different world. He was

257

involved in the quiet work of teaching theology, the kingdom of heaven that seemed so utterly distinct from the kingdoms and republics of political battles, even when the battling people ranged themselves under banners with religious-sounding names like Catholic and Protestant. He read the news stories and was horrified, but he never became involved in any sort of political or quasi-political activities, even when one of the bloodiest riots took place in Newry, a scant four miles from his seminary. His job was to give his students the best he could and try to get them to think—think about Jesus Christ, who had said, "My kingdom is not of this world," and, "Render to Caesar the things that are Caesar's, and to God the things that are God's."

He couldn't keep out of it altogether, not after the "Bloody Sunday" in Derry on January 30, 1972, when British troops fired into a crowd of Catholics, killing thirteen young men who were marching unarmed in a demonstration that had been billed as nonviolent but forbidden by the authorities. That was when many Catholic Irish in the Republic wished they had an army strong enough to invade the North and restore order; but they didn't, and their government saw no prospect of success in any such policy. The illegal IRA recruited men to go where the government's army wouldn't go, and a mob in Dublin burned down the British embassy in a gesture of fury and frustration.

The funeral of the thirteen young men became the greatest "nonviolent demonstration" the North had ever seen, and this time the army and police protected it, and the rioters stayed home. From all over Ireland, Catholic priests gathered to represent their parishes among the mourners, and Father Peter O'Rourke was among them. He described it later as "a horrific experience, the most awful bitter day of my life" and remembered being comforted by the families who lived in the little side streets near the church and invited the visitors in for a cup of tea after the service was over, although they didn't know them, except to see by their black suits and dog collars that they were priests. And it comforted him afterward to march in a

258

silent protest in Newry after he got back; a solemn procession to the church in which no word was spoken, no music sounded, nothing was heard except the footfalls on the pavement. The affair was in the hands of Caesar's men; there was nothing a priest could do to stop it or change what was happening.

Peter had changes of a different sort to cope with in the new theology courses he was designing for Dromantine. He had studied the subject in Latin; now he was teaching it in English. When he found himself lapsing into some Latin phrase, he had to translate it, because most of the students hadn't studied Latin in school. And the liturgy was different; in the old days the priests on the faculty at Dromantine used to say their own Masses separately and privately every morning at side altars on each side of the church, whispering the words softly in Latin with their heads bowed, facing the wall, their backs to everyone else. They would take turns saying Mass at the high altar for the students, but even there the procedure was the same; the priest whispered the Mass in Latin with his back to the students, and they found the words in their own missals.

Now the altar was turned around, and all the priests of the faculty stood behind it together every morning, facing the students, to concelebrate the Mass in English. Everything was said aloud, and the students chorused the responses, of which there were many more than there had been in the old liturgy. Suddenly the Mass was a dialogue between priests and people, as it had not been since the early years of the Church, when there was no Catholic or Protestant, only the brotherhood of Christians and those outside who had not been converted.

There was a new emphasis in the liturgy, too, on the "joy of the Resurrection" instead of what Peter called the "killjoy religion of the Calvary Christians." This too, he told his students, was a return to early Christian ideas, brought about by the reforms of Vatican II.

"In the early Church," he said in his lectures, "the Eucharist was an expression of joy. There was a very clear realization that the definitive deed of salvation had been accomplished by Jesus Christ in his death and Resurrection, and that therefore we had access with great joy to God the Father, and He was our father. There was a feeling of brotherhood, of fraternal sharing of celebration and joy, of community. . . ."

In the Middle Ages, for reasons that Peter developed elaborately in his courses, a new attitude developed, by which the emphasis shifted from Christ's Resurrection to his suffering on the cross. "The idea was of God the Father demanding strict justice, a kind of Shylock if you like, and therefore willing to sacrifice his own Son, demanding his pound of flesh." It was the "god of retribution" concept that Peter had first recognized in Nigeria, and he called it "a very low stage in man's ascent to God, the process of evolution."

The medieval concept had been slow in reaching Ireland, for the influence of Rome was not great on that remote island, which had its own traditions of Christian teaching going back to Saint Patrick and Saint Kevin of Glendalough. Nearly three centuries of persecution beginning in Elizabethan times succeeded in breaking up the Catholic Church in Ireland even if it did not convert the faithful. When the priests returned to Ireland in strength in the nineteenth century, they came mainly from France and brought with them the Puritanical teachings of Jansenism, and the emphasis on the Cross of Mount Calvary. The idea was alien to the Irish traditions of rather earthy enjoyment, the singing and dancing and carefree attitudes that had carried them through centuries of oppression; but in the Great Famine of 1847–52 people were readily convinced that their misery was in some way retribution for their sins.

"The Great Famine profoundly affected the soul of Ireland," Peter said. "Death stalking the land killed the joy of it, and a killjoy religion took its place."

Peter hoped the new Vatican II theology would do away with the killjoy ideas, and he threw himself into his work with tremendous enthusiasm. He drew up new reading lists for his students, sending them to the library for the works of the most liberal of modern theologians; he developed lectures on the new ideas, introduced seminar discussions where such a teaching device was unheard of, and worked into the late hours of the night reading his students' papers and pursuing his own studies. He was full of ideas, and prayed that once his students started thinking they would never stop.

After five years at Dromantine, Peter taught for another year at Maynooth, and then took time off to study for his doctorate in theology. He went first to the University of Chicago, for the stimulating experience of studying Catholic theology in a non-denominational university, and the opportunity to visit Pat and Bill in America. Then for six months he was in Rome at the Gregorian University, and found it unbelievably backward by comparison—doddering old men messing about with little pieces of paper, great scholars in their day but long since past it.

When he got back to Ireland the doctorate seemed less pressing, and he found himself doing a combination of part-time lecturing and pastoral work, sometimes at Knock Shrine and sometimes on temporary assignment filling in for a country pastor who was ill or away from his parish for some other reason. He was in a small parish in County Mayo when I went to see him, the winter after our meeting at Knock, and found him restless and unsure of what he wanted to do next. Not that the decision rested with him; his bishop could call him at any time for a new assignment.

"It's part of the game, you have to be ready for it," he said. "If you asked me personally what I would like to do, I think I would like to have my hand in both camps now, the pastoral and the academic, but it's hard to find that in an institutional-ized way. Perhaps I'm looking for the Garden of Eden, you know. But I think they are such a happy relationship because there's a terrible danger of the academic sort of going off on a line of its own and forgetting about the grass roots, and on the other hand the person in the parish is inclined to despise the academic, he's all airy-fairy, he's all theory. But I think we need both."

In the years since he started teaching at Dromantine, Peter had worked his way through the crisis of faith that confronted many priests after Vatican II, and caused a number of his friends to leave the priesthood altogether. The new ideas and liberal viewpoints that emerged from the council were a source of great hope and joy to Peter and his friends, but then the reaction set in, and there was a general putting up of fences, a feeling that reform had gone far enough. The crunch came with Pope Paul's pronouncement against birth control in *Humanae Vitae*, which was issued in the summer of 1968, just when Peter came to Dromantine to teach.

"*Humanae Vitae* brought to a head the forces that were there at the council," he said, "the essentialists who were mildly aware of changing circumstances but said the essence of the Church was going to remain the same, and the existentialists who said that Christianity after all is in the world, and while there is a fundamental to Christianity that can't change, the world is changing and circumstances are changing, and therefore we must change our approach to things."

The birth-control issue was a purely theoretical one to the theology teacher, and it wasn't until later years when Peter was hearing confessions from troubled wives and husbands that he gained more insight into its impact on people's lives. But he knew there had been no consensus on the subject at Vatican II, and the commission of experts that studied it before Pope Paul issued *Humanae Vitae* were by no means united in support of the pope's decision.

"Pope Paul argued that contraception was against the natural law," Peter said. "But here were a whole lot of people who didn't think it was against the natural law. So what kind of natural law was it supposed to be when huge bodies of Christians couldn't see that it was against the natural law?

262

Pope Paul couldn't possibly expect that there would be universal agreement—it was in fact a crisis of authority.

"I think it was the last act—perhaps I'll be proved a false prophet here, but I think it was the last act of the monarchical Church, the last time the pope on his own would issue a statement on such a serious matter, yet expecting everybody to accept it and obey it. It was the last attempt to uphold the pyramid idea, the pope at the top and then the passive base of people at the bottom.

"I think there is a new notion of the Church, the concept of the local Church; instead of reacting to vibrations from Rome they'll be sending vibrations to Rome. This is going to take a long time, but there are world forces going on that are going to put us all in our place, whether pope or bishops. Take the concept of democracy the way it changed the whole world. I think there are comparable movements going on today within the Church."

This optimistic thought hadn't solved the problem Peter was facing, the dilemma of authority versus conscience. Some of his friends had solved it by leaving the priesthood; should he do the same? What good was he doing, teaching liberal theology to young men headed for Nigeria, where they would be up against the old conservative, hierarchical society of bishops? And what good was the new liberalism if the reaction could set in so quickly, and the whole thing be demolished by a monarchical act of the pope?

A cloud of depression obscured the high hopes with which Peter had started his work as a teacher, and it brought back to him some of the sense of darkness, of desolation, he had known when he had been a seminarian at the same Dromantine College.

He remembered a line from the Exercises of Saint Ignatius Loyola, which he had studied during his novitiate at Kilcolgan before he was twenty: "Never make an important decision in times of desolation." This was certainly a time of desolation, so he put off the decision. And by the time the desolation passed, he had found his answer and knew he wouldn't have to leave.

Many of the priests who left, he said, did so for the very human reason of companionship—they wanted to get married. "And," he added, "it was also a fact that a lot of the priests left because they didn't say their prayers."

He paused a moment, as though wondering if I understood what he meant, and went on, "There's no point in some cases bringing out high ideas for what they did, it's a fact, you can't stay in the business without the help of prayers. I know this from myself, I mean I have slipped up in it so I know. You can't survive in our business without some lifeline of faith. You could, well, you might drift for a few years and seek compensations, and some of them are quite pleasant, but . . ."

He seemed uncertain how to go on, so I prompted, "The Church isn't the lucrative career it used to be, nor the road to power . . ."

"Not now," he interrupted. "Financially it's not worth it now; you're in the wrong place if you're in it for money. I have a job surviving, I can't even afford a housekeeper."

"Still, there must be men who go into it because it's the best job they can get, especially in Ireland, and maybe they don't realize how tough it's going to be."

"You're dead right, there were a number who entered who shouldn't have. And now that they're gone, the Church is really better off without them. But there are people who could have survived in it, through the prayer life, and that is the central fact."

I wanted to know if in his parish work he had found any evidence that the changes in the Church—the return to the "joy of the Resurrection" instead of the "killjoy religion"—was having any visible impact on people's lives.

"Well, I would have to put question marks on that one," he said. "Certainly there hasn't been any dramatic change."

"Not dramatic, of course, but any impact at all?"

"There's a much more joyful mood in the celebration of Mass, etcetera, the involvement of the people in it is the big breakthrough. And the most obvious is the charismatic movement that's growing here in Ireland."

"I don't mean people's behavior in church, I mean their daily lives."

"Well now, I don't want to be knocking pubs because I take a drink myself, I enjoy a drink, but I'd say a lot of Irish people get a lot of their joy in the pub rather than in the church."

He looked at me with a rather solemn, sad expression, and I wondered if he was thinking about his father. Peter had talked often about the Irish "pub culture," as he called it, and tended to blame the Church for "conniving" with it, especially in the days before Vatican Council II, through misplaced emphasis on sinful sex. Traditionally the Church had identified the body with evil, and physical pleasures with evil, so any emotional feelings that involved physical reactions seemed evil too. Husbands and wives might have large families yet lead lives of quiet desperation, never able to reconcile their impossibly unrealistic notions of right and wrong, good and evil, pleasure and sin.

The pubs provided an escape from these pressures, and from the feelings that many an Irishman was reluctant to express—feelings of intimacy, of love and hate, of joy and despair, of hope and fear and pleasure and anger, feelings that were all right if they were handled in a superficial way, but could be disturbing and frustrating and even terrifying to someone who thought they might be occasions of sin and didn't know how to deal with them. There was a superficial kind of friendliness and companionship to be enjoyed in a pub, and it seemed to Peter a symptom of spiritual sickness, a way of denying healthier and deeper feelings.

Whether it came from the "pub culture" or not, the Irish seemed to me an uncommonly cheerful people, though surely they had as much to worry about as anybody else. I asked Peter if he thought this cheerfulness was real, or simply a habit of expression.

"I think you're on to something there," he said. "I don't have the answer. I have my doubts myself. Definitely there is a basic core of cheerfulness that is real. But I've often wondered if some of it wasn't a sort of façade."

"Some of it of course is training isn't it? And habit. Yet it is a good habit to be in, and good training to have."

"I'd prefer to be trained that way than be trained to be morose," Peter laughed, "if I were given the choice."

"Well, I wonder if this habit of cheerfulness comes from the Church training that this is what you're supposed to do, that the goal of life is joy and resurrection. The teaching of the secular world is very different—your goal is winning the competition, everyone for himself."

"Yes," said Peter, "and as somebody said, in a rat race the rat usually wins." He quoted a line from a popular country-and-western song then at the top of the charts in Ireland: " '. . . where nice guys get washed away like snow in the rain, and hustle's the name of the game . . .' There's a lot of popular philosophy in that, to an Irishman," he said.

"But is it related to the meaning of the Church in the lives of Irish people?"

Peter thought about it a moment. "Yes," he said slowly, "but I think there's a kind of tug-of-war going on about that. We're entering a technological age, and you know all the jargon about that."

"Sure, Ireland's come out of its isolation now, you're entering the twentieth century, the international business world, and you have to compete on the same terms as everybody else."

"You have to, yes. There is a necessary competition for survival. But in Ireland there is probably more a spirit of cooperation rather than competition. People do not see other people as threats to them, people who must be made to get out of their way, or who might beat them in competition. They see people rather as fellow human beings, or perhaps even further, to see

Jesus Christ—you know, if you give a cup of cold water, you've done it to Me.

"That is there, in the very best example of Irish Catholicism. This idea of seeing the other person literally as an image of Christ; it's a very strong ingredient of Irish Catholicism, though perhaps it was lost for a while."

"You mean this could be the source of the Irish cheerfulness —the habit of seeing a little bit of Christ in everybody?"

"Oh, it is, yes, most definitely."

It seemed a very remote, intangible explanation, yet somehow believable and satisfying. I went back to my first question, the impact of the new liturgy of joy and resurrection. Would it be enough to keep this attitude alive in the tug-of-war of modern Ireland? Or was it too soon to tell?

"No," said Peter, "you can't dig up the tree and see how it's growing. I can't answer. I'd just express a hope that it will."

19.

The Lonely Country

It *was* a lovely mild day in January when I left Castlebar after my visit with Father Peter, to drive the fifty miles to Rita's home on the shore of Sligo Bay. The sun was coming and going through broken clouds, and there was a softness in the wind that would have suited a Connecticut April. The snowdrops and early primulas were already in bloom outside the cottages I passed, and spears of daffodils showed a good six inches above the ground; purple Veronica blossomed in the hedgerows, and clumps of gorse were tipped with candle-flame yellow.

I took the scenic route across the wild, brown, empty upland bog to the shore of Lough Conn, and then under the steep hillside littered with boulders that seemed to be growing out of the ground like massive cabbages, bare gray on top but sheathed with white lichens and mosses in a thousand different shades of green. The road led through Ballina and along the

Moy River estuary to Killala Bay, where the waves of the Atlantic had built up the sandbars at the river mouth into fantastic sculptured castles forty or fifty feet high.

I splashed along the damp road on the bluffs above the beach, through the empty towns of Enniscrone, Kilglass, and Easky, with their neat seaside villas, wondering what busy places they might be in the summer season; there was no other car on the road that morning, and whoever I passed on a bicycle or on foot would give me a friendly wave, a welcome to a stranger, and I would wave back. At last I turned south with the low winter sun in my eyes to rejoin the main road at Dromore West, with a view of humpbacked Ox Mountain instead of the sea.

At Saint Columbanus's Church, standing high on the flat ground with its back to the mountains, I was in Ballycarrick and had to start asking the way. The church, like so many in rural Ireland, was far and away the biggest building to be seen, dominating the landscape with its high peaked roof of gray slate above pink plastered walls, edged at the corners with square-cut blocks of gray granite rising from ground to roof like a binding to hold the structure together and give it a neat, finished look. A red-brown calf with short ears and shaggy hair was grazing in the long winter-gray grass under the brambles and ivy that grew over the cut-stone wall around the churchyard.

The obvious place to ask for directions was O'Riordan's pub, a little farther along the road beyond the graveyard, so I stopped there for lunch. This was where Master O'Rourke used to go after Mass on Sundays, but none of the O'Rourkes went there anymore. One of the farmers at the bar knew Rita's husband, Tom Brennan, and where they lived—there was a left turn beyond the telephone kiosk, which I remembered as being near Mary's new house on the main road, and not far from the old farmhouse where Mary and her mother had both been born, and where Mary and Joe had been brought up by Aunt Annie and Uncle Pat, and Rita had gone as a teen-ager, after the old ones died, to help Mary with her children for a few years. The roof had fallen in on the old place and it was hard to find among the ivy and brambles that hid it from the road, but the new house was easy to spot with its neat plot of lawn and low stucco wall in front.

Mary had been quite ill before Christmas, and spent a couple of weeks in Baggot Street Hospital in Dublin for tests. The doctors had found no cure for the pains in her chest, the upset stomach, the loss of appetite and weight, and she had been very shy and found talking a burden. She was lonely and depressed; for nearly thirty years she had devoted herself solely to her seven children, and now they had all grown up and left home except the two youngest boys, teen-agers, who would soon be going, for neither of them showed any interest in the family farm.

Rita's bicycle was leaning against the wall in front of Mary's house as I drove by; it was her habit to look in on Mary every day when she wasn't well, to cheer her up and make sure she had everything she wanted. Rita thought of Mary as old enough to be her mother; they were the eldest and youngest of the O'Rourke sisters, with eighteen years difference in their ages. But they weren't expecting me that day; I had simply written notes on my Christmas cards to say I hoped to be in Sligo soon, and Rita had replied with a cheerful invitation to come anytime. Rather than burst in on Mary unannounced, I went on down the road, looking for the turn that would take me to Rita's house, where I could see her husband and find out what was what.

Outside the modern glass and concrete school that had re-placed the old building where Eoin O'Rourke used to teach, the narrow lane was blocked by a bus picking up children, and I had to wait until it was safely loaded and lumbered past me toward the main road. Farther up the lane three children in the road waved at me, but I hardly paid attention as I waved back, for I was looking for the next turn I was to make, and trying to remember the landmarks the farmer in the pub had given me. It never occurred to me that two of the children were Rita's Padraig and Belinda, who could have shown me the way if I had offered them a lift.

I was still looking for landmarks when I saw Tom Brennan in a neighbor's yard, helping him build a concrete wall between heavy wooden frames. They looked up and waved, as everyone else I passed that day had done, but Tom showed no sign of recognition until I parked the car at the gateway of his house and walked back to him. Then he set down his end of the long board he and his friend were carrying, and came to shake my hand in great excitement.

"You've come back!" he exclaimed, as though he hadn't believed the promise on my Christmas card. "Herself will be home directly—she's over at Mary's looking after her, but she'll be coming now because the children will be home from school and want their tea."

His face was wind-reddened over a broad grin, and his brown eyes sparkled with pleasure under the brim of his floppy hat. Tom was the one man I had met in Ireland who habitually spoke in a loud voice, almost shouting, as though from the habit of calling to his animals in the fields, or perhaps he was a little deaf and had to shout to hear himself. He brought me up to date about Mary—she was up one day and down the next, seemed to be getting along well and had improved a lot since Christmas, but wasn't ready yet to see visitors. Tom wanted to know where I'd been and what I'd been doing since July, and I said it was a long story and I'd tell him about it when Rita got home.

"You've left your friend there holding his end up without you," I said, and Tom spun around to see his neighbor patiently standing with one end of the long board in his hand, the other resting on the ground where Tom had dropped it. With great apologies he brought me into the yard to introduce me, and his friend dropped his end of the board to shake my hand, and whispered a soft Gaelic name I couldn't identify.

"Now you walk along down to the sea for five minutes while I finish this job, and by that time Rita will be home and you'll have a cup of tea with us," Tom said.

I left them there and followed a muddy track down the slope between the stone walls, watched by the silent cows with their solemn, unblinking eyes, to a ring of stones guarding the clear pool of a spring; the long grass around it was so deep in surface water that I could go no farther. Just beyond was the sea, at high tide now, quiet in this sheltered cove and almost violet blue under the slanting rays of the winter sun.

The air was mountaintop clear, and all morning there had been a kind of dawn light in the sky, pink and gold on the undersides of the high clouds as the sun climbed the little way it had to go, this far north in the winter; now at three in the afternoon the sunset colors were beginning, and beyond the whitecaps of the outer bay the steep flank of Ben Bulben on the distant headland was shining like burnished copper. In another hour it would be twilight, and if the good weather held and there was no rain, the sky would be luminous long after sunset, the dark hills silhouetted against it until half-five or almost six.

A gust of wind lifted my coat and my feet were getting cold. I turned back toward the house, lifting my eyes to a line of oak trees along the road, their main limbs so thickly wrapped in ivy that they looked like evergreens, and the bare smaller branches and twigs that reached out beyond the ivy looked oddly out of place against the sky. Farther up on the ridge the tall pines were shaped by the wind, standing with their backs to the sea, their branches stretching landward like long arms with many fingers, the tips level at the top, sheared off by the wind as neatly as a Dublin hedge. Song sparrows and chickadees whistled at me from the brambles, and once I thought I heard a thrush. What an extraordinary country, I thought, as far north as Labrador or Hudson's Bay, yet here was a New England April in the middle of January.

"Lovely day for the time of year, isn't it," said Tom when I got back to the house.

"Tremendous," I said. "But they tell me a mild January is followed by a cold February. Is that true?"

"Sometimes it is, sometimes it isn't," said Tom. "How would they know? People like to say these things, you know, but that doesn't make them true. We get some bitter cold here sometimes, could be January or February, and a little snow most winters, but if there's a bad storm you remember it. That's how we date things here."

"The last time we had a big snow was 1947," said Rita, who had come home as Tom said she would, and was setting out the tea things on the kitchen table. "I was six years old."

"It's rain and wind more often," said Tom. "We had a good blow the week after Christmas, it pulled some of the thatch off the roof. Did you notice it as you came in?" Indeed I had, a big gash over the front door, showing yellow against the gray brown of the heavier thatch around it. I wanted to ask whether the yellow color was new thatch hastily applied to plug the hole or simply the color of the old inner layers that hadn't yet weathered like the other thatch on top. But I didn't have a chance, because just then Padraig and Belinda came in.

They had indeed been in the group of three children I had seen outside the school, and they looked so like their father and mother that it seemed impossible I had passed them without noticing. Belinda, nearly eleven, had her mother's chestnut hair and big brown eyes, and both children had their mother's oval face and generous mouth, though the children's faces were rounder and their eyes seemed larger, as children's eyes so often do. Padraig, nine and a half, had his father's apple-red cheeks and lean features, the strong chin and straight nose, though his smile was a shy copy of his father's big grin, and in his neat school clothes he looked more like a little businessman than a farmer's son.

They took their places on either side of the big iron kitchen range, Padraig in the straight-backed chair next to the table and Belinda on the settee under the window. They sat quietly, hands in their laps, and laughed when I told them why I hadn't stopped to give them a lift home from school. They couldn't understand why I thought there could be anybody else but them on that lane.

"There aren't any other children here anymore," said Rita. "There's nobody. Only the one who takes the other turning, and an older boy who lives beyond us. That's all."

"There's one more now," said Padraig. "There's a new baby at the Kellys' since last week."

"But he's not in school yet!" said Belinda scornfully. " 'Twill be another five years before he walks home from school with us." And I began to realize something that hadn't occurred to me before—this beautiful countryside could be a lonely place.

It was a theme that recurred often that afternoon, as Tom and Rita chatted over their teacups after the children went out to play. Tom was looking forward to the new chemical plant that he said an American company was planning to build in Killala, because it would create jobs and bring more people to the area, or at least stop so many from moving away. It was running into opposition from environmentalists, who feared the effluent from the plant would pollute the river and kill the fish in Killala Bay.

"There's always somebody who objects to things," he said, "whatever it may be. One plant isn't going to kill all the fish in the sea. There's too much of it."

"What if you get more than one plant coming here, after the first one has polluted the river? Pretty soon you could be in the middle of an industrial area instead of all this beautiful scenery."

"Scenery!" he exclaimed, spitting out the word with impatient contempt. "We get tired looking at it. What we want is neighbors, not scenery!"

He waved his arm toward the back window, where his cow sheds partially blocked the view I had been admiring from his fields. He was right; you could search the horizon out there from end to end and not see any people—only the fields, the cows, the sea, and the distant mountains. The neighbor whose wall he was helping to build was the only one he had.

"Now the tourists come here for the scenery, and they're welcome," he went on. "We're glad to have them, it's a nice change to see some new faces in the summer. But they don't stay long. When you came along the strand road, you came through Enniscrone and Easky, didn't you?"

"Yes."

"I'm sure you didn't see many people on the road as you came."

"No, I didn't. I thought . . ."

"Those towns are empty now. If there were people there they would be out on the road and you'd see them. But there's no one there anymore."

"I thought it was because of the season. They're summer resorts, aren't they?"

"No, no! Oh, they get a few tourists there in the summer, but those are towns where people used to live, you know; they were busy places but now everybody's moved away."

"Why? Where have they gone?"

"They've gone looking for jobs. There's nothing here now, you know, but farming, and the young people these days, they're not so interested in that. They see people with factory jobs coming home on the weekends with nothing to do but play golf or whatever, only working five days a week, and only from nine to five those days, and it looks like an easier life to them. On a farm you work all the time, seven days a week, up before the sun summer and winter—"

"And up all night sometimes, too," Rita interrupted. "When

there's something wrong with the animals, one of the cows is sick, they're as much care as children sometimes."

"That's true," said Tom. "Up all night with them sometimes. But you see, on a farm you enjoy what you're doing all day long, and you've got something when you've done it. A factory job is all right for a young man, but all you're doing is working the machines for somebody else, and what happens when you're older, and have nothing for it. You've made your money and you've spent it as you went along, it's all gone in the pub or whatever, and a lot of them don't get married; it's an empty life as you grow older. But the young people, they think it's easier and they go for it.

"You see what's happening in rural Ireland, it's vanishing, it's empty. Back years ago now, before the famine, there were no real towns in Ireland—Dublin and Cork and Sligo and a few more, but they weren't the big places they are now—but there were eight million people in Ireland then, nearly all of them living in the country. Now everybody lives in towns and cities and there are only four million people altogether. So the countryside is empty."

Tom looked down at his hands, the long red fingers interlaced in his lap, and was silent for a moment, as though he'd made his point and there was no need to say any more. Rita took it a step further.

"I'm not talking about myself, I enjoy the farm life," she said, "but Padraig, what's he going to do? I doubt if he'd ever stay on the farm. And I'd definitely not encourage him either. The farm is always there for him, but with him getting secondary school, and then going on to a real education and all—let him see for himself what he wants to do. But I think to come in and start on the farm when he finishes the national school, like people used to do, that we would not approve."

"Is he interested in the farm?" I asked.

"Oh, yes, very interested. He helps his dad, and he has his own cows, he looks after the cows, comes out and feeds them in the morning, and puts them in in the evening. At the calves now, he'd be able to go out into the field and show you the cows that had the calves. He is very interested, but I wouldn't like him to get too involved in it."

"By the time he's ready, farming may be very different in Ireland," I suggested.

Rita shook her head skeptically. " 'Twould take it a while now, I'd say, to be different," she said.

"If the price of beef and butter go up," Tom began, and left the sentence unfinished. "If you'll excuse me now," he went on, getting to his feet, "I don't like to leave you, but there's a lot of work waiting for me out there and she'll tell you all you want to know." And with a friendly grin he clapped his hat on his head and was out the door.

If the country life was so lonely, I wondered, why had Rita chosen it? Her elder sister Mary hadn't had much choice; she had been sent to live with her aunt and uncle on the family farm when she was a child, now more than forty-five years ago, and her life had been arranged for her, as was the way in those days. But Rita was a modern girl; she'd been to London, seen the outside world, made her own choice. The three middle girls, Gertie, Tess, and Brigid, had left Sligo for a busier life in more crowded and prosperous England. Why was Rita still here?

"I don't know really," she said with a laugh. "I just like the country. I did not like the town, definitely. I'd been in London, when Pat went over, my younger brother, and I went with him. I worked in a factory in London, bookbinding, working the machines for a year, and I didn't like it. I lived with Gertie in Tottenham; she was married and had two children then, Mary and Stephen, and I suppose I got enough of the taste of town life. So I came home, and I stayed with Mummy then, and I met my lover. I decided that I'd stay at home altogether, get settled down in Ireland. We got married on Easter Monday, the year after I came back from London."

"Are you glad you did that?"

"Oh, yes, I am. I have no regrets, no regrets whatsoever. Now Gertie might be a different type, she's settled in England, she hasn't been home since the year Tony died, God rest him. Her husband is English, he was only in Ireland once and he doesn't like it, or he's afraid, he thinks it's all the same in the North and the South, he probably thinks that the twenty-six counties are the same as the six. Gertie likes to know all about home, but she's English now, too. Well, naturally I suppose where your bread is—but I don't know if she really likes it.

"Myself, now, I enjoy the country farm life. Even though as I say it's a seven-day week, I enjoy it. If you have good, open fields, fresh air—well, I suppose if we had running water and all this kind of thing in the rural areas it would be great, and we haven't them so far. But there's not an awful lot more you could wish for."

I looked around Rita's neat kitchen, with the begonias blooming in the deep embrasure of the front window, and the picture of Pope Paul on an illuminated scroll imparting the formal papal benediction on her marriage, flanked on either side by color photographs of her bright-eyed children. I began to see what she meant. There was peace in this house, whatever else might be lacking.

"Of course it's a different run of country altogether from what it was years ago," she went on. "We had a very happy youth, all the lot of us together. There were kids on every road. When you came home from school you'd have someone to play with going home. Whereas now there's nobody. Padraig and Belinda, they're the only two kids that's walking down the road from school now, all the rest travel on the bus. Only the last few years they started the bus, since the three schools amalgamated up here. There wasn't enough kids left to fill the three of them, and they have to have the bus because so many kids come from so far away now. Definitely the population drop in the rural areas is shocking."

I wondered if Rita would like to live where there were more

people, but she didn't think so. "It's going to be very sad for the coming generation," she said, "but then where would you go unless you go into a town or something? And I would not want to do that, certainly not. But it's going to be sadder for the next generation. They're going to have nobody at all. Of course they'll have cars and what have you, we never had a car or a bike. We had to go on foot everywhere we were going.

"There's a dancing class that I'd love to send Belinda to, but it's up too far, and I couldn't get her to it. There's no other one from here around that would be going to it. I would definitely love them to go, even Padraig too, to learn the Irish dances, but there's no transport, no other child."

There had been no Irish dancing lessons for Rita in her childhood, for that matter, and no big iron range to cook on and keep the house warm with a fire that lasted all night. There had never been much meat in the "home stew" that was cooked in the big pot hanging from the crane over the open hearth fire, but in Rita's recollection those days were still the good ones.

"Sure, to come home to that pot of Irish stew in the evening, you thought it was marvelous!" she said. "To come home now to it you wouldn't look at it. But at that time it was a treat, because you knew no better. There was none of us undernourished.

"We all had our little chores in the evening when we came home from school, go to the shop, go to the well, get in the turf for the fire, and the usual bits and pieces. We hadn't the farm work, that didn't affect us, except we had the one cow. Always a cow, with milk for the house. And we used to do the churning. In the summer we always had milk; we had too much milk, because that turned me against it. A cow would give you a full big bucket, two and half gallons in the morning and two and a half in the evening. We used to put down a bit of a garden, enough of potatoes to keep us going, and cabbage and turnips and whatever it was, ordinary countryman's feed. 'Twas happy, I wouldn't have changed it now. You didn't know what you were without, you had just to go to school and if someone next to you had a new outfit on and you had to go in the same outfit, day in and day out, it didn't seem to worry you."

"I don't suppose you were the only people like that in the community," I said.

"No, we were not. But then again there were very few large families by the time I was in school; in the general run there were only four or five kids in any family, and you didn't call that large at that time. I think we have a large family now with two! Every family experienced it somewhat, but it was— you didn't seem to move with the Joneses then. You didn't give two hoots. You just got up in the morning and if there was bread and butter on the table you'd just eat it and you went off to school and brought your bit of lunch with you, come home in the evening maybe for your potato and onion and drop of milk and you're still as happy as Larry. You never worried about tomorrow, you didn't!"

From the little I'd seen of Padraig and Belinda, it seemed that their attitude was not very different. True, they didn't have as many playmates, and when they came home there was nothing after their chores but "do their homework, watch the television, kick the ball around the place, and that's it," as Rita said. They were getting a lot more out of their schoolwork, in a modern school with separate classrooms and library, and more teachers, so there were only about a dozen children to a classroom instead of forty or fifty. They were learning subjects Rita had never had in school—nature study, science, the new math—so she couldn't help them with their homework; but they really loved school and hadn't missed a day of it except when Belinda had her appendix out.

Rita was worrying about what would happen when they became teen-agers. The only youth club for miles around was run by a nun and two helpers, with tabletop games and a weekly class in handicrafts, and an occasional hop, but funds were low, and Sister Finbarr didn't have enough time for it.

Every year there were more empty houses, as families died or moved away; there weren't even enough cattle anymore to stock the land fully. The land was all in use, but the animals would be moved from one field to another at different times of the year, and the empty fields left to recover slowly by themselves; that way they didn't need so much fertilizer. And in the loneliness of the countryside it seemed to Rita that the coming of television only made people lonelier.

"You never see people going to each other's houses now for a nice visit; what we used to call rambling—television has done away with rambling. If you go into a house, the television is left on there, someone in the house wants to see the program and they won't turn it off. You just have to sit down and look at it with them. It's done away with all that warm, homely life here. The radio never did—you can have the radio on and still talk, whereas if you have the television on you cannot talk. And television has done away with card playing. That was a great go years back, but you won't get a child to play cards now, they don't even know what you're talking about."

Rita kept their television set in the kitchen, where she could exercise a strict discipline. The children weren't allowed to watch it until they finished their homework, and only then if there wasn't too much violence in the program. If Rita saw something she didn't think fit for the children, she would switch the set off, even if she herself was interested in the program. The children accepted her decisions; as Rita said, "They know no other way. If they touch the switch to turn on the television, they won't touch it a second time."

Belinda was a great fan of "The Little House on the Prairie," and so soft-hearted that whenever anything happened to the people in the story, an accident to one of the children, or an illness of the mother or father, she'd get terribly upset, and Rita would have to remind her that after all, it was only pretend. Padraig would sometimes watch "Hawaii Five-O," but all he really wanted to see on television was sports, and there wasn't enough of it for him.

Ireland had only one TV channel of its own, and Sligo was too far west to pick up British television from Northern Ireland or Wales, as a good antenna in the Dublin area would. But Padraig knew which evenings there would be a half-hour sports show, and if there was a big soccer or rugby match on a Saturday afternoon he'd watch every minute of it and you wouldn't get a word out of him. The big match of the day was always replayed on the late show Saturday nights, and if it involved Leeds, Padraig's favorite among the First Division English football teams, Rita would let him watch it, because he was a great supporter of Leeds. Padraig would go to bed at nine or half-nine as usual, and if Leeds was on the late show Rita would wake him up for it.

"Of course the television has broadened their outlook, somewhat, anyhow," Rita said. "Television is fine, but it can be an awful hindrance in a house, because when that thing is on, even the husband and wife are not sitting down to talk at night. Whereas if there's no television, there would be more communication. If you sit down there, you're going to look at that damn box, from whatever time it's turned on, and there's no conversation. You just get into that rut, and it's nothing but a rut. When they were on strike before Christmas there was no television in the evening, it didn't worry you, we had to sit down and talk. You'd think you'd miss it, but you don't."

There had been a lot of excitement in Ireland that summer and fall about the possibility of building another transmitter and opening up another channel, and the big argument had been about whether the second channel should simply buy its programs from the British, so that the rest of Ireland could enjoy what the Dublin area already had. Naturally, Dublin viewers argued in favor of setting up all new Irish-produced programming for the second channel. Rita scoffed at that.

"It's all imported what they have on now," she said. "Very, very few shows are produced at home now, except the news and some of the sports—most of that comes from England, too, that's where the big matches are. Take 'Kojak,' that's supposed to be the most popular television show in Ireland, and 'Hawaii Five-O' and 'The Little House on the Prairie,' you could keep naming them. They're all imports. And when you have that on one station how are you going to get material for the second? They just won't."

As it happened, the project was postponed, because the government didn't have the money for it. Television was mainly government-supported in Ireland, through an annual license fee; mornings were devoted to school programs, and on weekdays the popular shows began at four o'clock in the afternoon and were over before midnight. There were some commercial sponsors, but their markets were limited and scattered. Farm implements and fertilizers didn't generate much advertising revenue, but they sold better in Ireland than luxury cars or hair sprays. And whether it was the Catholic Church, the government, or popular taste that kept sex out of the television shows and commercials, nobody seemed to complain about it.

The children burst in from outdoors as we were talking, and it was time to be on my way. Rita pressed me to stay for the evening meal, but the rain clouds were moving in, and I wanted to find the way to Sligo Town before it got too dark. She followed me with the children to the front gate, and when I had turned the car in the narrow lane they were still there, waving good-bye. Tom and his neighbor looked up from their work on the nearly finished wall to do the same. I waved back, and a moment later my rear-view mirrow showed Padraig running across the lane to his father, as though to help with the wall now that the work was nearly done.

20.

Perspectives

W$\mathfrak{h}$en Betty and I left Ireland that summer to come home, the government was debating new measures to combat terrorism, the British ambassador had been killed by a bomb outside his home, and the banks were on strike. Inflation was out of control, the pound had lost a third of its value, the tourist hotels had been emptied by bombs and bomb scares. If we hadn't been in Ireland long enough to know better, we would have thought the country was in terrible shape.

We thought we understood, after fourteen months, some of the contradictions that make Ireland such a mystifying place— or if we didn't fully understand, at least we were aware of them. The terrorists, for example, were a product of the fighting in Northern Ireland, which was British territory, beyond the reach of any Irish laws against terrorism. But new laws would have to be passed, not least as a courteous gesture to a friendly nation whose ambassador had been killed on Irish soil. Perhaps they would set an example that the British might follow in their own territory.

For eight years the British had been unable to stop the fighting in Northern Ireland, but they didn't have much incentive to try very hard. The agony was hurting Ireland more than Britain, and anyhow it involved only 1½ million people out of Britain's 55 million. It was costing British lives, but it was a good training ground for the British army; it was a burden on the British taxpayers, but not as heavy as some others. Certainly the British didn't want to get rid of the burden by letting the Irish take over; that would be giving away the last remnant of the once-great British Empire, their last foothold on an island they had tried for eight hundred years to rule.

Besides, if Northern Ireland became part of Ireland, would it be any easier to restore order there? Many people, even in Ireland, thought it would not; most of the people we talked to were sure it would, but as long as the British were in control the Irish couldn't put it to the test.

Inflation and unemployment in Ireland involved the same kind of contradictions; they depended on actions of the British government as much as the Irish, and sometimes more. When the English pound went down on world markets, the Irish pound went down with it, and our dollars went further in Ireland. But prices went up, and so did unemployment, and these effects were even worse in Ireland than in England, because Ireland was smaller and more dependent on imports. That was the trouble, it seemed—the Irish economy was just too small. It couldn't defend itself against England's problems, and it couldn't cut loose and stand on its own.

A lot of Ireland's other problems seemed to arise from the profound differences between the traditional Irish scale of values and the demands of the modern world economy. We had a taste of that during the bank strike, a phenomenon that could hardly be imagined in a modern industrialized nation.

What would happen to the American economy if the banks were closed by a strike? It didn't bear thinking about.

Our Irish friends told us not to worry; such things had happened before, twice in the last ten years, and Ireland had survived. Banks are not a particularly Irish institution; they were brought to Ireland by the British in the old days, and have not achieved anything like the position that they occupy in countries like America. Bill O'Rourke never used a checkbook in his life before he came to America, and some of his brothers and sisters in Ireland still don't. They keep their money in postal savings accounts, and during the bank strike Betty and I learned to do the same. Our problem was how to get money sent to us from our bank back home in Connecticut; nobody there could imagine what a bank strike was like, and they had no way of dealing with it.

I had written to them before the strike began, explaining the situation and suggesting an alternative way of sending me my monthly remittance, but somehow the message didn't get through. They persisted in trying to send me money through my bank in Ireland, which was closed by the strike. The result was a tangle that took five weeks to unravel, and then only because I learned how to reach the manager of the struck bank by telephone when I couldn't get past his barred doors. He got to know me well enough during those five weeks to trust me.

I was finally able to produce for him a cable from my bank in Connecticut explaining what they had done, and he was willing to believe that he would get the money eventually, though he didn't have it yet. On that assurance, he wrote me a check on a New York bank, and arranged for the manager of the Dublin office of American Express to cash it for me. It was in the nick of time; Betty and I had barely five pounds left in the post office between us, and owed money all over Dublin.

The problem wasn't so unfamiliar to our Irish friends, for they had been through it before. In the two previous bank strikes, those who used checks had been able to get them accepted by the companies they dealt with, because people trusted one another to be honest and keep track of their affairs. But the second strike had lasted six months, and at the end of it too many checks turned out to be worthless. Some people had made mistakes, taken chances, sustained losses, and their bankruptcy meant losses for others. One of our friends found himself two thousand pounds overdrawn when he finally got his bank statement, so he converted it into an installment loan, canceled his checking account, and never used checks again.

When the third bank strike began, the one we lived through, all the chain stores announced that they wouldn't accept checks from anyone. Whether they stuck to this resolve we never found out, but everyone told us that checks weren't being accepted anywhere, unless your credit was well established with a shop, a pub, or one of the foreign-owned banks that weren't on strike. We were using cash, as long as it lasted, but in the crunch we were glad of the shops that knew us and trusted us.

The economy suffered, of course, and the loudest complaints came from the banks themselves and the smaller importers and exporters, who were having the same kind of trouble we had. Bigger businesses shifted their accounts to foreign banks, which expanded their services to accommodate them; government financial services were made somewhat more flexible, though there were plenty of complaints that the government wasn't doing enough. Small domestic businesses and professional people went on as usual, trusting their customers and clients, sending bills at long intervals and waiting patiently for their money. The strike ended after nine weeks, which wasn't all that bad, and most people seemed pleased that the strikers hadn't gained anything by it.

One of the keys to the situation seemed to be that the Irish like to trust one another, even when they know it may cost them money. Most of them don't believe that anyone's economic self-interest should be pursued to the point of hurting other people, which is what the bank strikers were doing. They don't like "materialistic" ideas; they are accustomed to a relatively low standard of living. As Peter O'Rourke said, they prefer a "spirit of cooperation rather than competition." They love competitive sports, but few of them would accept the Vince Lombardi view that winning is everything. The idea of competitive business enterprises is relatively new to them; they'll do it if they have to, but they don't like to be too aggressive about it.

At least the O'Rourkes don't, and while their viewpoint isn't as widely shared as it used to be, the tradition they represent is still the strongest in Ireland. Like the nation itself, the O'Rourkes are coming to terms with the outside world, but in their own ways. And as their experiences have shaped their lives, contact with the outside world is slowly shaping the development of Ireland.

If the old schoolmaster and his wife could see their children now (and many in Ireland would say that from heaven they can), they would, I think, be pleased. None has become rich, or is likely to; but they live comfortably enough, and help others. They have made their own ways, each with dignity and independence, in a vastly different world from the one they grew up in; they all remember their childhood with pleasure, and have kept the faith they were taught.

Maire fulfilled in her lifetime the ideals of the Irish country women of her generation, and did so more generously than most. To bear sixteen children, and care for them so well that only one died before her and only one other soon after, was an achievement to be envied. It was a life of constant work and some hardships, but she didn't think of it in those terms; she believed she was doing what God wanted her to do, and that was enough. All her children grew up to be missionaries in a sense, like Matt, carrying her faith and her ideas of life to the four corners of Ireland, and to England and America as well as Africa, as the disciples of Saint Kevin of Glendalough carried his teaching to Europe in the Dark Ages. It was one of the themes of Irish history, and is still an Irish ideal.

Maire's children no longer live quite the way she did, nor

believe exactly what she believed; the faith she taught would seem primitive to them now, and inadequate to the modern world. But the core of it is the same: keep God's commandments as well as you can, and accept the troubles of life without complaint.

Eoin, too, would say that his life had been a good one, though his drink and his passion for politics—the weaknesses of his flesh—brought him to an untimely death at sixty-one. His dedication to freeing Ireland from English rule was as typical of the men of his generation in Ireland as Maire's dedication to raising children was typical of the women. The Irish Republic he dreamed of became a reality the year after his death, and if the reality did not exactly match the dream, it was a sufficient achievement for one generation's work, and Eoin had done his share.

From his little country school came teachers, preachers, and politicians taught by him to do more than set fire to customs houses. His own sons and daughters lived more comfortable lives than his, and five of his ten sons gained for themselves more education than Eoin had ever received or been able to give. His death was a turning point in the lives of all his children, and the way they responded did credit to what their father had taught them and done for them. Only Mary, the eldest daughter, and Mick, the second son, seemed to fall behind as they grew older, hurt by changes in the Irish way of life that they couldn't quite keep up with.

Mary followed her mother's example perhaps too closely, and never knew any other. Like her mother, she was brought up by Aunt Annie and Uncle Pat, but they were great-aunt and great-uncle to her, a generation removed and already old-fashioned and set in their ways when Mary came to them. Mary was modern enough to consider seven children a large family, and take steps to have no more; but this one change in the established pattern didn't lead to the other changes that were taking place in modern families. Like her mother, she devoted herself entirely to her children, and had no other interests once the first was born.

As Mary's children grew to be teen-agers they didn't stay home to look after the younger ones and dig potatoes or work in the fields, as her brothers and sisters had; there weren't as many younger ones to look after, and there were new opportunities for secondary school or jobs away from home. So Mary's children gradually left home, and at an age when her mother had still been surrounded by babies, Mary was lonely again, as she had been in her childhood. Her husband was not an educated man like her father, he was a simple farmer, and none of her sons showed any interest in staying to work the farm.

With loneliness came depression, and by the time Mary was in her fifties she became so withdrawn that she could barely talk to her own brothers and sisters when they came to see her, and spent long periods in bed, refusing even to eat. She still grieved for her mother, eight years after her death; when the family picture was taken after the mother's funeral, Mary had been the only one unable to manage a smile for the camera. She began to imagine that she was dying of cancer, as her mother had done, and spent a week in a hospital in Sligo, and then another week in another hospital in Dublin, undergoing tests. They showed no sign of cancer, and no other physical problem to account for the pains Mary felt in her chest, her upset stomach, and her inability to eat. Mary was sure the doctors must be wrong, but Una, Charlie's wife, with her experience of nursing, convinced her that they were right. Mary went home feeling more cheerful, but it didn't last; no sooner was she home than she fell again into despair.

Rita visited her regularly, to try to cheer her up, and from time to time Peter came up from Knock, Charlie from Dublin, and Joe from Galway. It was psychiatric help Mary needed, they were sure, and her case wasn't so different from those of many other country mothers of her age. It took a while for Mary to overcome her resistance to that idea, but if rural Ireland was a rather fertile ground for such afflictions, it was also well provided with facilities for dealing with them. There was a very good psychiatric hospital not far from Sligo, and one day Mary let Peter drive her over there to see what it was like. She stayed a few days, and then, feeling much better, went home; the old terrors returned, and this time she went back to the hospital promptly and without protest. She was in and out a good many times after that, and her brothers and sisters were still worrying about her when I last saw them; but the improvement was continuing, and the prognosis was good.

Mick's trouble was loneliness of a different kind. He never married, and none of his brothers and sisters knew exactly why; perhaps the right girl just never came along. Since he was eight years old Mick had carried the family responsibilities that Mary had been spared when she was sent to live with spinster Aunt Annie and bachelor Uncle Pat; it was Mick who had given the babies their bottles when there was no older sister at home to do it, and who ran the household for his mother after the father's death, when the mother was so ill. He had stayed with the mother while his brothers left home, one by one, to seek their fortunes or further their education, and in the end he grew up to be a bachelor, like Uncle Pat.

Mick followed Charlie and Tony to Dublin only when everyone else had gone except the four youngest, of whom Chris, at fifteen, was old enough to take charge. By that time Mick was twenty-six, and for the next couple of years he was as busy with the girls in Dublin as Charlie, or more so. He did a line for a while with a dark-eyed girl from Galway whom he'd met at a Legion of Mary hop, but it didn't last; and after that there weren't so many others. He put more time into sports, and played on the football team at the bakery; and he became very popular in the pubs he went to.

Mick had a ready wit and a good singing voice, and he was generous with his money, standing rounds to anyone who wanted to join him. As long as he could enjoy the fellowship of the pubs, he liked this way of life, and kept it up for nearly twelve years. But his health couldn't take it—he had chronic bronchitis, made worse by the heat and dust of the bakery where he worked, and so many years of night work, winter and summer. In his late thirties he had a stomach ulcer, and his doctor told him he'd have to give up the drink.

Then the loneliness began. He couldn't spend his evenings in the pub drinking lemonade and orange squash, for that was as depressing to his friends as it was to him, and the taste of the stuff turned his stomach. He began to lose touch with his old friends, and didn't know where to look for new ones.

He spent some weeks at Toberpatrick first, recovering from the operation, but that didn't help; everyone he knew in the district had gone, and there was nobody home but his mother and Tony, whose illness took all his mother's time and care. Mick went back to Dublin and moved into Charlie's digs with him, but the following year Charlie got married, and Mick was alone again.

For a brief time Mick decided his doctor might have been wrong, and maybe one little drink wouldn't hurt. But the result was so catastrophic that he never tried it a second time. Whether it was the medication he was taking, or the effects of the operation, or the long period away from alcohol, nobody in the family knew, but one Saturday night when he was going home from the pub he collapsed in the street, and his friends took him to the hospital, unconscious. When he came around, his doctor came straight to the point.

"I've done what I could for you, Mick," he said, "but if you're going to do that again, don't come near me. It will be no use." That floored Mick, and he never took another drop.

Mick took a liking to the landlady at Charlie's digs, a woman about their mother's age, and he stayed there after Charlie left to get married. He was her only tenant, and he used to do odd jobs for her around the house, and walk the dog when she didn't feel up to it, and make her breakfast when she was ill. She was company for him, and they drank a lot of tea together in the evenings, which was the best substitute he had for the old days at the pub. She helped him forget his grief when his mother died, only a few years after he'd given up the drink and the friends he had had. Mick visited his married brothers and sisters often, too, bringing presents for the children and playing with them as he used to play with the little ones at home. They all loved him; he was the nice uncle of the storybooks, who always had time for the children and delightful surprises in his pocket.

Mick got used to this life after a while, and quite enjoyed it; after all, it was an extension of what he'd done when he was younger. Now that he didn't spent his evenings in the pubs, he had more time for reading, television, and the radio; like all the O'Rourkes, he had an inquiring mind, and soon was as well informed on public affairs as his better-educated brothers. But he didn't do anything about getting a better job than the maintenance work in the bakery he'd been doing for twenty years; in his forties now, with no family responsibilities, he didn't see any reason to.

What Mick didn't realize was that jobs don't go on forever in the modern world, not even in Ireland. He was forty-seven when the bakery where he worked was bought by a larger company, and in the resulting economies and consolidations he was one of the men to be squeezed out. The plant where he worked was closed; his job ceased to exist, and the new owners had no other for him. He was out on the street, with no pension and precious little separation pay, and no idea of how to find another job.

Mick had never had to look for work before; when he was twenty-six he'd taken a job his brother Charlie fixed up for him, and it was the only job he'd ever had. Now at forty-seven it was different. Charlie's brother-in-law, by this time an executive of a large meat-packing company, arranged for Mick to be given a job at one of the company's plants, but Mick was too embarrassed to accept it. Charlie offered to take him to the plant for his interview, and Mick reluctantly agreed, but he told the interviewer he had something else in mind, and would let them know. Whatever else it was, the job never materialized, and after that Charlie decided there was no sense trying to push him. Joe was clipping "men-wanted" ads from the papers and sending them to Mick, but he didn't follow them up.

It was demoralizing, and nobody in the family knew what to do about it. Mick had his pride, they could see that and sympathize with it; but he was becoming depressed and withdrawn. In some ways his problem was worse than Mary's, but it couldn't be treated the same way.

A few months after Mick lost his job, his landlady died, and then the house where he'd lived for nine years was sold, and he had to find other digs. The old lady had been his closest friend, almost his only friend outside the family, in those years; now he had lost her as well as his home, his job, his health, his old companions, and the drink that had been his comfort and entertainment in happier years.

He didn't worry about money—he'd never done that, any more than his mother or his brother Jimmy when Jimmy was a bachelor, because money didn't mean anything to him. He spent it or gave it away when he had it, and when he didn't he went without. The welfare payments he got from the government were enough to keep body and soul together in a one-room bedsitter in Harold's Cross, a respectable working-class section of Dublin near the canal, and occasionally he would get temporary work as a night watchman or hotel porter. But he saw less and less of his brothers. Charlie and Una were always inviting him to the house for a meal, but when he couldn't afford to bring little presents for the children, he wouldn't come. The same reticence kept him from visiting Chris in Roscommon or Joe in Killimor, though in the old days he had spent a week or two with each of them at least once a year. Now he didn't have the fare; they'd have sent it to him, but he wouldn't have accepted it.

Mick turned fifty without any real improvement in his way of life; his brothers wondered what he did with himself all day long, but he wouldn't tell them. When Joe went to Dublin for the football final every year he would go to see Mick, but Mick wouldn't talk. It was as though he felt lost in the modern world; he couldn't get a job because unemployment was high and his few skills were obsolete, and while the government provided for his material subsistence, it gave him no comfort. He was no longer so close to the family he had grown up in and helped to raise; the others had made their way in the world, and either raised families of their own or become part of the Church. Mick had done neither. Perhaps one day something would turn up; meanwhile, there seemed nothing to do but wait.

The other O'Rourkes had less trouble with their adjustments. Joe, the eldest after Mary, found his career as a policeman disappointingly dull, and sometimes wished he had more education, and could advance to a more stimulating post. But these were complaints that had to be dragged out of him; on the whole he was pleased with life. He had supported his mother in her widowhood, and helped his godson and younger brother, Willie, achieve his ambition of becoming a priest. He had modernized the family home after his mother's death, and kept it open, as his mother wished, as a home place for the three priests. More than that, he had made it a kind of base for the whole family to return to when they wanted, and it had become a bond that held them all together, kept them in contact with one another, more than most Irish families of that size and generation. It was a bit of the old tradition worth preserving, a way of keeping brothers and sisters in touch with one another, helpful to Mary in her illness, and company for Rita in her isolation. Perhaps one day it would be a help to Mick.

By the time Joe was in his fifties he had finished paying for the improvements at Toberpatrick, and was reconciled to the idea that he wouldn't be promoted to a more interesting station than Ennis. He moved out of rented quarters for the first time in his married life, and bought a house of his own, a nice new modern one on the outskirts of Killimor, with huge floor-to-ceiling windows in the sitting room looking out on the blazing yellow gorse of the bogland and the distant hills of the Burren, and picture windows in the kitchen facing the rolling pasture land, the green and white hawthorn hedges, and his own plot of potatoes, onions, parsnips, and cabbage. It was a comfortable home, with wall-to-wall carpets and electric fridge and cooker, but he kept an enamel turf-burning range like Rita's in the kitchen as well, for the comfort of its warmth and for security in case the electric power should fail. His daughter sang in the choir and his two sons served Mass as altar boys, but he didn't think they'd grow up to be priests, or policemen either.

Charlie was the most prosperous of the older group, and the only one engaged in a business of his own. He added a new kitchen to his home after the boys were born, equipped with freezer and washer-dryer as well as fridge, and put in central heating. The old kitchen became the family room, with a couch next to the tea table for watching television; the front parlor was for company, including sometimes Charlie's business clients. The guest bedroom was almost always occupied, for Charlie's home became the Dublin headquarters of the O'Rourkes, where Matt came first on his home leave from Nigeria every two years, and Pat stayed whenever his business brought him to Ireland, and Bill stopped in every year on his vacation before going to Toberpatrick; for the other O'Rourkes in Ireland and England it was only natural to stay with Charlie and Una whenever they came to Dublin.

Charlie's home was almost more of a center of O'Rourke family affairs than was Toberpatrick, though it wouldn't have worked if Toberpatrick hadn't been there as a kind of country guest house for the busy season, with Rita to be hostess and housekeeper. As it was, Charlie and Una had all they could handle, and Charlie's work kept him busy till nine or ten every evening, and much of his weekends too. He tried to take Mondays off, but it wasn't always possible.

Jimmy Gertie, and Tess, the middle ones, and Brigid, who

followed them to England, had settled for a less demanding life. Though they turned their backs on rural Ireland, they took their Irish culture with them, and didn't find life in England particularly different. They had moved from the country to the city, and joined the new middle class that the English called "working class," but that was it. Jimmy had returned to Cobh not because he didn't like England, but because his mother-in-law wanted her daughter near her. Once settled there, he didn't want to move again; he knew all his neighbors and they knew him, and there was no loneliness and nothing much to worry about. His three sisters in England felt much the same, and so did their husbands and children.

Chris, a year older than Brigid, had followed the example of his eldest brother, Joe, and discovered like him that a policeman's lot could be a pretty dull routine. Joe's role as father figure and head of the family had meant more to Chris than to the others, for Chris was only eleven when Eoin died, and by the time he was thirteen almost all his elder brothers and sisters had left home—Peter, Willie, and Matt to their religious schools, Tess to be married, Gertie to Mrs. Flynn's in Westport, Jimmy in the navy, and Charlie to Dublin. In the next two years Tony and Mick left as well, and Joe used to come up from Galway to help Chris with the vegetable garden and the turf cutting, and coach him in his responsibilities as eldest of the four remaining children.

When Chris went to Dublin at age nineteen he tried the post office first, like Tony, but with Joe's example the Garda looked like a better career, and he joined up as soon as they would take him. He took his job seriously, and acquired a respect for the skill and effort a professional criminal puts into his work; but there weren't many of them in Roscommon. When he came across one it would be a "traveling criminal," the hardest kind to catch because they're here today and gone tomorrow.

In his late thirties, Chris, and his blonde wife, Kay, lived in a neat two-story home rented from the county council, with four energetic little sons, two of them old enough for school. Chris didn't think of police work as his main goal in life; he'd been in the Garda eighteen years and it looked as though he'd be able to retire young enough to have a second career, though he didn't yet know what it would be. Meanwhile, he enjoyed the community work that people expect of policemen; things like spending off-duty hours at sports clubs for youngsters, to keep them out of trouble and teach them good citizenship. Like his brothers and sisters, he enjoyed the feeling that when he went out on the street everybody knew him, and he knew everybody he met; there was never any lack of friends.

The three priests led quite different lives, in some ways more diverse and stimulating, and developed personalities quite different from one another and from the rest. Peter, the theologian, was contemplative, intellectual—too much so for Joe's taste— but passionate in the way he wrestled with his doubts and dilemmas, the moral challenges his penitents brought him, the contradictions he saw between the teachings of the Church and the demands of life in the modern world. He accepted the disciplines of the Church because he was a part of it and because he believed in Christ. But he was never able to believe in the Church in the same way he believed in Christ. The distinction was important to him, and it produced conflicts within him that were dramatic in their way, though they weren't often visible to outsiders.

Matt, four years older than Peter, had been trained for the priesthood at the decision of his parents and his Aunt Doty, who had put up the money. His was a different kind of vocation, and his brothers and sisters never inquired what it meant to him. They saw him briefly once every two years when he came home on leave, but he normally visited Rome and other parts of Europe on the way, spent a few weeks on retreat as soon as he reached Ireland, and for the rest of his leave watched football matches. He was a demon for promptness, a very un-

Irish characteristic that made Rita think he must have trouble getting the Nigerians to come to Mass on time. He was always on the go, never sitting still for more than ten minutes at a time, hurrying to get outdoors and play ball if there was no game to watch. His letters from Nigeria were few, brief, and uninformative; as Joe said, you could throw them away without reading them and you wouldn't miss much. He didn't enjoy his year in Australia, apparently because he found it too stuffy and civilized. He preferred the informality of Nigeria, where he could spend most of his time in a T-shirt or bare-chested. He didn't talk much of his experiences, but they were obviously very different from Peter's.

Willie, the middle one in age and the last of the three to be ordained, had neither Matt's restless energy nor Peter's inner conflicts. He'd had his share of both before he was ordained, and worked his way through them. He liked the way of life he found in America, and he devoted much of his time to such practical aspects of the ministry as career guidance for high-school students and pastoral visits to the aged and infirm. He was pleased when the American church adopted a regular salary system for parish priests and their assistants, including deductions for Social Security and the corresponding promise of comfortable retirement. This was obviously an improvement over the system that had supplied his first pastor in Bridgeport with so much ready cash, and it also meant more opportunities for promotion, since the old pastors wouldn't hang on so long.

For a few years after Vatican II there was even talk of allowing priests to marry, but it didn't get very far. On theological grounds it could easily be justified, for Saint Peter had been married, and so had many of the early priests in the first centuries of Christianity. Celibacy had come later, and many in the modern hierarchy thought it caused more trouble than it was worth. But Bill thought it would be a long time before that changed. The Catholic laity weren't ready for the idea, because the tradition of celibacy had been established so long ago. The Church couldn't afford it, because married priests would need higher salaries to support their wives and children, and would the parishioners feel they were getting extra benefits for the added cost? Protestant churches, which allowed their clergy to marry, were having as much difficulty recruiting them as were the Catholics, so it wouldn't solve the personnel problem. Besides, with today's divorce rate, how could you stop married priests from becoming divorced priests? The Catholic Church already had enough trouble over divorce.

Like Peter, Bill thought the Irish church needed to rethink its attitudes toward sex, and he didn't think the American church had all the answers either. But again like Peter, it wasn't a problem that touched him personally. He had accepted celibacy when he was called to the priesthood, and at forty he had no desire to change. He knew many priests who had left the ministry to get married, and he didn't envy them.

Nor did he think he'd ever leave America to go back and live in Ireland. There were benefits he'd gained here that he wasn't willing to lose. If he ever lived long enough to retire, he thought he'd go to Florida; he'd been there often enough, and he liked the sunshine. He liked the old folks he'd met there, too; he found them very congenial.

Patrick, the youngest of the O'Rourkes, was the most modern in his way of life, a business executive comfortably settled in his wife's native Connecticut, in an air-conditioned suburban home on a quarter-acre plot with two cars and two children. He hadn't broken his ties with Ireland, and indeed he had become more closely involved with Ireland and Irish-Americans since his marriage than he had been before. That was not a conscious choice, but a response to the demands of his business career.

With his experience in the airline business, it was inevitable that a young Irishman like Patrick, eager to climb the ladder, would sooner or later become involved in the complex of travel-and-tourism enterprises run by CIE, one of Ireland's semistate bodies and the parent corporation for Aer Lingus, the Irish international airline. It happened soon after Pat's marriage, and it made a big change for him. Until then he had not thought much about being Irish; he had left home at twenty, and after a few years of working in America and serving in the National Guard he thought of himself as an American like anyone else.

His new job involved him in organizing package tours and charter flights to Ireland, and the Irish-American associations in New York and Boston were his best market. He was astonished to find how many there were, and a little suspicious of them at first. So much wining and dining, such long after-dinner speeches, such hearty displays of friendship and sentimentality—all seemed rather phony, and very different from anything he'd known in Ireland. But he found they were very nice people, very Irish in their own way, loyal to Ireland and to their own organizations. And they were willing and able to spend a lot of money in Ireland on their package tours, which was good for Pat's business and good for the Irish economy.

At thirty-three Pat had lived more than a third of his life in America, and considered it home. But he hadn't been naturalized and wasn't an American citizen. He thought that someday he probably would be, but he saw no reason to take that step yet, and no one was asking him to. For that matter, his wife hadn't been converted and wasn't a Catholic, though their children were, and Pat never asked her to take that step either. These differences between them didn't seem to matter; they were part of the diversity of American life.

There was still a trace of Irish in the way Pat talked, though you might not recognize it if you didn't know Ireland. If his background showed in some of the things he did, they were not noticeably different from his neighbors' habits. There were some fine pieces of Waterford crystal on display in his dining room, and he drank tea when some others might drink coffee; he was as gentle and affectionate with his children as any Irish father, and three-year-old Michael was as often in his daddy's lap at the tea table as his cousin Liam was in Uncle Charlie's lap in Dublin. The roses in the garden behind the house were a credit to Pat's training in horticulture, and the stone fence he had built to shelter them looked a little different from other Connecticut stone fences, but only to the knowing eye. A small plot was devoted to potatoes and onions and cabbages, like the garden that had won him a prize at Toberpatrick when he was fifteen; his neighbors, if they bothered with such things at all, planted tomatoes and corn, and Pat planned to experiment with these crops when he had time.

The only times Pat consciously thought of Ireland were in connection with his business or letters to his brothers and sisters, mainly about plans for vacation visits to Toberpatrick. The business relationship was important; that's where his future was. Pat was still climbing the business ladder, though he tried not to let that interfere with family life. More important, perhaps, was his feeling that if recession or inflation ever knocked a big hole in the package tour and charter flight business, he could expect his Irish employers to find him another job in Ireland more easily than he might find one in America. He was working for a semistate body, a blend of private capital and government funds in which the government holds the controlling interest, and that gives the company a certain social obligation. It is still the Irish philosophy that people need jobs, and if private capital can't provide them, the government has to. That might be inefficient from the business standpoint, but it suits the Irish tradition. Mick's trouble had been that he worked for a small privately owned company, and when it was bought by a bigger private company, Mick was squeezed out. Pat didn't want anything like that to happen to him.

Here the story ends, not because it's finished but because the rest of it hasn't happened yet. Pat has more to learn about America, and is busy learning it; Ireland is also learning about the outside world, of which after so many centuries it is once more a part. Pat is in his early thirties, and the Republic of Ireland is six years younger; even the Irish "free state" that preceded it was born only a year before Pat's sister Mary. As nations go, the new Ireland is one of the youngsters, though her traditions are among the oldest.

The new Ireland has already taken on characteristics that make the old descriptions obsolete. It can no longer be defined by the old clichés, neither the sentimental ones about leprechauns and smiling colleens nor the bitter ones about rowdies and drunkards, men who fight too bitterly for hopeless causes, clowns and buffoons who live absurdly unreal lives in worlds of their own imagination. These images are hangovers from history, formed when the Irish were a subject people, and their reputation was shaped for them as much by the hostility of their rulers as by the nostalgia of their exiles. The Irish are a free people now, and no more prisoners of their history than any other nation.

Today they are dealing directly with the outside world, making their own decisions and adjustments to the world's demands. In the process, Ireland is changing, yielding more to America's influence now that the British is declining, and learning from other countries too. The changes are neither rapid nor wholly one-sided; the Irish are careful not to give up any part of their old traditions that they value, and those who come from the outside world to do business with them often find, when the long process is over, that they too have gained something of value from the experience. And that, after all, is only fair.